Round Aberdeen, from Deeside to the Deveron

Walks and History

Boar's Head Press 003

Also in this series:
Round Inverness, The Black Isle and Nairn;
Round Moray, Badenoch & Strathspey

First published in April 2000
by Richard Gordon
at
Rosebank, Cairnfield, Buckie, Banffshire AB56 5EL, Scotland

Re-order from above address or tel. 01542-836087

ISBN 0 9533096 2 2

Note

Description or mention of walks and routes in this book do not guarantee or constitute a right of access.
Permission for access should be sought as appropriate or if in any doubt whatever. Every care has been
taken to guarantee the accuracy of this guide but, given constant change in the physical landscape, road
systems, telephone codes, etc., the author/publisher will not be responsible for any loss, damage or incon-
venience caused by inaccuracies, nor for accidents incurred while using this guide.

Acknowledgements

Thanks are due to Bill Smith/Storycards for permission to use the original artwork as duplicated on the
cover and internally. For Storycards catalogue/information contact the above address or: The
Schoolhouse, Urquhart, Moray IV30 3LG

All photographs by the author

Scanning, typesetting and cover printing by
Posthouse Printing, The Park, Findhorn, Moray IV36 OTZ
Contents printing and binding by Short Run Press, Exeter

Contents

North East Scotland

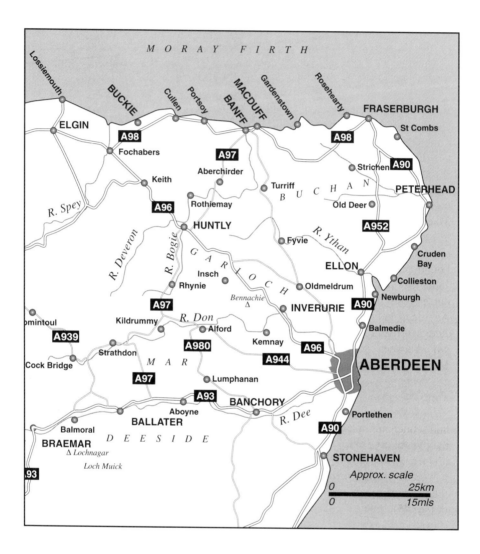

This map covers the region travelled in this book, and shows the main routes, towns and villages. However, it is for illustration purposes only and should not be regarded as more than a general outline.

Happy walking!

Foreword: How to use this book

The third in a series that began with *Round Inverness, The Black Isle and Nairn* (1998) and continued in *Round Moray, Badenoch and Strathspey* (1999), this journey explores Aberdeen and the land about, from Stonehaven to Cullen, Braemar to Buchan, and the land in between. With some 60 walks described, and using back roads as much as possible, the tour is divided into six sections.

The first (with many route directions which some may wish to skip) explores Aberdeen and its immediate neighbourhood; the second follows Deeside to Braemar and beyond, and the third (with side-trips to the Lecht and Cabrach) follows Strathdon east to Inverurie. Section four covers the Garioch from Inverurie west past Bennachie to Strathbogie, then returns east to follow the Ythan from its estuary at Newburgh past Ellon to Haddo and Fyvie. Starting at Huntly, the fifth section explores Deveronside north to Banff, the coast west to Cullen, and the backland in between. Finally, section six travels through Buchan: first via the coast from Macduff to Fraserburgh, then through the Howe of Buchan (again west to east), and last the coast from Fraserbugh south to Peterhead and Cruden Bay.

En route we visit hills, moors, forests and rivers, rocky shores and cliff-bound beaches; battle-sites, haunted places, symbol stones, stone circles and hill-forts, old kirks and castles, fisher-towns and forgotten hamlets. We hear tales of curse, feud and tragic love, and meet Calgacus, Canute and St. Drostan, Lords Aberdeen and Byron, the Bonny Lass of Fyvie, the wizard Thomas the Rhymer, the fiddler-brigand James Macpherson; Robert the Bruce and the Marquis of Montrose who between them sacked half of the Northeast, and George Keith, 5th Earl Marischal, who singlehandedly built half of it. The Black Colonel of Inverey goes on the rampage, as does Black Airtir of Strathgirnock, and of course there's the Turra Coo (**87**).

With frequent side-trips off main road and beaten track, the route-selection and sequencing may seem arbitrary to some, but the mosaic-like texture of much of the region, especially Buchan, makes this hard to avoid. In any case, the book needn't be followed step-by-step, and for ease of cross-reference is written in short chapters, each dealing with a specific route, walk, visit or subject. Cross-references to related sites or subjects are inserted as bracketed numbers in **bold type** – i.e., (**45**) or (see **45**) – meaning chapter-numbers, not pages. So Easter Aquhorthies stone circle (**60**) cross-refers to Loanhead of Daviot (**66**) and other such sites; the Bell family masterpiece of Craigievar (**55**) to other Bell-designed castles: Crathes (**20**), Castle Fraser (**58**), etc.

Of the mostly-circular walks, some explore high or remote ground, but few are strenuous, this tour being for folk who prefer fresh air and discovery to heart attack or broken neck. It's also for those who enjoy seeking out hidden places as well as those better-known; places which, perhaps due to their very anonymity, retain a spirit less apparent in more popular and exploited destinations. Deeside is beautiful, but so too is Monymusk (**58**) by the Don, or sleepy Rothiemay (**83**) by the secretive Deveron, or (in a very different, wilder way) the cliff-hemmed shoreline hamlet of Crovie (**96**).

As to access, Scotland has no law of trespass as such, but those working the land may see things differently to those seeking rural or wilderness recreation. Most folk are reasonable, but a few can easily spoil it for others by leaving gates open, littering, failing to control dogs, and so on. So, please follow the country code and, though as far as I know walkers are welcome on all routes described, if in doubt ASK FIRST, especially during the stalking and shooting seasons. Many rely for a living on the land: it and they deserve respect. To learn more about trespass, rights of way and public access, write to or call The Scottish Rights of Way Society (24 Annandale St., Edinburgh EH7 4AN; tel. 0131-558-1222) to obtain their *Rights of Way: A Guide to the Law in Scotland*.

Also, especially in remote areas, wear good boots, dress appropriately, take food, and tell someone where you're going and when you expect to be back. If walking cliff-bound shoreline, check the tides first. The weather can change fast: a compass is always useful, and the 1¼ in-1 mile (2cm-1km) Ordnance Survey map is essential. Map references cited are read from the top (eastings) first. In the text these are given to pin-point sites and to clarify junctions. Heights are given both in feet and metres (metric height x 1.0936 x 3 = height in feet).

Population figures given are as revised by Aberdeenshire Council in 1996 from the 1991 census.

Note: Few photos are captioned. If their subject is ambiguous, inserted at the appropriate point in the text is (see photo) or (as shown below), etc.

As for Bill Smith's paintings (thanks, Bill), the cover shows the Maiden Stone under Bennachie (artistic licence invoked). Section 1 opens with Aberdeen's Wallace Monument, section 2 with the Dee at Ballater (**33**), and section 3 with Kildrummy Castle (**49**). Section four is introduced by the moonlit recumbent and flankers of one of Aberdeenshire's megalithic circles (**60**), and section five opens with Fourman Hill above Rothiemay (**84**). Lastly, the Buchan section opens with cliffbound Pennan on the Moray Firth coast (**98**), and the back cover photo is of nearby Crovie (**96**), equally cliff-hemmed.

Also please note: all road numbering is as redefined in 1997, and not necessarily as on existing OS maps; i.e., the route from Stonehaven to Aberdeen and north to Ellon is now the A90, not the A92 as formerly.

Section 1

Aberdeen & Neighbourhood

1. Introduction: The Lay of the Land

Inhabited since Mesolithic times nearly 10,000 years ago, and now home to over 500,000 people (70,000 more than in 1970, with almost 220,000 living in Aberdeen, Scotland's third-largest city), the Northeast is a land of contrasts defined as much by its rivers as by its hills, moors, straths, haughs, fields and coastal plains.

Flowing east from the Central Highlands, both Dee and Don leave behind their wooded, hill-hemmed valleys for fertile lower ground before converging on Aberdeen and the sea. Further northwest, at Huntly (**80**) the moor-born Deveron takes up the Bogie then meanders secretively north past Turriff (**87**) to the Moray Firth between Banff (**88**) and Macduff (**96**), while, rising east of Huntly, and marking Buchan's southern boundary, the placid Ythan flows east past Fyvie (**78**) and Ellon (**75**) to join the sea by Newburgh (**73**). Buchan, Scotland's hard elbow into the cold North Sea, has no great rivers; yet two east-running streams, the North and South Ugie Waters, offer welcome oases before meeting near Peterhead (**110**).

These very different waters fertilise lands with little in common save a violent past. For centuries prominent families – Farquharsons, Forbeses, Frasers. Gordons, Hays, Keiths, Leslies and others – fought for control from Braemar to Buchan, where place-names like Cruden Bay (*croju-dane*, 'slaughter of the dane': **111**) recall earlier Viking raids. Even older, the region's many Iron Age hill-forts, as at Tap o' Noth (**51**), Bennachie (**68**) and Dunnideer (**69**), offer further evidence of a hard and often violent past.

The Northeast's first recorded battle was fought *c.*AD83 at Mons Graupius (**16**), Agricola's Romans defeating tribes led by the legendary Calgacus. At Nechtansmere in Fife in 685, the Picts of the Northeast defeated the Northumbrian Egfrith. Later, for nigh on two centuries the Vikings ravaged the coast, while Macbeth's death at Lumphanan (**25**) in 1057 ushered in 233 years of Canmore rule. Thereafter the Wars of Independence saw the Northeast raked first by England's Edward then by Robert the Bruce (**64**). Aberdeen was torched in 1336, but spared from the Lord of the Isles by the bloodbath at Harlaw (**65**) in 1411. With the 1562 Battle of Corrichie (**23**) nearby damaging the Gordon cause; in 1571, 1639 and 1644 Aberdeen was again the scene of conflict (**2**). Only after the failure of the 1745 rebellion did life begin to get easier…at least, for some.

Less brutally, the Northeast is rich in Iron Age and older Neolithic remains, including Aberdeenshire's unique recumbent stone circles. Dated back to *c.*3000BC, these are so-called because the largest stone lies horizontal between two vertical flankers, as at Clune Hill and Mulloch (**19**), Easter Aquhorthies (**60**), Loanhead of Daviot (**66**), Rothiemay (**83**) and Strichen (**106**) – monuments as mysteriously evocative as the region's many Pictish symbol stones (**67**), erected *c.*AD500-*c.*850 and the land's earliest surviving representative art.

Later came castles, towerhouses, and Renaissance chatêaux. Drum (**18**), Crathes (**20**), Kildrummy (**49**), Craigievar (**55**), Castle Fraser (**58**), Fyvie (**78**), Huntly Castle (**80**) and others display great invention, especially those built *c.*1550-

1630 by the Bells of Mar and Leipers of Buchan. The 18th century saw advances in farming techniques and the foundation of planned villages, as at New Aberdour (**98**), New Pitsligo (**100**) and New Deer (**101**). With battle and bloodfeud fading into the past, the 19th-century herring boom put Northeast ports on the map as Aberdeen and the larger towns developed suburbs. So 'modern' times arrived, and today folk make a living by farming or fishing (both occupations in peril), in forestry and other land-related pursuits, in commerce and the professions, or in the North Sea gas and oil business centred on Aberdeen.

Known as the 'Silver' or 'Granite City', and though its parks and gardens have often won the Britain in Bloom competition (and in 1999 the world title), this busy port has its detractors. In *Kingdom by the Sea* (1983) US author Paul Theroux resurrects the clichéd 'mean Aberdonian' while, in *Notes from a Small Island* (1995), Bill Bryson mentions Aberdeen restauraunt stairs 'that looked as if they had recently been used for a motorcycle rally'. Yet the real joke is that *Aberdonians* created the image of the 'mean Aberdonian' – a dry wit characterises the folk of this region where life has never been easy...

2.   Aberdeen Past   *(History)*

Sited as it is between Don and Dee, the meaning of the name 'Aberdeen' may seem obvious. The Brittonic 'Aber' implies a settlement at the mouth of a river, in this case the Dee (Gaelic *deva*, an ancient goddess); and 1900 years ago Ptolemy named the site 'Devana'. Cut and dried? Not quite. Some say *aber-devan* means 'at the meeting of two rivers'. Others argue for *aber-Don* or *aber-Den*, the second after the Denburn, now mostly built over.

Of two early settlements, 'Aberdon' or 'Aulton' (*allt-ton*; 'village by the stream'), now Old Aberdeen, was a Donmouth Pictish church community made a burgh of barony in 1494 – the name 'Old Aberdeen' arose when anglicising map-makers confused the Gaelic *allt* with the Scots *auld*. As for 'Abirdeon', this merchant community sited near the modern city centre was made a royal burgh by David I (1124–53) and chartered by William the Lion *c*.1171. Isolated from the rest of Scotland by mountain and sea, by then the burgh already traded salted fish, wool, hides and meal with Europe. The first town centre was the Shiprow by the waterfront, but by the 13th century for greater security it was moved to the Castlegate, now Castle Street, a quarter-mile east of the Kirk of St. Nicholas – protector of sailors and Aberdeen's patron saint.

The city's second oldest kirk, St. Nicholas (01224-643494) is mentioned in 1157, but the site is more ancient. Originally built outside the burgh boundary in the Norman style, and once Scotland's largest parish church, today it is divided in four, St. John's Chapel (partly 12th-century) having been converted into the Oil Industry Chapel. Outside, a doric-columned façade invites entry from the hustle and bustle of Union Street to the peaceful kirkyard.

By Old Aberdeen's Seaton Park and the Don's wooded banks about the Brig o' Balgownie (**4**), is the Cathedral of St. Machar. It's said St. Columba (*c*.521–597) sent Machar from Iona to find, near the sea, a riverbend curved like a bishop's crook, which here he discovered on the Don. So Aberdon became an early Christian centre, David I later transferring to it the see of Mortlach (Dufftown). Begun *c*.1140, the cathedral fell into ruin; the present twin-towered granite edifice (open all year: 01224-485988) dates from *c*.1320, Bishop William Elphinstone's (1431–1514) central tower collapsing in 1688. With its heraldic ceiling and robust design, St. Machar's is solid rather than beautiful.

Chancellor of Scotland, in 1494 Elphinstone also founded King's College in the Aulton, James IV having petitioned Pope Alexander IV for the foundation bull on grounds that in North Scotland were: 'men who are rude, ignorant of letters and almost barbarous'. King's College Chapel (1500–05) followed, remaining (with the Imperial Crown of King's College tower), a splendid example of late Gothic exuberance. And in 1593, George Keith, fifth Earl Marischal (**13**, **100**, **110**), founded the Protestant Marischal College. With its arresting fretted granite pinnacles and facade designed by A. Marshall Mackenzie (**36**, **41**, **49**), the present building on Broad Street (begun in 1844 by Archibald Simpson) was opened by Edward VII in 1906 and, after Madrid's Escorial, is the world's largest granite edifice. So, until 1860, when the colleges merged, Aberdeen had as many universities as all England!

Long gone, Aberdeen Castle was probably a courtyard fort. Dating from *c*.1249, in 1264 it was repaired by Richard Cementarius (Richard the Mason; see **18**), who in 1272 became Aberdeen's first Provost. In 1308, after Robert the Bruce defeated the Comyns at Barra (**64**), Aberdonians massacred the castle's English gar-

12

rison and their password, 'Bon Accord', became the city motto. The grateful Bruce, now Robert I, granted Aberdeen land at Mid Stocket, and in 1320 ordered that the Brig o' Balgownie be built. Paid for by Bishop Cheyne of St. Machar's, in 1605 the Brig Fund was established by Sir Alexander Hay, becoming so well endowed that in 1831 it funded the building of the five-arched Bridge of Don, now carrying the A90 north. As for city bridges over the Dee, earliest and most westerly is the seven-arched Bridge of Dee (1520–27), which daily siphons traffic from Anderson Drive onto the A90 south to Dundee and Perth.

Torched by the English in 1336, Aberdeen was often in the wars. Provost Davidson fell at Harlaw (**65**) near Inverurie in 1411; the Gordons defeated the Master of Forbes at the Craibstane (936056) near the Denburn in November 1571 (**44**); and during the first Bishops' War in 1639 Covenanters led by Montrose took the city, installing a garrison. Later Montrose (**15, 54, 78**) changed sides and, on defeating the Covenanters at Justice Mills (also site of the 1571 battle, now under the streets) in September 1644 his Highlanders ran amuck, slaughtering 'eight score' citizens – an atrocity thought so shocking that, when Montrose was executed in Edinburgh in 1650, his severed arm was sent to Aberdeen and nailed to the Tolbooth door. In 1690, during the rising in favour of the deposed James VII, Highlanders again threatened the city, but General Mackay chased them to Cromdale, routing them there by the Spey. In December 1715 the city fathers unwisely welcomed the Old Pretender: when he fled back to France the Earl of Erroll and George Keith 10th Earl Marischal (**109**) lost their estates. Finally, during the '45 Cumberland billeted his men in Robert Gordon's College (**7**).

3.   Aberdeen Today   (*History, Description*)

Thereafter both 'old' and 'new' Aberdeen grew, expanding north and west and in 1891 uniting. The granite canyon of Union Street (named for the 1801 union of Britain and Ireland) ran west via Union Bridge over the Denburn, now carrying the Inverness railway line. From Union Street's east end after 1800 King Street ran north; from its west end Holburn Street took the road south. Meanwhile the city's granite industry also expanded. Appalling author Lewis Grassic Gibbon (Leslie Mitchell; 1901–35) as he walked by the 'immense granitic monuments' of Allenvale Cemetery, this hard, sparkling stone graced Napoleon III's tomb and Rio de Janeiro docks before demand declined. With 127 quarries in the Northeast in 1900, the greatest was in Aberdeen at Rubislaw (912054; above Anderson Drive and Queen's Road). Before it was closed in 1971 a hole 500 feet deep, now wired off with danger signs everywhere, had been gouged out.

19th century Aberdeen also built clippers like the *Thermopylae* which, racing the Clyde-built *Cutty Sark*, proved itself the world's fastest. Later, the city's fleet of steam trawlers and the railway meant that fish sold at the docks reached Billingsgate in London next morning. Today, failing fish stocks and pollution put this trade too at risk, and the oil business now drives the city's expansion in a way not to everyone's taste.

Since the oil boom began *c.*1970, Aberdeen's house-prices and skyline have soared. Old kirks and colleges are eclipsed by concrete office-blocks and multi-level car-parks. The road system, as elsewhere, is a mess. At peak rush-hour Anderson Drive, part of the city's ring road, is choked, with plans for a new, more westerly bypass on hold. Bland new estates smother the Dee's north bank (**12**), while Union Street's old shops are gone, replaced by banks, building societies and burger joints.

That's the debit side. Yet Aberdeen has more to offer than the shopping malls and leisure facilities of any city its size – theatres, galleries, museums, old kirks and restored historic houses. As if to make up for so much dreary weather, the city is enriched by its parks and gardens, from Union Terrace Gardens to Seaton Park (**4**) in Old Aberdeen and, by the Dee, Duthie Park with its celebrated Winter Gardens (**6**). Even Anderson Drive is planted with roses. How they cope with the exhaust fumes is anyone's guess.

Starting at the Castlegate, Aberdeen's historic centre, the following tour avoids most of the city centre. The information centre (St. Nicholas House, Broad Street; 01224-632727) will fill you in but, in brief: Aberdeen Art Gallery (Schoolhill; 01224-646333) displays work old and new; Aberdeen Maritime Museum (Provost Ross' House, Shiprow; 01224-585788) presents exhibitions and events relating to the city's marine heritage, and the Gordon Highlanders Museum (St. Luke's, Viewfield Rd., 01224-311200) commemorates this famous regiment. Provost Skene's House (Flourmill Lane; 01224-641086) recreates 17th and 18th century period style, as does James Dun's House (Schoolhill; 01224-646333), while the steep-staired Tolbooth Museum (01224-621167) near the Mercat Cross in the Castlegate presents the city's civic history.

Once the main approach to the castle, the Castlegate has been Aberdeen's hub since at least the 13th century. Sited at the top, east end of Union Street, its focus is the 1686 Mercat Cross, an open-arched hexagonal burgh cross placed here in 1842. With the site of the old castle occupied by high-rise flats, Virginia Court and Marischal Court, nearby stands the neo-baronial Salvation Army Citadel (1896), its tower commanding views over the Castlegate and west along Union Street's one-mile length of modern city centre traffic congestion.

Yet not very far away a much older and quieter world may be found...

4.   Round Old Aberdeen   *(Walk)*

With Justice Street then Beach Boulevard running east to the beach-front Esplanade (**5**) from the Castlegate, also from the Castlegate the old 'Spital Brae' leads north to Old Aberdeen. Start west up Union Street and at Broad Street turn right past Marischal College's fantastical façade. Continue up Gallowgate, King's Crescent and College Bounds to the High Street's university buildings. Students come and go, but here in the Aulton the Cathedral, the Chanonry, crown-topped King's College, King's College Chapel and other peaceful nooks and crannies endure, though besieged by concrete and steel. With its high Gothic exterior, carved oak rood screen and other fittings, the Chapel is especially impressive.

At the top of High Street, cross St. Machar Drive and walk up the walled, tree-shaded old Chanonry to St. Machar's Cathedral (see **2**).

Alternatively, drive or take a bus from Castlegate up King Street and past King's College to the vast College of Agriculture. Here, turn left onto St. Machar Drive, which cuts through the Aulton to the Great Northern Road (Inverness A96). 300 yards up St. Machar Drive, opposite the top of High Street by Old Aberdeen Town House (1788), turn right up the Chanonry. Park on the Chanonry or by the cathedral, as you can.

From St. Machar's start east along the doglegging Chanonry, turning south past Dunbar Hall of Residence. The high-walled brae descends under under crow-stepped gables to cobbled Don Street. Turn left (north) up Don Street past a right turn onto Cheyne Road to the outer wall of Seaton Park and a junction. Here a right turn to King Street and left up this busy road leads to Bridge of Don. Just before it turn left on a wooded riverbank path (Donmouth Local Nature Reserve) half a mile to the Brig o' Balgownie. Or, preferably:

At the junction mentioned above keep left up the Seaton Park wall, not far, to park gates. Once in the park turn right, then right again onto a wooded, climbing path by the wall and railings flanking Don Street. Just past a fine walled garden amid rich shrubbery above the park's broad flat haugh, turn right down steps to a sunken tarmac cycleway, this below Hillhead Halls of Residence. Turn right up this track back to Don Street, rejoining it at Seaton Stables and following it north past the halls of residence. Then descend the wooded brae past Cottown of Balgownie's restored old houses to the narrow, 14th-century Brig o' Balgownie (see **2**), its buttresses and single pointed arch spanning the wooded gorge above a dark river-pool.

Sited at the east end of the Don's last steep-banked, crook-shaped bend, from each end of the bridge (pedestrians only) paths descend through tangled trees to the riverbank, allowing further exploration.

Here young Lord Byron (**77**), a fatherless only child riding his pony, shuddered at an ancient prophecy of Thomas the Rhymer (**78**), that from the Brig o' Balgownie should fatally fall: '*...a wife's ae son/And a mare's ae foal.*' Later at the Linn of Dee (**40**) the future poet almost *did* fall fatally, but survived to fall instead for the fast life for which he became notorious.

Having contemplated this lovely if indefinably dreich spot, return 50 yards up the Don Street brae to an iron gate in the Seaton Park wall. Through it follow the top of the wooded riverbank west, below the halls of residence and round the horseshoe bend, now bearing south under fine old beeches. The path descends to a flat riverside haugh, Kettocks Mill visible the far side of the brown stream, St. Machar's twin spires soon visible above the trees ahead. Follow the river until, by a carpark, it bends west. Here, keep left up to a gate by St. Machar's, or turn right past the carpark on a rough riverbank path and, where this fades, climb left up to Tillydrone

Road. Turn left, then left again down a cobbled lane past the Wallace Tower, a 1616 Z-plan tower house resited here in 1963; and so back to St. Machar's.

This easy, attractive circuit is about three miles.

5.   To Footdee & Girdleness   *(Route, Walk)*

Facing the docks at the mouth of the Dee, Footdee (*Fittee*) is – or was – a fishing village of terraced houses designed in 1808 by the city architect, John Smith. From the city centre it's reached via quayside roads or by the Esplanade.

From Old Aberdeen and St. Machar's, follow the Chanonry back to St. Machar Drive and turn left over King Street onto School Road. At the edge of King's Links, turn south on what is now Golf Road to Pittodrie, home of Aberdeen FC. By the golf driving range turn left up to the Esplanade's broad curve and its 360° panorama – south over Aberdeen Bay to Girdleness Lighthouse (972053), east past anchored ships and out to sea, north past Donmouth up the miles-long beach to Newburgh Bar (**73**), and west over the city skyline of tower blocks and church spires. Continue south past the ice rink, Beach Leisure Centre and Codona's Amusement Park down to Footdee. Turn left down New Pier Road, then right to park at the end of Pocra Quay. Here by gas tanks and anchored ships, there are fine views of Victoria Dock, Albert Basin and the mouth of the Dee.

To visit Girdleness on the south side of the estuary, return up New Pier Road and turn left then immediately right up York Street. Take York Place or Wellington Street left to Waterloo Quay, following the busy waterfront via Regent and Trinity Quays to Market Street, just short of the railway station. Here turn left past the docks and over the Dee via Victoria Bridge into Torry, a grimly functional suburb of which Aberdonians say, if hit by hard luck, 'I dinna come fae Torry onywye.' It's clear what they mean. Now follow the curve of canyon-like Victoria Road east, past Torry Research Station, to its junction with St. Fittick's Road. Here, with the sign indicating St. Fittick's Road currently half-hidden by overgrowth, bear sharp left down the lane to Greyhope Road above the estuary.

Turning right (east), and now under Balnagask Golf Course with clear views over the estuary to the clanging docks and city beyond, follow Greyhope Road to a left turn up to a carpark by ruined Torry Battery (964056). Built in 1860 against the threat of invasion by the French under Napoleon III, bombed during World War II (five men were killed), it was last manned during the Suez crisis of 1956 and largely demolished in 1958.

From here (with other carparks further on), drive or walk a three-mile circuit round the lighthouse. A shoreline path rejoins the road just before the lighthouse, beyond which the road curves west above Nigg Bay, descending to St. Fittick's Road. Here, still by the windswept golf course, turn right past a ruined kirk on open heath to the left – presumably St. Fittick's. Past housing to the left the road rises over a crest to a fork. Here the left turn is not a continuation of St. Fittick's Road, but Victoria Road, bearing west back past Torry Research Station into Torry. The lane continuing ahead is St. Fittick's Road.

Descend to Greyhope Road and turn right, back to the carpark.

6. Duthie Park & Beyond *(Routes, Short Walks)*

If roses are your game, then Duthie Park's the name. With its ponds and pagoda, obelisk and Celtic memorial cross, this neat small park on the north bank of the Dee off Riverside Drive and in the heart of the city offers two unique attractions – the 'Mountain of Roses', a sculpted knoll in summer ablaze with the blooms of over 100,000 bushes and, by it, the Winter Gardens, where tropical exotica flourish all year round (as shown in the photo at the end of this section).

Erected in 1899 and reopened in 1970 after 1969 gale damage wrecked the old glasshouse roofs, today the Winter Gardens extend over two acres under glass arcades surrounding an open central square and courtyards. These feature hardier northern plants not requiring the warm equatorial damp of the exotica which, maintained in the hothouse corridors, offer year-round pleasure, especially when the winter blues get you down. And it's all free. To find towering Jurassic ferns, bright tropical tree-parasites, terrapins swimming in bubbling warm pools, cacti and carp and a Japanese Garden, you don't have to visit the Amazon or Africa – Aberdeen, improbably, offers similar wealth.

A mile south of Union Street, from the city centre Duthie Park is reached via Holburn Street and Great Southern Road, which cuts through it. From Torry and Victoria Road, cross the Dee and turn left, following North Esplanade West over the roundabout by Queen Elizabeth II Bridge, and so onto Riverside Drive. Or, in Torry, turn left off Victoria Road along Menzies Road to a roundabout. Bear right over the Dee via Queen Elizabeth II Bridge, turning left on Riverside Drive.

Sited by a bend in the Dee, Duthie Park has plenty of parking-space. The Winter Gardens are reached by crossing its lawns.

Now, as we start out of Aberdeen, a *caveat*: the next few chapters are dense with route-directions for folk unfamiliar with the city and surrounding area. Those who know their way about, please bear with me, or simply skip.

Continuing west over Great Southern Road past King George VI Bridge and the long narrow riverside green popular with dog-walkers, where Riverside Drive nears Bridge of Dee turn right to Holburn Street, then left to the roundabout north of the bridge.

Here, for the A90 south to Stonehaven (**13**), or the South Deeside B9077 to Banchory (**21**), turn left over the Dee. For Garthdee Road and Inchgarth Road west past the Scott Sutherland School of Architecture and Gray's School of Art to Cults (*Coutts*: **12**) and the North Deeside A93 west to Braemar (**38**), continue over the roundabout. For routes further north and west, turn left up Anderson Drive. This ring road rises north past St. John's Terrace (A93 west) and Queen's Road (B9119 west to Alford; see **11**); crests at Lang Stracht (A944 west to Alford); then descends to a roundabout above the Don.

From this roundabout the Great Northern Road/A96 breaks northwest through Bucksburn past Dyce (**7**) to Kintore (**8**) and Inverurie (**62**). Over it from Anderson Drive the Parkway continues the ring road, crossing the Don via Persley Bridge then climbing east to the Ellon Road (A90 north towards Peterhead; **110**, and Fraserburgh; **100**).

Now follows an outline of these routes, the land immediately outside Aberdeen that they cover, and description of several rural walks near the city.

7.   Leaving Aberdeen: North by Northwest   *(Routes)*

Starting with the northerly route: from the Castlegate King Street bisects Old Aberdeen before as the A956 it crosses Bridge of Don. Rising past the Exhibition Centre and taking up the Parkway ring road, now become the A90 dual carriageway it leaves Aberdeen past Denmore Industrial Estate. Shedding the B999 west to Tarves (**72**), it enters rolling open land and sweeps past Balmedie (pop. 1253) and Balmedie Country Park. Reverting to two lanes, west of the Balmedie Beach dunes it bears inland. Six miles north of Aberdeen the Cruden Bay/Peterhead A975 breaks right through Newburgh (**73**) and over the Ythan past Forvie National Nature Reserve (**74**). The A90 continues north past the hamlet of Foveran and over the B9000 (right to Newburgh, left five miles to Pitmedden: **72**). Bypassing Ellon (**75**) and shedding the A952 north through Buchan via Mintlaw (**105**), it continues to Fraserburgh via Peterhead through a bare land redeemed by huge skies.

From King Street, the A96 route northwest follows West North Street, Powis Place, Powis Terrace, and Great Northern Road. Crossing the Anderson Drive/Parkway ring road at the roundabout above Persley Bridge, as Auchmill Road it enters Bucksburn. At the first traffic lights in this industrial and residential sub-urb, the road forks. The Inverurie-bound A96 continues west (**8**); the Oldmeldrum A947 breaks right (north).

18

Passing through Stoneywood and Dyce east of Aberdeen Airport, the A947 sheds Dyce Drive, which loops west and south through Kirkhill Industrial Estate past the airport entrance to meet the A96 a mile west of Bucksburn. Crossing the Don and wriggling under a disused railway bridge past the B977 to Hatton of Fintray (see below), the A947 continues north through Newmachar (pop. 1755), an exposed village with a 1791 parish kirk, then swings west past Straloch House (860213).

Hidden amid its wooded policies and built in 1780, the house occupies land chartered to Henry Cheyne in 1348. Bought by the Gordons of Pitlurg near Glass (**83**) in 1600, here lived 'the Great Straloch', cartographer and historian Sir Robert Gordon (1580–1661), the first graduate of Aberdeen's Marischal College (**2**). His son John (c.1615–86), minister of Rothiemay (**83**), compiled surveys and maps of Edinburgh and Aberdeen; and his grandson founded Aberdeen's Robert Gordon's College – a busy family!

Four miles beyond Straloch, amid nondescript open land the A947 meets the A920 from Pitmedden, this just short east of Oldmeldrum (**64**).

Backtracking, from the A947 the wooded bank-top B977 follows the Don west four miles before bending south past Hatton (*Hall-town*) of Fintray's 1821 parish kirk. Named after a hall and grange erected here c.1200 by the Abbots of Lindores in Fife, the hamlet has that tranquillity so often found at old monastic sites. From it the B977 breaks west three miles to Kintore (**8**) or five miles to Inverurie (**62**). Continuing south, the B979 crosses the Don at Boat of Hatton then, bridging the railway, in another two miles enters Blackburn (pop. 1171) by the A96.

Just south of the railway a lane breaks left (east) up a wooded slope to a junction (834145). The left turn continues east above railway and river then descends to Dyce Drive (above). The right turn follows the western slopes of the Hill of Marcus and Tyrebagger Hill, both forested higher up, then drops to the eastern roundabout of the A96 Blackburn bypass. Here, with traffic roaring down from the crest of the ridge between Bucksburn and Blackburn, a left turn uphill leads, in a mile, to carparks for walks up Tyrebagger Hill north of the A96; and Elrick and Brimmond Hills south of the road.

8.   Tyrebagger Hill & Beyond   *(Route, Walks)*

Continuing west through Bucksburn past Kepplehills Road (see **10**), the A96 reaches a roundabout. Here a left turn up Hopetoun Grove (signposted to Forrit Brae) climbs to Eastside of Craibstone (880102), where another left turn leads west over a back-road city 'bypass' (**10**) at Newhills, and on to a junction at Ashtown. Here, two miles from Bucksburn, a left turn up a brae wooded one side soon brings you to a Brimmond Hill carpark (859101; see **9**).

Leaving Bucksburn, in a mile a right turn at the next A96 roundabout leads via Dyce Drive to Aberdeen Airport. Continuing west past Craibstone Agricultural

College, in another mile a left turn to Newhills/Kingswells is the start of the 'bypass'. Beyond it, the A96 climbs to a wooded crest under Tyrebagger Hill. Just before the crest turn right onto the eastbound lanes, looking out for fast oncoming traffic. In a few yards turn left (north; signposted Kirkhill Forest Wayfaring Course) to a carpark. Here amid the pines a laminated map outlines cycle and orienteering routes, also walks waymarked orange and white. The latter, to the tower atop this broad low (844127; 820ft; 250m) forested hill, is the longer.

I cannot describe either, having sought my own circuit through this mostly viewless forest via confusing unmarked trails. These demand a compass, and the walker should watch out for mountain bikers – I was almost hit by one. On a steep and rocky pine-knotted path he sped by inches away, bounding from root to root, kamikaze-style. Nor are these paths quiet. On the final stretch the noise was incredible. Half-glimpsed A96 traffic roaring, planes bellowing, helicopters clattering, fellow-strollers barking at their dogs. There was a brief view south to Brimmond Hill's radio mast-capped top – but, on the whole, Tyrebagger Hill is about as peaceful as the interior of the garage its name suggests. Still, there's better to come...

Just beyond the A96 turn to the Kirkhill Forest carpark, on the left a turn leads to Elrick Hill and Brimmond Hill. First, though, let's look at the continuing road past Blackburn to Kintore.

Until 1999, the A96's token strip of dual carriageway ended just east of Blackburn. The next six-mile stretch to Inverurie usually involved 80 vehicles crawling behind tractors both ways, through Blackburn past the B994 to Kemnay (**59**), and then through Kintore. Now Blackburn, a ribbon of housing where the B979 from Hatton of Fintray joins the old A96, is bypassed by dual carriageway, as is Kintore (pop. 2247).

At the edge of the ancient earldom of the Garioch (**61**) and sited on easily-flooded Donside haughs, Kintore became a royal burgh in 1190, but was later over-shadowed by Inverurie, three miles away, and from which a Neolithic processional causeway ran to Kintore's Castle Hill. With the site of a Roman marching camp nearby (786164; see **16**), a mile to the south is the ruined 14th century tower of Hallforest Castle (777154), once a Keith (Earls Marischal) stronghold; and two miles north over the Don is Balbithan House (813188) a harled three-storey 17th century L-plan towerhouse. Bisected by the long dogleg of School Road and Northern Road, which between them until lately carried the A96, Kintore itself is notable for the external double stairs of its Town House (*c*.1740).

Beyond Kintore the landscape is dominated by the Mither Tap of Bennachie (**68**) – the first outcrop of the Highlands and Aberdeenshire's most potent landmark.

But there's a way to go yet before we get to Bennachie...

9.   Elrick Hill and Brimmond Hill   (*Walks*)

Offering panoramic views, this six-mile circuit includes easy climbs up both hills, plus forest walks and a 'Sculpture Trail'. The circuit can also commence from the

Brimmond Hill carpark (see **8**), or be shortened to include just one hill or the other, or adapted to include low-level forest rambles (via the Sculpture Trail or the Four Hills Walks; see below).

From the crest of the A96 and almost opposite the Kirkhill Forest turn the B979 (Kirkton of Skene 4) departs southwest. Follow it into dense forest past a carpark on the left to the main roadside carpark (850111). Start east up the way-marked Sculpture Trail, bear right at the first fork, curve downhill, then cut right (south) over a burn (brown and yellow waymarkers). Climb a rocky path (brown), keeping left, to Elrick Hill's open heather slope. Where the now eastbound path levels off, take the second (brown) fork on the right, uphill to the summit copse (850103; pictured below from Brimmond Hill) with its fine views.

With Brimmond Hill (855092; 873ft; 266m) ahead, descend Elrick Hill's steep, ferny south slope via concrete steps to a small carpark. Continue up the track over a back road to overgrown steps above which, through gorse and fern, the path crosses a stile onto Brimmond Hill's grassy slope. With Bennachie to the west and Hill of Fare (**23**) southwest beyond Kirkton of Skene (**11**), climb diagonally left of the summit radio mast. At the pasture's fenced crest, cross a gate left (a stile not far below) to the service road. Past an adjacent gate, climb the road to the summit with its broad views east over Aberdeen, south past Westhill (**11**) and Kingshill Wood to Deeside, the distinctive nub of Clachnaben (**22**) beyond, and southwest along Brimmond Hill's heathery whaleback.

A path follows this southwest ridge to a carpark (845087) on a back road near Westhill: from it longer circuits may be worked out.

Return northeast down the service road to the back road crossed earlier, and at the junction is the carpark (859101; **8**) above Ashtown as previously described. Cross the road to a kissing gate signposted to the Four Hills Walk. The path beyond descends the edge of the wood north to a short track joining open ground currently

21

being converted into a golf course. Bear left just inside the wood past Greenwelltree (856105) and a path to the right. Where the path forks by a burn, keep right of the burn to the next fork. Here turn left over the bridged burn (brown/yellow way-markers) past a track on the left to a signposted path, also on the left. Follow this west through mature woodland back to the carpark.

The cranes seen to the west on the first part of the Elrick Hill climb belong to Sparrow's Offshore Training Centre, the lane to it climbing from the southern end of the carpark. Via paths beyond this yard and by passing under Clinterty Home Farm (844104), you *can* circle the west side of Elrick Hill, gaining an overgrown path to the minor carpark (see above) on the south side – but the route smacks of privacy and involves fence-straddling, gorse and other obstructions.

10.   Back-Road Bypass & Forest Walks   *(Route, Walks)*

If driving, say, from Stonehaven (**13**) to Huntly (**80**) there are various ways to avoid Aberdeen and the crawl up Anderson Drive to the A96. Furthest out is the Slug Road (A957: **16**) from Stonehaven to the Deeside A93 at Crathes (**20**). Closer in, the B979 crosses the Dee at Milltimber and continues north from Peterculter (**12**). Closer still, and here described north to south, is the route via Newhills, Kingswells, and Countesswells to Bieldside or Cults on the A93, where a left turn west leads to the B979 at Milltimber. This route also offers access to several forest walks.

From the A96 a mile west of Dyce Drive turn south on the minor road sign-posted Newhills/Kingswells. Descending past ruined St. Mary's Chapel, this turns hard right past Chapel Farm and a wooded lane signposted 'Four Hills Walks – West Woods'. The busy brae climbs a mile past a right turn to Ashtown and Brimmond Hill, crosses the Ashtown-Hopetoun Grove road (**8**) to Bucksburn, then descends past a cemetery and left to a junction at Holmhead (874093). The continuing road returns via Kepplehills Road to Bucksburn; the right turn south passes west of Kingswells, a green belt housing estate with fields either side. Crossing the Denburn, it meets the A944 west to Alford and Donside.

Over the roundabout and now climbing south through farm and woodland, the continuing Cults (two miles) road descends to a rural junction at Countesswells (871043). Just before it, opposite Loanhead a carpark (869046) gives access to way-marked walks through conifer and mixed woodland – short, level circuits.

At the junction (opposite the drive to Countesswells House) turn right then left to forest walks at Foggieton (869038), a mile north of Bieldside. By Countesswells golf course, these too are short walks through mixed woodland. At Rotten O'Gairn (852045), a mile west of the Foggieton turn, is a short walk amid conifer woodland. Beyond this point the minor road runs west to join the B979 between Westhill (**11**) and Peterculter.

Turning left (east) at the Countesswells junction, the road descends past a junction with Countesswells Road, continuing south to Cults and the A93, so completing the 'bypass'. Turn right (west) three miles to cross the Dee at Milltimber.

Meanwhile tree-shaded Countesswells Road runs east by Hazlehead Park two miles past Robert Gordon's College playing fields before, as Seafield Road, meeting Anderson Drive south of the routes west to Alford and Donside.

11.   The Road to Alford   *(Routes, History)*

For the more northerly of these routes west, from Anderson Drive follow Lang Stracht past the industrial estate and out of the city. Just east of Kingswells the road (now A944) bends south over the Denburn to take up the B9119.

For the B9119 ('Highland Tourist Route to Inverness'), two roundabouts south of Lang Stracht turn west off Anderson Drive onto Queen's Road. Past the Hill of Rubislaw (**2**) follow this tree-shaded avenue past Hazlehead Park (Alford 23) into open country.

Two miles beyond Kingswells roundabout (Cults left, Bucksburn right: see **10**) is another roundabout. Here the B9119 (to Echt, Torphins and Tarland) diverges left four miles to Garlogie, site of an old woollen factory, where the B9125 breaks southwest to Banchory (**21**). A few yards along the B9125 a rural left turn leads to Cullerlie Stone Circle (784042). On flat ground south of the Leuchar Burn, within the older Bronze Age circle are eight inner circles of kerbed rubble. Folk were cremated here, probably (as at Daviot: **66**) long after the circle's real or original purpose was forgotten. This lane continues south past a right turn to Drum Castle (**18**), joining the A93 west of Peterculter (**12**).

From the roundabout the Alford A944 continues through Elrick and under Westhill (pop. 9260). On south-facing slopes with Deeside views, Westhill Garden Suburb (1972) is one of the oil boom's more attractive legacies. With hills ahead, the B979 departs south (Peterculter 4), then north to the A96 through Kirkton of Skene, its parish kirk dating from 1801, and part of the barony Robert I granted Robert Skene in 1318. Held by Skenes until 1827, one of Robert's descendants was a notorious warlock who allegedly drove his carriage over the frozen Loch of Skene, a placid stretch of water now skirted by the A944.

Between road and loch, a towerhouse lodge guards the two-mile driveway to grandiose Dunecht House (751078). Begun in 1820 for William Forbes, in 1845 it passed to the Lindsays, whose Lancashire coal-field wealth led to extensive additions. In 1880 Lord Lindsay's body was stolen from a vault under the huge barrel-vaulted chapel. Building work ceased and the estate was sold, its purchase in 1912 by Lord Cowdray (**15**) leading to further elaborations.

West of the loch and past the entry to Skene House (766098), an old tower-house converted into a baronial mansion in 1850, the A944 intersects the hamlet of Dunecht. Here a staggered minor crossing carries the B977 north, past a left turn to Castle Fraser (**58**), to Kintore (**8**); and south to Echt past the rounded Barmekin of Echt (725072; 899ft; 274m). Within five concentric lines of defence, the large Iron Age fort (**51, 68, 69**) crowning this hill is reached via the track running west from the road past Upper Mains.

Beyond Dunecht the A944 courses wooded land past lanes turning north to Monymusk (**58**) and Kemnay (**59**), and south to Midmar (**24**). With Bennachie now visible to the north, the road traverses broad flats south of Cluny Castle (688127; private). A Z-plan edifice built c.1600 by a Bell of Midmar, it was rebuilt 1836–40 for Colonel John Gordon of Cluny. Owner of vast local estates and half the Outer Hebrides (from which he cleared 2000 folk), he died rich in 1858. With battlement-ed towers and Graeco-Renaissance interior, the pile reflects the vanity of its owner, who was: 'as eccentric as any member of his family and a good deal less pleasant than most of them' (see **80**).

With the B993 turning south at Ordhead to Torphins (**24**) and Deeside, and the L-plan towerhouse (c.1550) of Tillycairn close to the north, the A944 climbs past the B933 northeast to Monymusk and Kemnay, then from wooded Tillyfourie Hill (**57**) descends to the fertile Howe of Alford, and to Alford (**54**) itself, snug on its Donside haughs.

12.　To Peterculter and Maryculter　　*(Routes, History)*

From Lang Stracht, Anderson Drive descends south past King's Gate, Queen's Road and Seafield Road to traffic lights by the Amatola Hotel. Here the North Deeside Road/A93 to Braemar starts west via St. John's Terrace.

Though leading to the glories of Royal Deeside, the first seven miles of this route consist of housing projects and traffic crawl through suburban Cults, Bieldside, Milltimber and Peterculter, the last being 'rural' Deeside's only industrial community. Here, hidden under the A93 near the Leuchar Burn's confluence with the Dee, paper mills founded in 1750 by Bartholomew Smith still produce high-quality material for luxury publications.

Beyond Peterculter the open country begins at last. The transition occurs where, on shedding the B979 north to Westhill, the A93 crosses Bridge of Culter above the Leuchar Burn. On a rocky shelf of the gorge below is a painted statue of the outlaw Rob Roy Macgregor (1671–1734). Dating from 1926 and the third such effigy, it recalls his flight over the burn after a secret visit to Aberdeen – which happened, though not here. But why spoil a good tale?

With the A93 now rounding Newmill Hill and approaching Drum Castle (**18**), a mile south of the road and above the Dee at Normandykes (829994) is a Roman camp from Agricola's campaign of *c*.AD83. Another is found at Raedykes (**16**) above Stonehaven – our next visit after the south bank run to Maryculter.

From the Amatola Hotel, continue south over Bridge of Dee (**6**) to a roundabout. Here, right of the main A90, the South Deeside Road/B9077 breaks west via Leggart Terrace, reaching open country in half a mile. Though busy with impatient BMWs, this winding, wooded riverside route is paradise compared to the A93.

A mile beyond a side road striking south via the Blue Hill (467ft) to views of north bank suburbia and an indicator identifying remote Cairngorm peaks, the B9077 passes Banchory House (910026), rebuilt amid woodland policies in 1840 by 'Tudor Johnnie' Smith in imitation of extensions he'd made to Old Balmoral Castle (**36**). With a 12th-century motte in the grounds, the house is named after the parish, Banchory-Devenick or Lower Banchory (Gaelic *beannachar*, 'mountainous'?). The town of the same name (**21**) lies 15 miles upstream in the parish of Banchory-Ternan. It was 400 years after the 5th-century St. Ternan that Devenick founded his church at Nether Banchor and, to serve its descendant, in 1837 the parish minister Dr. George Morrison built St. Devenick's Bridge, a suspension bridge connecting the south bank with Cults. Known as the Shakkin' Briggie, in 1958 floods ruined its foundations and it is now unused.

A mile further on in the parish of Maryculter, behind the spire of St. Mary's (884007) is Blairs College, a Catholic seminary set up in 1827 in a formerly Menzies-owned mansion. Dating from 1897, its present buildings house a trove of illuminated manuscripts, early printed books, and historic portraits including a Hilliard miniature of Mary Queen of Scots; 'the Jewel of Blairs'. A chain ferry nearby once crossed the river north to Bieldside; while until *c*.1187 both banks were one territory, Culter. Granted Culter land south of the Dee by William the Lion (1165–1214), the Knights Templar (**20**) dedicated a chapel, long ruined, to their patroness, St. Mary – thus Maryculter; while on the north bank Peterculter got its name from a chapel dedicated to St. Peter.

In another mile and in quick succession the riverbank road passes the wooded entry to Kingcausie (864999), an old mansion house in grounds acquired by the Irvines from the Knights of St. John in 1535; a right turn takes the B979 over Maryculter Bridge (1895) to Milltimber, and a left turn leads to Storybook Glen, a 'Family Theme Park' (01224-732941; March–October). Here the Dee loops north under Peterculter, encircling the meadowland of Templar's Park, now a camp-site with Maryculter House and surviving riverside fragments of the old Templar chapel nearby. Here too (849997) the continuing B979 breaks south past Kirkton of Maryculter over bare high ground 11 miles to Stonehaven, while the B9077 runs on towards Banchory via Kirkton of Durris and the junction with the Slug Road/A957 by Durris Bridge, opposite Crathes (**20**).

13.   To Stonehaven   (*Routes, History, Walks*)

From Bridge of Dee the four-lane A90 sweeps rapidly out of Aberdeen, following the main line railway and jagged coastal cliffs through rough bare farmland 15 miles to Stonehaven (pop. 10,430). Along the way it passes old fisher-towns clinging to the edge of the land – Cove, Findon, Portlethen, Downies and Newtonhill; all with growing populations of folk in love with the vast views out to sea and with the wild, grand, windy coastline itself. From Newtonhill and the Burn of Elsick's deep defile south past the Burn of Muchalls this coastline boasts many evocatively-named stacks and offshore rocks – May Craig, Brown Jewel, Tily Tenant, Long Meg and Red Man among them.

Nearing Stonehaven, the A90 sweeps west round the burgh, *en route* cross-ing the B979 and Cowie Water before running under the Slug Road north to Deeside. South of Stonehaven it forks, the continuing A90 dual carriageway bear-ing inland to Dundee via Brechin and Forfar, the A92 breaking east and following the coast to Montrose.

Alternatively, if crossing the Dee at Milltimber, from Maryculter turn south up the B979. Three miles longer, this lonely high road climbs past old steadings to brief woodland by Netherley – a signpost, no more – where a lane breaks east to Newtonhill. On over bare heath the road passes a minor left turn (866894) west to Raedykes (**16**), then descends under the A90 into Stonehaven.

With its red sandstone buildings overlooking the bay between Garron Point and Downie Point, the town occupies a tableland, Cowie Water to the north and the Carron to the south. The old fisher town of Cowie being originally separate, Old Stonehaven occupied the Carron's south bank about and behind the harbour.

Largely established by George Keith, 5th Earl Marischal (a busy man: see **2**, **100**, **110**), and made a burgh of barony in 1587, in 1600 it became Kincardine's county town. Torched by Montrose in 1645 and in 1651 occupied by Cromwellian troops besieging Dunnottar Castle (**15**), Stonehaven languished. But in 1648 Colonel David Barclay – a Quaker and Covenanter made Governor of Strathbogie the year before – had bought the nearby estate of Ury. Thus began the Barclay con-nection. His son Robert ('the Apologist', for his defence of Quakerism) was a friend of William Penn, founder of Pennsylvania. Returning rich from Jamaica in 1760, the Apologist's grandson Robert 'the Strong' Barclay laid out a new town just east of now-ruined Fetteresso Castle (843856).

A medieval L-plan towerhouse, this Jacobite fortress and Keith shooting-lodge in the Carron valley was sacked by Montrose but rebuilt in 1671. Here in 1715 the Old Pretender stayed incognito. Forfeited to the crown in 1720, like nearby Dunnottar the castle and its grounds were snapped up by the predatory York Buildings Company. Later bought by Admiral Robert Duff of Premnay, in 1808 it was rebuilt, but after World War II declined to ruin. Local lore whispers of a secret tunnel from its grounds to Dunnottar; the same being said of Cumberland House, now no more, where Stinkin' Billy lodged in 1746. It's also said that the burgh's Green Lady haunted both castle and house…

Enriched by the 19th-century herring boom, today Stonehaven's house-hemmed harbour shelters only pleasure craft. On the quay, built of red sandstone and the town's oldest building, the crow-stepped 17th century Tolbooth houses a museum; and at the end of the High Street by the Bridge of Stonehaven are the mercat cross and tall 1790 steeple.

With its pleasant air and dramatic Dunnottar so close, this is a popular resort, its information centre (66 Allardice Street; 01569-762806) open April–October. Both new town and old have an intimate feel. Walk east from the High Street via Dunnottar Avenue then southwest by the A957, and on the right are the Woods of Dunnottar, with walks up to two miles in circuit. Further south along the A957 and before it meets the A90, on the right a lane signposted 'access only' leads to a carpark, also on the right.

Other walks about Stonehaven – to Dunnottar (**15**), ruined Cowie Castle and the cliff-top ruin of the Chapel of St. Mary (885874) – are detailed in Archibald Watt's popular historical guide to the area (see bibliography).

Stonehaven also hosts one of Scotland's three surviving fire-festivals.

14.   Stonehaven: 'The Fireballs'   *(History, Folklore)*

Every Hogmanay Stonehaven celebrates a now-rare custom as local men proceed up the High Street swinging fireballs round their heads. Made of tallow rope and combustible waste held in a sphere of wire netting, this old pagan rite was once intended to ward off Auld Clootie. Similar festivals occur at Lerwick in the Shetlands (the Up-Helly-Aa), where the last Tuesday in January a replica longship is torched, and at Burghead in Moray, where each January 11th the Brochers welcome the old New Year by burning the Clavie (see *Round Moray…*).

Once, such festivals were essential to collective life (see **104**). The greatest was held at Beltane (Mayday), one of the four main annual Celtic festivals. The others were Lugnasad (harvest); Samhain (Hallowe'en); and the lambing festival, Imbolc, early in February. The Beltane (Gaelic *Bealltuin*; 'Bel's Fire', Bel being a British sun-god) celebrated the return of spring. Central to the rite was the kindling of *tein eigin*, 'forced fire' which, taken into every house, was sustained as the hearth-fire through the coming year, the old year's fires being put out the night before. Beltane customs survived in Scotland into the 19th century but are now lost, save in the custom of girls washing their faces in the dawn dew on Arthur's Seat in Edinburgh. Called 'bone-fires' in the Northeast, they were kindled until c.1800

27

(often on May 2ⁿᵈ) by farm workers, who then danced 'southways' round them.

Many reports survive. Before dawn, after putting out the old fires, folk climbed a local hill, playing music to keep evil spirits away. A trench was cut, turf seats set by it and fire-wood or peats put in the trench. At dawn the unmarried girls (hair loose, all knots undone) washed their faces in the dew as, three by three, the youths took turns to whirl a spindle in an oak log until the new fire came. The bone-fire (thus 'bonfire') being lit, folk danced round, crying 'Fire! Fire! Blaze and burn the witches!' To jump three times through the fires or run three times between them, was said to ensure the harvest.

Then the Beltane oatmeal cake was broken and eaten, pieces being thrown to the spirits said to preserve horses, sheep and cattle. In places cakes were rolled downhill at noon: a broken cake meant death or misfortune. Elsewhere, pieces were drawn blindfold from a bonnet: whoever got the charcoal-blackened piece was mock-sacrificed to the fire.

Once, such sacrifices did occur. In the druidic era Beltane was celebrated by forcing criminals or war-captives into a wickerwork cage shaped like a giant man or god, maybe Bel himself. Then this 'Wicker Man' (as in the cult movie) was torched. The more victims burned, the greater (it was believed) the coming fertility; the ashes of the dead being scattered on the soil like Growmore. Christians ended such horror, but then burned so-called witches instead, and in greater numbers; even as in rural areas the symbolic sacrifice continued.

Later the new fire was carried down to houses carrying crosses of rowan or juniper over the door, these put up to reject evil during the hours when the hearth was cold. Cheese and butter, made at dawn by old wives to keep the fairies away, were distributed: more fires were lit and cattle were driven between them to prevent the murrain.

All something to remember the next 5ᵗʰ of November.

15.   Dunnottar Castle   *(History, Visit, Walk)*

A mile south of Stonehaven is a spectacular fortified sea-cliff promontory. On a grassy plateau circled by cliffs 160 feet high, Dunnottar Castle's semi-ruined red sandstone walls, gables and mostly-intact towerhouse occupy an offshore crag connected to the mainland by a sunken narrow tongue of land – St. Ninian's Den. Access requires a steep descent then a climb up the crag to the ruined fortress.

As dramatic as any site in Scotland, Dunnottar early hosted a Pictish fort or *dun* (thus the prefix); the *Irish Annals* for the year 681 recording a siege of *Dunfoithir*. Here in 900 Donald King of Scots was slain by marauding Danes, and 34 years later Aethelstan, the first acknowledged King of the English (as a self-identified nation) also laid siege.

Much earlier, here in the 5ᵗʰ century a Celtic church was allegedly founded by St. Ninian; later in 1276 William Wishart of St. Andrews founded a parish church. Whether as sanctuary or fortress, Dunnottar always mattered.

In 1297 William Wallace slew an English garrison put here by Edward I; in 1336 Andrew de Moray besieged a renewed English presence. Regained by Scots, from the late 14th century the site was owned by the Keiths, who built the L-plan

towerhouse. New work by the Earls Marischal in the 16th and 17th centuries created the 'Palace', also fortifications which held off Montrose (**2, 54, 78**) in 1645 but fell to Cromwellian artillery in 1651–2 after an eight-month siege, Scotland's Honours (royal regalia) and Charles II's private papers having been smuggled to safety.

One tale is that the wife of a local minister and her maid carried them out past the besieging army in broad daylight, having got permission to enter the castle to visit the governor's wife and bring out flax. With Crown, Sceptre and Sword hidden in bundles of flax they fled unsuspected. Another account is that the regalia were lowered by rope down the Castle Rock to an old woman gathering dulse on the shore, and she carried them off hidden in her creel.

Surrendered to the English on 24 May 1652, the castle became a jail in which, in 1685, 147 Covenanters were held in atrocious conditions in the Whigs' Vault. With many dying, in 1689 it was the turn of Aberdeen Jacobites. The 10th Earl Marischal (**109**) inherited the castle, but joined the 1715 Rebellion and so forfeited Dunnottar to the notorious York Buildings Company, which stripped it of its lead. The ruin now belongs to the Cowdray family, and is open to the public (daily 9–6; Sundays 2–5; entry charged).

From Stonehaven you can walk or drive to Dunnottar. If driving, with the coastal back-road from the old town currently closed to southbound traffic due to erosion, take the A957 southwest past Woods of Dunnottar, then turn left onto the

A92 Montrose road, then left again to a small carpark. Follow the footpath east some 400 yards to the castle.

If walking, from the old town climb the brae above the harbour and follow it over the Black Hill to the castle carpark and path. Or, from the top of the brae where the road bends west (878853), bear south over the promontory's open, grassy neck. Past Downie Point the path skirts Strathlethan Bay then cuts over a neck of land west of Dunnicaer (*Dun-na-caer*, 'little hill fort', an offshore stack with a hole from its head to the sea below) and Bowdun Head. Meander on round the cliff-top, or take the direct route. In any event, with the castle ruin prominent ahead over Castle Haven bay, you won't lose your way.

16.   Raedykes & Mons Graupius   *(Route, History)*

The Roman historian Tacitus is taciturn about where Agricola, his father-in-law, fought the battle which, due to a later scribal error, gave the Grampians their name.

Fought *c*.AD83, the Battle of Mons Graupius is the first recorded in Scottish history. Abandoning successful guerrilla tactics (by night they'd almost destroyed the Ninth Legion: the enraged Agricola had called them 'spiritless cowards'), Caledonian tribes under Calgacus ('spearman') faced Roman auxiliaries in open battle and lost. Yet soon enough the Romans withdrew south of the Forth-Clyde line more-or-less permanently, leaving the hard northlands to warrior folk they later called *Picti*, ('painted people': see **67**).

In *The Agricola*, Tacitus has Calgacus declare: *'Battles against Rome have been lost and won before, but hope was never abandoned, since we were always here in reserve. We, the most distant dwellers on earth, the last of the free, have been shielded until today...'*. Did Tacitus *invent* this legendary figure to make Agricola look good? And where was the battle fought? At Durno (**66**) near Bennachie? Under Kempstone Hill northwest of Stonehaven, or at nearby Raedykes? By Sillyearn Hill near Keith in Banffshire? Tacitus says Agricola: 'reached Mons Graupius, which he found occupied by the enemy.' The Caledonian front line was on a plain; behind them: 'other ranks seemed to mount up the sloping hillside in close-packed tiers.' He uses the phrase *summa collium*, 'the top of several hills', which fits Bennachie's long tor-studded ridge. He adds that the Romans had built a camp nearby, which also fits Durno/Bennachie – but says nothing of the Romans crossing a river: the little Urie, between Durno and Bennachie.

Yet a battle *did* occur amid the Roman advance northeast from Inchtuthil in Glenalmond, and they left traces of their marching camps throughout the Northeast – at Raedykes, Normandykes (**12**), Kintore (**8**), Durno, Ythanwells (**71**), Muiryfold by the Knock (**86**), Bellie by Fochabers, Thomshill south of Elgin and, probably, Easter Galcantray in Strathnairn – apparently as far as they got.

Besides Bennachie, the chief contender for the battlesite is Raedykes.

From Stonehaven, follow the A957 three miles northwest. Called the Slug Road because it twists and turns like a slug's trail, it crosses the A90, follows the wall of the Ury estate, then twists over the Cowie Water. A mile on, by a sharp wooded bend over Cowton Burn (838891), turn right up a steep brae to a junction. Bear right, north past South Raedykes. Where the lane bends sharp right, a rutted track continues to derelict Broomhill (845902). Walk this track by the camp's eastern ditch past Broomhill to stony Garrison Hill (628ft) where, 1900 years ago, the legions fortified their 93-acre camp

With a deep broad ditch and turf rampart topped by sharp wooden stakes, this four-sided camp commanded the hilltop and every approach. Yet apart from the ditch, most obvious in the northeast corner, there is little to see – a low bare hilltop, stone dykes, sheep grazing. Imagination is required.

Returning past South Raedykes to the junction above the Slug Road, turn hard right uphill to open moor, past West Raedykes to Nether Aquhollie. Beyond the latter a track breaks right to the upper moor. Up it, by the fence on the left, is the Langstane (824908), a standing stone with Ogham notches down one edge. Named after Ogma, Irish god of eloquence, this Celtic alphabet of the early centuries AD

used horizontal or slanting strokes cut in wood or stone. This stone may have been a boundary-marker, the Ogham incisions stating treaty-terms between tribes. Nobody knows.

Half-a-mile east of the Langstane, near the bare top of Campstone Hill (833906), are four kerbed ring cairns with round inner chambers. Reached from West Raedykes, these 'Druid Circles' far predate the first arrival of Celts (and druids) in Scotland *c.*700BC. Yet, associated with Bronze Age Beaker Folk (*c.*2000BC), they're *young* compared with other cairns, many larger and more complete, as at Clava and Corrimony near Inverness, dated over a millennium earlier.

Back at the Slug Road/A957 turn right,

climbing Durris Forest west of the radio masts atop Carn-mon-earn (1240ft; 378m), then zigzag steeply down past a left turn at Blairydryne (749926), a turn leading west under Mulloch Hill to the Nine Stanes (**19**). From Blairydryne the Slug Road descends to Deeside where, above the B9077 and the Dee, the Slug Road as such departs left towards Banchory as a minor road, and the A957, no longer deemed sluggish, crosses Durris Bridge to Crathes (**20**) and the A93.

Winter Gardens, Duthie Park, Aberdeen (see 6)

Section 2

Royal Deeside

17.   Introduction: By Royal Appointment...

Deeside had been known to early tourists like the Welshman Thomas Pennant (**34**) and to health-seekers visiting the spa at Pannanich above Ballater (**32**) since the later 18th century, but it was the arrival at Balmoral (**36**) in 1848 and their purchase of it in 1852 by Queen Victoria and Prince Albert that sealed the popularity of this beautiful region.

If not for bad Speyside weather it might have been very different. Five years after their first Scottish visit, in 1847 the royal couple came north to Ardverikie by Loch Laggan, with nearby Cluny Castle also in the running as a long-term residence. Yet at Ardverikie that year it rained incessantly while, east of the Cairngorms, the sun shone on Balmoral. When in 1848 they returned, it was to Deeside's drier, more equable climate.

Born 4000 feet high in the Cairngorms at the Wells of Dee on the summit plateau of Braeriach (4248ft, 1296m), from the edge of the Garbh Coire ('Rough Corrie') the infant Dee plunges 500 feet east into the notorious Lairig Ghru (*Lairig Cruaidh*, 'hard pass', or *Lairig Gruamach*, 'gloomy pass'). Under the crags of Ben Macdhui (4296ft; 1309m), it picks up the Lairig Burn from the Pools of Dee at the top of the pass (974014; 2733ft). Running south under Carn a' Mhaim and joined by the Geusachan Burn, it enters Glen Dee, curves southeast over the rocky shelves of the Chest of Dee to White Bridge (022885) and, taking up the Geldie, bends east to the Linn of Dee (062896; **40**).

By now well on its 85-mile way to the sea, here at last it meets the dead-end road from Braemar (**38**). Spouting through a narrow gap under the bridge Victoria opened in 1857, it winds on through broad haughs past Mar Lodge (096899), taking up the Quoich (**41**) and, under Morrone's high ridge at Braemar, the Clunie Water from the south. Still vigorous, by Invercauld House (174924; **37**) it's spanned by Caulfeild's 1753 Invercauld Bridge. Past Balmoral and north of Lochnagar (**34**), next it's joined by the Gairn (*garbh-abheim*; 'rough stream'), its longest tributary. Taking up the Muick at Ballater (**33**), it continues under the fairytale suspension bridge at Cambus o' May (**32**) past Muir of Dinnet by Loch Kinord (**29**). Met by the Tanar near Aboyne (**26**) and winding past Kincardine O'Neil under the three-arched Bridge of Potarch (**24**), at Banchory (**21**) it's joined by the Water of Feugh, its final substantial tributary. Now leisurely, it loops under Peterculter (**12**), and flows on through Aberdeen to the sea at Footdee (**5**).

The Dee has many moods. In its bare upper reaches a wild mountain stream, east of Braemar it twists and turns over grassy haughs and through narrow gorges under forested slopes, until after Banchory the land about opens out. *En route* the views change constantly, from wild grandeur to the intimately lovely. 'If a river flows in Paradise,' wrote angler W. B. Currie, 'it must surely be the Dee.'

True? Let's find out, starting two miles west of Peterculter at Drum.

18. Drum Castle *(Visit, Walks)*

Sited in the parish of Drumoak (said to be Deeside's driest) amid the 117-acre Old Wood of Drum, Drum Castle (974004; National Trust; 01330-811204; open May–Oct., grounds all year) is a mélange of different styles, with Jacobean and Victorian additions to the original Tower of Drum. It could have been a mess – yet, amid broad-leafed lawns, all its parts fit harmoniously. With gardens and woodland walks, it's found by turning north off the A93 on a minor road to Garlogie (**11**; the castle signposted), this just before Mains of Drum. In half a mile turn left into the grounds past the East Lodge.

Dating from *c.*1290 and built as a watch-tower in the Forest of Drum, a hunting-ground of early Scots kings, the square battlemented keep is 70 feet high, and consists of three vast vaults set atop each other. With corners rounded to resist battering-rams and basement walls up to 12 feet thick, from the basement dungeon and store-room (built about a well 18 feet deep), a stair in the wall climbs to the great hall, originally entered by ladder from the ground below. Above it, the 'large hall' has a pointed vault typical of the master mason Richard Cementarius, Aberdeen's first Provost (**2**) – his mark was found on the fabric. On the roof an up-and-down walk runs behind high battlements, niches cut in them to let archers rain arrows on attackers below.

An old rhyme speaks of: *'six great barons of the North:/Fyvie, Findlater and Philorth/.../Pitsligo, Drum and Delgatie.'* (For the others, see **78**, **93**, **108**, **100** and **87**). Until bequeathed to the Trust in 1976, for 653 years Drum had been Irvine-owned, Robert I having granted the Forest of Drumoak to his armour-bearer, William de Irwin. A tradition grew that the laird's first name must be Alexander. So, when the 'good Sir Alexander' Irvine, 3rd Laird of Drum, died in single combat with

a Maclean of Duart at Harlow in 1411 (**65**), his successor and brother Robert changed his name to Alexander.

Timber from Drum was probably used in the roof of St. Machar Cathedral (**2**) in 1435, and in Aberdeen's first large ship (the 'Bon Accord'; 1606). In 1619 the 9th laird, a benefactor of Aberdeen's Marischal College, added a large new house to the tower. Besieged in 1640 during the Civil War by General Monro, in 1644 Drum was plundered by Argyll's Irish kerns, but survived to tell the tale. In 1871 David Bryce redesigned the courtyard and, with an inner floor removed, the old tower became a library. It remains unharled and unadorned, as when first built, and no less impressive for it.

With tearoom, shop and play area, Drum Castle is a popular spot. An SSSI (Site of Special Scientific Interest), the old oakwood, with Deeside's largest winter rookery and sheltering many wildlife species, is carefully nurtured.

A mile further west, above a sharp bend in the Dee the A93 bisects the hamlet of Drumoak, then continues three miles to Crathes Castle (**20**). From Drumoak a lane over the Dee reaches a B9077 crossroads (803974; to Woodlands of Durris). Continue over it to visit the stone circle on Clune Hill, followed by a visit to the Nine Stanes of Mulloch.

19.   Clune Hill & The Nine Stanes of Mulloch   *(Route, Walk/Cycle)*

From Maryculter (**12**) the B9077 follows the Dee west past wooded estates. Where the river breaks north, the road starts over a broad haugh to the crossroads at 803974. Turn left (south), then at the first junction right, past Durris House to another junction (798963). Here keep left up to a third junction by a phonebox (803957). Bear right past a sharp bend over a bridge and park by a main forestry track. Follow this, finally turning right to the top of Clune Hill with its 5000-year-old recumbent stone circle (794949).

Flanked by tall red granite pillars and oriented just east of south, the nine-ton grey granite recumbent was dragged to the top of the hill. Quite a feat, but at Old Keig (**57**), a 53-ton slab was moved 11 miles! One of over 90 unique to the Northeast (see **60**), this circle was already old when, *c.*2000BC, lately-arrived Beaker Folk (**16**) built a ring cairn inside it and another next to it, with further small burial cairns nearby.

Back at the B9077, continue west two miles under a web of hillside lanes to the lovely wooded den at Kirkton of Durris (*door*), over the Burn of Sheeoch (*fairy burn*) and on a mile to the A957 (**16**) at Bridge of Durris, the tower atop Scolty Hill above Banchory (**21**) visible ahead. Here turn left up the A957 Slug Road two miles to Blairydryne (749926: **16**), and right on a west-running lane (Strachan 5). In 100 yards a junction on the right marks the return of this four-mile road-loop. Follow the south-facing lane past Mains of Blairydryne above the Burn of Sheeoch, forested hills beyond, the scenic sweep vast. Now under Mulloch Hill, after two miles

(724912) a belt of forestry mounts to the road opposite a track into dark woodland, not far into it a carpark and picnic area near the Nine Stanes of Mulloch.

Once consisting of eight red granite boulders plus the 16-ton recumbent and its flankers, with one stone lost and another a stump, this circle got its name when excavated almost a century ago – the recumbent was discounted. Why? Probably dating from c.3000BC, the ring is a flattened oval, within it a large ring cairn. Cremated bone, charcoal and pottery were found about the cairn's central pit.

Under the wood past a left turn west down to Strachan (*Straa-an*: **22**) on Feughside, the continuing lane loops north then east round the hill's upper slope. Enjoying fine views of Hill of Fare (**23**) north of Deeside, continue past a left turn to Banchory and, by West Mulloch, another circle (723922). Half-a-mile short of the end of the loop at Blairydryne, a left turn at Standingstones descends northwest through mixed woodland past Tilquhillie Castle (722942); a private, well-concealed 1576 Z-plan towerhouse with a vast central keep. This is an old Douglas property.

From a junction (720945) below Tilquhillie, a sharp right turn descends through pleasant woods over the now-minor Slug Road to the riverside B9077 two miles east of Banchory. Turn right a mile to Durris Bridge, Crathes Castle peeking above trees over the Dee. A left turn over the Dee leads through Crathes to the A93 (Braemar 45). Turn left half-a-mile, then right (north) to Crathes Castle.

Beyond the junction at 720945, the lane descends to the B9077 at the narrow 1790 Bridge of Feugh by the Falls of Feugh (701950). Here from a wire-caged pedestrian bridge over the Feugh's final gorge you can watch salmon leap the falls. By the tollhouse over the bridge turn right (B974) over the Dee into Banchory (**21**).

20.   Crathes Castle   *(Visit, Walks)*

After Balmoral (**36**) Deeside's main attraction, Crathes Castle stands three miles west of Drumoak (**18**) and two miles east of Banchory. From the A93 a mile-long drive winds past woodland ponds and waymarked walks to this 16th-century confection of decorative corbelling, turrets and crowstep gables (734967: National Trust; 01330–844525; open April–Oct., grounds from 9am, castle from 11am).

In 1323 Robert the Bruce granted nearby Drumoak to William de Irwin. With the grant came the hereditary office of King's Forester – an office already given to Alexander de Burnard. So, a month after the grant to Irwin, Burnard got the neighbouring barony of Leys. Saxons encouraged north 200 years earlier by David I (1125–53), the Burnards had long occupied a castle built on an Iron Age crannog (**29**) on the Loch of Leys between Banchory and the Hill of Fare. Not until 1553 did the 9th laird, Alexander (now *Burnett*) hire Bell of Midmar (**24**) to start a masterwork completed in 1594.

If less exuberant than the other great Bell family masterpiece at Craigievar (**55**), this L-plan towerhouse is impressive, especially for its interiors – the vaulted tower-room's bare stonework; ceilings with painted beams portraying mythic heroes, musicians and heraldic devices, each with descriptive texts, vivid and colourful. And there's a mystery here. The Chamber of the Nine Nobles depicts Hector of Troy, Alexander the Great, and Julius Caesar; also Joshua, David and Julius Maccabaeus from the Old Testament; plus the Christian heroes Arthur, Charlemagne, and Godfrey de Bouillon. Each is eulogised in a black-letter rhyme and the series, painted in 1602, ends with:

Gude redar tell me or you pass
Whilk of these myn maist valiant was?

The mystery here may lie with Godfrey de Boiullon, in 1118 co-founder of the Knights Templar. Some connect the arrest in France in 1307 of this proud, secretive order, and the flight from torture of excommunicated Templars to Portugal and Scotland – where, it seems, they gave the excommunicated Robert the Bruce vital aid at Bannockburn – with the later growth of Scotch Rite Freemasonry. The Templars had property in Aberdeen and at Maryculter (**12**); later, when slain at Killiecrankie in 1689 Viscount Dundee was found to be wearing a Templar cross under his armour. Given that the first Scottish lodges date from the very period of this painting at Crathes (built by a master-mason), might it be that the answer to the question in the rhyme is – Godfrey de Bouillon?

Nearby the Chamber of the Nine Muses exalts the classic virtues of intelligence and art (so as to decipher the Nine Nobles?). The Green Lady's Room, as in all the best Scots houses, belongs to the ancestral household ghost – over a century ago the skeletons of a woman and child were found walled up behind the fireplace.

Round the castle the fine woods offer five waymarked trails. Colour-coded pamphlets describe each, from the 4-mile Ley Way to the Viewpoint Trail, which shouldn't take more than half-an-hour. But watch out for the Green Lady!

From Crathes (and the Milton Art and Craft Gallery by the A93 just west of the castle entry), the minor Candieshill road climbs north towards the Hill of Fare via the Mill of Hirn's crow-stepped gables (729995). Subject of Scott Skinner's best-known composition (see **21**) and now a recording studio, this architectural oddity is worth the diversion, as is this lush back-land. A mile further north and past Hirn the road joins the B977, this near the 1951 monument to the 1562 Battle of Corrichie (**23**).

21. Banchory & Scolty Hill   *(Visit, Walk)*

18 miles west of Aberdeen and Deeside's largest community, Banchory (pop. 6539) occupies the Dee's north bank by its confluence with the 20-mile-long Water of Feugh. Snug under forested hills with the bald dome of Scolty Hill (677939; 983ft, 299m) a mile to the south, here the Dee leaves the hills. In the parish of Banchory-Ternan (the kirkyard with its round watch-tower lies south of the A93 on the site of a monastery founded perhaps in the 5th century by St. Ternan), modern Banchory

dates from 1805, and lies not in Aberdeenshire but Kincardine, this because a Burnett of Leys wanted his Crathes Castle lands in the same shire as Muchalls Castle near Stonehaven.

With a small museum and an information centre (Bridge Street; 01330-822000) open April–Oct.), like other Deeside resorts Banchory profits from the royal connection. Here author Somerset Maugham recovered from TB; here too, as commemorated by a tablet in the High Street, lived master-fiddler Scott Skinner (1834–1927), the 'Strathspey King' and composer of 'The Miller o' Hirn'.

Of many walks about Banchory, one offering wide views involves climbing Scolty Hill, high above the forested fork created by the glens of Dee and Feugh.

From High Street cross Bridge of Dee south past the gateway of Banchory Lodge Hotel. If walking all the way, here climb steps up to a lane and turn right. If driving, continue round a bend then turn hard right onto a lane signposted Auchattie/Scolty Hill. This climbs west 600 yards to a fork above the Dee. Bear left up a second fork where a wide unsurfaced track signposted to Scolty Hill continues south up the forested slope to a carpark. Past a pole-gate take the on-going track deeper into Blackhall Forest, gently up and down half-a-mile southwest to a fork (682946). Here keep left, following waymarkers up to a gate (680946). Beyond the gate turn left 200 yards to an indicated path on the right. This climbs through larch

and birch to an open bracken slope, then continues up by fenced forestry to the tree-line. With fine views back over Banchory and the Dee a short further climb gains the tall slender tower at the top.

Visible far and wide, the tower commemorates General William Burnett (1762-1839) of Banchory Lodge. Pausing for the views – north to the Hill of Fare (**23**); east down Deeside towards Aberdeen; south over Feughside to the Mounth and Clachnaben (**22**) – start back via a track west of the tower. Rocky and eroded, this descends over open heather, curling north-west to a junction (675944). Bear right, round the hill's north flank down through scattered silver birch to the gate at 680946, and return as you came. From Banchory the distance there and back is about five miles; from the carpark, about three. In parts the ascent is steep, but no problem if you're reasonably fit.

22. Feughside, Clachnaben & Peter's Hill *(Routes, Walks)*

With its distinctive summit tor, Clachnaben ('stone on the mountain'; 61485; 1900ft, 589m, shown opposite) is eight miles southwest of Banchory and two miles west of the B974 at Bridge of Dye. A there-and-back moorland trek with a final 1000-foot climb, it offers a good introduction to the wilderness beyond. As for the tor, it's said the Devil hurled it at his nagging wife, crushing her under it forever.

From Banchory the B974 follows the Water of Feugh three miles southwest to the village of Strachan, with its primary school, single shop and bungalows. Here the road forks. The B976 continues west up Feughside (see below), while the B974 breaks south over the Waters of Feugh and Dye up wooded slopes past Glen Dye. Continuing over Cairn o' Mount (649806; 1475ft; 450m), it descends past St. Ringan's Cairn and over the Clatterin' Brig 15 miles to Fettercairn. A military road (**45**), in 1296 amid the Wars of Independence this ancient route over the Mounth was used by England's Edward.

Amid forestry three miles south of Strachan, the B974 crests then briefly enters open ground by two cottages on the left. These face a Glendye Estate track (652867) running west towards Clachnaben (pictured opposite). Reach Bridge of Dye and you've gone too far.

Parking where the track starts, follow it west on a wooded slope falling left to a field. Note the 'no feeding horses please' sign on a gate where a dyke begins. Above Glendye Lodge descend to a junction facing open moor. With Clachnaben ahead turn left down the rocky forest-side path past a lodge entrance to an estate noticeboard by a grassy sink. Cross a bridge to a fork (842862) and bear right, following the burn up its glen over Miller's Bog, bald Mount Shade (1662 ft, 507m) to the north. In under a mile the track, now climbing, reaches a stand of conifers. Bear right up the plantation's drier northeast side. Beyond it a rough path crosses a burn to the saddle between Mount Shade and Clachnaben. Turn left to the summit tor. Of solid granite and 95 feet high, it is best climbed from the north, the south side being precipitous, wet and treacherous. Save on Sundays, avoid this walk during the grouse season (12 August–30 Sept).

Returning north on the B974, in two miles a road (650891) breaks left to cross the Feugh at Whitestone. From Strachan the B976 runs west two miles past a medieval motte at Castlehill of Strachan (657922) to the Feughside Inn by Whitestone. Here a right turn climbs northwest between Glack's Hill and the Hill of Tillylair to a carpark (633944: forest walks and mountain bike trails). With fine views up Deeside, this lane descends another four miles to the hotel and 1812 bridge over the Dee at Potarch (**24**).

Beyond Whitestone the B976 crosses pleasant riverside haughs to Finzean (*Fing-an*, 'the fair place') in the wide (31,591 acres) parish of Birse. One laird who lived here was Joseph Farquharson RA (d. 1935), celebrated as 'Frozen Mutton' Farquharson because he specialised in painting snowy scenes featuring sheep, doing so from inside a portable glass-fronted shed!

40

Here the road forks (616925), the B976 continuing northwest to Aboyne (see **26**); the dead-end left turn following Upper Feughside west six picturesque miles to a carpark near Ballochan (524905) in the Forest of Birse. nearby, commanded by Birse Castle (518904; private), the Fungle track from Aboyne crosses the upper Feugh before joining the Firmounth road (**27**) to Glen Esk. Built late in the 16th century by the Gordons of Cluny on land once owned by the Bishops of Aberdeen, by 1800 the abandoned pile was a lair of cattle reivers, but Annie, Viscountess Cowdray, restored it in the 20th century.

A there-and-back walk up Peter Hill (578886; 2023ft; 617m) starts two miles up this dead-end road. Parking at the Sawmill, cross a bridge over the Feugh and take the farm road until, just before Wester Clune, a track branches right to join the shooting road climbing south of the Garrol Burn to the summit. Again, there is no access on shooting days.

23.   The Hill of Fare & Battle of Corrichie   *(History)*

Three miles north of Banchory runs the three-mile, east-west ridge of the forested Hill of Fare and its four tops: Meikle Tap, Greymore, Craigrath and Blackyduds, the latter the highest (1545ft, 433m). Here, about the boggy head of the Burn of Corrichie on the south slope, on 28 October 1562 Lord James Stewart, newly-invested Earl of Moray and half-brother of Mary Queen of Scots, defeated George Gordon, 4th Earl of Huntly (**80**).

In his time Earl of Moray, but stripped of that title in 1550; sometime Chancellor of Scotland and commander-in-chief of the Scottish army; and both

Sheriff and elected Provost of Aberdeen, the powerful Catholic Huntly opposed Mary's acceptance of the Reformation. She already mistrusted him when on 27 August 1562 his uncle, Bishop William, received her in Old Aberdeen. His wild third son, Sir John, had seized Findlater Castle (**93**) from Sir James Ogilvie, and in July had wounded Ogilvie in Edinburgh. Escaping jail, John now lurked at Findlater. Staying away, Huntly sent his wife to Aberdeen to plead with Mary, but Mary demanded that John surrender himself, Findlater and Auchindoun (**52**). Wishing only to enjoy his declining years, the grizzled old man agreed.

John surrendered but, hearing that his Stirling Castle gaoler would be James Stewart's uncle, escaped again. Trailed from the Garioch to Strathbogie by John's men, at Darnaway by the Findhorn Mary invested James as Earl of Moray, then on September 11 was denied entry to Inverness Castle by Huntly's oldest son, Lord Alexander Gordon. Persuaded by his father to open the gates, he was hanged for his pains. Driven away from Findlater, on 12 October Mary had Huntly and his son 'put to the horn' – outlawed.

Making a hasty back-door escape 'without boote or swerde', the ailing Earl raised just 800 men, mainly Gordons. Mustering them at Gordon's Moss near Garlogie (**11**), early on 28 October he faced Moray's larger army, amongst it Forbeses, Leslies and Hays. Forcing the Gordons up the Hill of Fare, possibly near the Meikle Tap (723026), Moray followed via the Vale of Corrichie. Gunfire-raked by mounted arquebusiers, the Gordons fell back to wet ground where, with their horse routed and John captured, in desperation they charged Moray's Lowland pikemen. Driven back to the bog, trapped with over 200 dead, Huntly surrendered. Humiliated, he was led to his captors, where: *'withowte ether blowe or stroke...he sodenlie fawlethe from his horse starke dedde...'*.

Captive, his sons John of Findlater and Adam of Auchindoun accompanied his body to the Aberdeen Tolbooth. Adam lived to wreak mayhem against the Forbeses at Tillyangus (**53**), Aberdeen and Corgarth (**44**) in 1571, but at the Castlegate on 2 October Mary and her court watched the Maiden's spade-sized blade slice off John's head. This primitive guillotine, or one like it, may be seen in Provost Skene's House (**3**).

The Gordon-Stewart feud led to the 1592 murder of the 'Bonny Earl of Moray'; two years later the 6th Earl of Huntly (born 1562) defeated the Protestant Argyll at Glenlivet. Exiled, when in 1597 Huntly returned James enforced marriage between the two families, also a Gordon-Forbes reconciliation, so ending two violent feuds in one.

Today the bog where 200 Gordons died is dense with sitka spruce. By the A977 three miles east of Raemoir (below), a 12-foot-high granite memorial (732014) erected in 1951 by the Deeside Field Club commemorates the battle. The Gordons remained potent but, after Corrichie, the Cocks of the North never crowed so loud again.

From Banchory's Station Road (A93), Raemoir Road (A980 to Torphins) climbs north past a right turn to Hirn (**20**) two miles to a T-junction by the wooded entry to Raemoir Hotel (693991). Here a left turn west on the Torphins A980 passes ruined Cluny Crichton Castle under the Hill of Fare. From Burnhead (687003) above the ruin a track climbs the hill, but I'm told that walkers may get a cool reception if met by the estate rangers.

From the junction the B977 runs east past the Corrichie memorial and under the wooded Meikle Tap three miles to a Y-fork (743021). Here turn north, past the start of tracks up the Meikle Tap, to the crossroads hamlet of Echt, and at Echt turn west on the B9119 (Tarland 18) through the pleasant old land of Midmar. With the Barmekin of Echt and the track (**11**) to its summit fort a mile to the north, this road runs west through farmland under the northern flanks of the Hill of Fare.

Under two miles west of Echt a farmtrack on the right leads towards Sunhoney stone circle (716056). Surrounded by ash, pine, maple and beech on a hillside northwest of the steading, this consists of nine stones about two flankers and the fallen, partly-broken recumbent; on it 31 cup-marks, maybe representing lunar observations. Within a later central ring cairn (see **11, 19, 60, 66**) cremated bone and the remains of a pyre have been found.

Next, south of Midmar Inn and the road, with all but its topmost towers hidden amid woods cloaking the Hill of Fare (amid them tracks up the hill), is Midmar Castle (704053; private). Designed probably by George Bell, this 16th-century Z-plan towerhouse is among the best by the Aberdeenshire School. Full of panache and flair, for over 50 years George and his sons John and David created uniquely exuberant buildings, as also at Crathes (**20**), Craigievar (**55**) and Castle Fraser (**58**).

Just west of the castle entry, with the Cunninghar motte nearby, the roofless, overgrown old kirk lies by the narrow, wooded road. Parking is tricky, but in the kirkyard a stone explains: *HEIR LYIS GEORG BEL, MEASON, DECEISIT IN BAL-OGY ANO 1575.* A few yards on a lane climbs right past the 'new' kirk (699065), its yard dominated by a megalithic circle, the recumbent and its flankers massive, as shown in the photo next page. Continuing past The Millers visitor and retail centre, in three more miles the B9119 crosses the Inverurie-Torphins B993 and continues west to Tarland (**28**) and Loch Kinord (**29**).

Turning southwest past the Hill of Fare on the B993, with mountain ridges ahead the road descends three wooded miles to Torphins (pop.1082), a crossroads village on the A980. Named after Macbeth's cousin Thorfinn Raven-Feeder, or maybe from *torr fionn*, 'white hill', it woke up when the Deeside Railway opened in 1859 and went back to sleep when the line closed in 1960. From it the B993 descends to the A93 just east of Kincardine O'Neil. With the first church here founded by St. Erchard in the 5th century, Deeside's oldest village huddles round the ruin of St. Mary's Church, and though bisected by the A93 retains its charm.

Turning left onto the A93 leads in a mile to the elegant triple-arched Bridge of Potarch (607973), a popular picnic-spot. Built in 1812 near the narrows over which in 1800 the brigand Cyard Young fled from justice (he was hanged a year later), when near complete logs being floated downriver rammed it, so undoing months of work. Over it the B993 enters the parish of Birse, continuing southwest through rich woodland to the B976 three miles east of Aboyne (**26**), while the A93 returns east five miles to Banchory.

25.   Macbeth Country: Lumphanan   *(Route, History)*

From Banchory the A980 climbs seven miles through Torphins, and past Pitmurchie House amid open land soon crosses the Beltie Burn to enter the parish of Lumphanan ('Cell of St. Finan') and the village itself. Here, where the A980 bends north towards Craigievar (**55**; 6 miles) and Alford (**54**; 11 miles) by the Macbeth Arms Hotel, may be found Macbeth's Cairn, Macbeth's Stone, Macbeth's Well and the Peel of Lumphanan.

Little in Shakespeare's play relates to the *real* Macbeth (Maelbaetha or Mac-Bethad, 'Son of Light': King of Scots 1040–1057). He probably never met three witches, was not a tyrant or wife-ridden usurper, did slay Duncan but not at Inverness, and died here at Lumphanan in Mar, not Dunsinane in Perthshire. To portray 'that dead butcher and his fiend-like queen', the Bard plundered the *Chronicles* of Scots 'historian' Ralph Holinshed, which (via Aberdonian Hector Boece's 1527 *History*) were coloured by the long rule of the dynasty birthed by Macbeth's nemesis, Malcolm Canmore ('Great Head' or, as some insist, 'Bighead').

The Canmores had reason to malign Macbeth. Kin of the slain Duncan, they were long plagued by his descendants, the unruly men of Moray.

Macbeth was son of Findlaech mac Ruaidri, Mormaer ('Great Steward') of Moray, named in the *Annals of Ulster* as *ri Alban*, meaning *a* (not *the*) king in Scotland. At odds with the southern House of Atholl, the House of Moray was potent. Born in 1005 near Spynie, or maybe at Dingwall, by birth Macbeth was Thane (*ri*) of Ross, becoming Thane of Moray by marrying Lady Gruoch, daughter of Boedhe, son of King Kenneth IV (995–1003). Another tale is that he slew Duncan then married his widow, 'Dame Grwok'.

At Torfness (Burghead) on 14 August 1040 Duncan fought Thorfinn the Mighty, Earl of Orkney (**92**). Of the House of Atholl, High King since 1034, that year he'd failed to take Durham, and Thorfinn had beaten him at Deerness: he was already in flight. Was Macbeth his general? He was Macbeth's cousin, but so was Thorfinn. Macbeth and Moray men had no cause to support him; and one tradition says the battle was fought to stop Duncan invading Moray. Defeated, he was slain *a suis occisus est* ('by his own people') at Pitgaveny by Loch Spynie, probably by Macbeth. Certainly his three sons fled the land. The 'usurper' ruled successfully, and by 1050 felt safe enough to go on pilgrimage to Rome. Hardly a case of 'uneasy lies the head'. But in 1054 Malcolm Canmore invaded from England and defeated him at Dunsinane, then in 1057 slew him here at Lumphanan.

After he died it was said: 'in his time there was fertility' (*fertile tempus erat*). But later Canmore chroniclers *had* to malign this last Celtic Scots king to be buried at Iona. If not, they'd have been jobless, or maybe headless – like Macbeth after Lumphanan.

Where did he fall? Leaving Lumphanan, the northbound B870 passes the Stothart Memorial Church (1870) on its wooded knoll then, soon after, a copse on a slope east of the road – Macbeth's Cairn (568051); a Bronze Age cist holding bones and charcoal when excavated in 1855. More likely is the Peel of Lumphanan (577037). From the pub take the Deskry/Aboyne road southwest past the old kirk on its mound to the right, below it Macbeth's Well. Outside the village, turn right to the carpark by the Peel (Latin *palacium*, 'palisade') – a flat-topped grassy mound amid earthworks and ditches. With a stone castle atop it built by the Durwards (the king's 'door wards' or ushers) of Coull (**28**), here in July 1296 Sir John de Melville of Raith in Fife submitted to Edward I. Was there a fort here in 1057? It seems the obvious spot for Macbeth's last stand, not least as nearby is Macbeth's Stone, allegedly the site of his decapitation.

Continuing past the Peel to a fork, with fine mountain views the left turn follows the old railway line, then descends to the A93 between Kincardine O'Neil and Aboyne. The A93 west passes the Loch of Aboyne before, in three miles, entering Aboyne itself.

26.   Aboyne & The Fungle   *(Routes, Hill-Track)*

11 miles west of Banchory, 10 east of Ballater (**33**) and well-sited in a loop of the Dee, Charleston of Aboyne (*Ath no fionn*, 'ford of the white cattle'; pop. 2375) owes much to Sir William Cunliffe Brooks, wealthy Victorian owner of 17th-century Aboyne Castle (525995) north of the village. Before his daughter married the 11th Marquis of Huntly, so letting him indulge his 'absolute passion for building and road-making', this had been a small poor place founded in 1670 by Charles Gordon, son of the 2nd Marquis of Huntly and that year made 1st Earl of Aboyne in reward for his Royalist loyalties. It lay amid richly-wooded land, but there had been no easy way to move the timber until in 1732 the Countess of Aboyne established a sawmill, so that in 1797 her name was given to an Aberdeen-built boat constructed entirely of Aboyne oak.

With broad leafy streets and the vast triangular Green of Charleston which every September hosts the Aboyne Highland Games inaugurated in 1867, Aboyne's northern edge is defined by the A93 which, halfway through the village, is met by the B9094 from Tarland (**28**) five miles to the north. Bisecting the village, the road south from this point bridges the Dee to join the B976 at Birsemore, seven miles northwest of Finzean (**22**).

From Finzean, the B976 climbs northwest under Glack Hill and Tom's Cairn to a 745-foot-high forested crest on Corsedardar Hill (595940). Here, left of the road near the large war memorial erected to the men of Birse and Finzean, is the Corsedardar Stone, a granite monolith broken during the road-making. Clamped together and replaced on its original site, it's said to mark where, in AD81, rebellious nobles seized, beheaded and buried the Pictish tyrant king Dardanus.

Beyond it the B976 descends over the Burn of Cattie and through the scattered hamlet of Marywell to meet the B993 from Bridge of Potarch (**24**), this amid a wooded strath. From Marywell a lane breaks south to Ballogie House (1856), beyond which tracks climb the moors towards the Forest of Birse and Feughside. With the dome of Morven (**31**) to the northwest, a left turn off the continuing B976 leads to Birse Church, a St. Michael kirk containing the Crusader's Stone, a grave-slab sculpted with two cross-hilted swords.

Next, with Aboyne now visible ahead, the last left turn before the riverbridge runs south past Birsemore Loch. At a lochside crossing the right turn follows the edge of the loch under half-a-mile to the Fungle Road. Further on, other tracks break southwest round Birsemore Hill's wooded flanks, in time also meeting the Fungle.

To reach the Fungle's signposted start from Aboyne, cross the bridge and turn right a few yards to a road rising left. Avoiding turns, follow it to the last house. Beyond this a track runs south a mile through dense woodland above the Allt Dinnie burn to the unusual house at The Guard (519995). In another forestry mile the continuing path reaches open moor, climbing then descending to the head of the Feugh near Birse Castle (**22**). Bear right round its grounds on a rough signposted path.

Getting rougher, this climbs bare hillside above a Feugh tributary burn to a water-shed. Meeting the Firmounth track, it descends to the public road at Tarfside in Glen Esk – a distance of some 14 miles.

27.   Glen Tanar & Baudy Meg   *(Route, Hill-Walk)*

Southwest of Aboyne, Glen Tanar sees the start of the Firmounth Road, another old route over the Mounth. With 5000 woodland acres (a third indigenous and self-seed-ing), the estate offers a visitor centre, waymarked trails, and the start of longer hikes.

This circular seven-mile walk over open high ground demands map, com-pass and appropriate clothing. From the bridge at Aboyne turn right (west) on the B976 a mile to Bridge o' Ess. Here, where the road bends sharp over Water of Tanar, turn left (see **32** for the continuing B976) past a Victorian tower two miles up the scenic glen to a woodland carpark. By the footbridge cross the Tanar to the Braeloine Centre (481965; April–September), where waymarked walks begin – a mile to St. Lesmo's Chapel; two to Knockie Viewpoint or the Fairy Lochan; three for the Old Forest or the Riverside Walk.

Follow the riverside track left over a broad flat haugh to the Chapel of St. Lesmo, sod-roofed and ivy-walled as shown below. On the ruin of the old house of Braeloine, it looks ancient, but was built 1870–72 by Cunliffe Brooks (see **26**). Arriving in Glen Tanar in 1869, first as tenant and later as owner, he employed 250 folk to tend the estate and rebuild its farms, cottages, and Glen Tanar House itself; but the chapel, with deerskin-lined pews and its altar a huge boulder dragged from the Tanar, is what catches the eye.

At a cattlegrid and fork beyond the chapel, bear right (south) to a second fork. Climb left (red and green waymarkers) under Old Scots Pine to a crossing above Glen Tanar House below by the river. Continue past a forestry gate onto the Firmounth which, a board informs, has been in use for over 4500 years. Broad and sandy, it climbs above glen and Fairy Lochs to a viewpoint board identifying wooded ridges and remote hills.

With forest above and bare slopes below, the track leaves Glen Tanar, curving south towards The Strone's (1211ft; 369m) wooded eastern flank. Before reaching it, and where the 1995 OS map shows continuous forest climbing left, the forest ends. Not far beyond (481942), a rough track breaks left (east) up Baudy Meg's bare slope (497937; 1601ft; 488m), a new plantation on the right. Steep at first, this track veers north of east towards older forest, then eases off round the top of it. With bulldozed tracks plunging into it from Baudy Meg's northwest slope, a pine-studded glen opens up below, the bare ridge of Black Craig beyond to the north.

Here, with little but heather and stunted or dead lone pines, there's little to feel bawdy about. Yet the ridged waves of distant forested slopes impress; and the track is fine and high as, closing in on the Black Craig, it reaches a junction (498942) between these two high moorland brows.

Turn left and, in a hundred yards, left again. At the second junction (499944), the OS map shows two tracks and a path dividing. The shortest way back to Glen Tanar is via the path – heather-swallowed, not obvious. Missing it in the pouring rain, instead I took the track north via Black Craig down to forestry on Red Craig where, amid churned ground just before the forestry ends, there is a left turn (494964). Yet again, forestry shown on the OS map has been felled.

This unmapped left turn leads 200 yards west then descends a logged slope to the Glen Tanar estate road east of the river (488963). Turn left past a pine-wooded lochan and the descending track from the path I missed, and so back to the fork above St. Lesmo's Chapel. Keep right past the chapel andso back over the Tanar to the carpark.

28.   North of Aboyne: Cromar and Culsh   *(Routes, History)*

To the north from Aboyne the B9094 Tarland road climbs past Aboyne Castle, in its grounds the Formaston Stone; a Pictish cross-slab (see **67**) with symbols and Ogham inscription. In another mile, on wooded slopes by Balnagowan (516005) are over 900 Bronze Age cairns – the 'Balnagowan Necropolis', among them the older Blue Cairn; a mound of boulders over 50 yards long. A mile to the west, above Dykehead and the A93, are St. Machar's Cross and Well (504998).

At the entry to Cromar's broad green plain is the site of Coull Castle (513023: see **25**); a Durward imitation of Kildrummy (**49**). With five circular towers above its courtyard, it was held by the English during the first War of Independence, and later torched and demolished. Just past it, three miles north of Aboyne at Bridgend (508024) a minor right turn to Coull Outdoor Centre and Coull

Loch is identified as a 'heritage trail'. Over a humpbacked bridge past Coull kirk-yard it climbs a bank above the plain, Morven (**31**) now prominent beyond. Past a junction left to Tarland opposite a track to Loch Coull House, it runs on under Craiglich (1562ft; 476m) to join the B9119 from Echt (**24**) at the Slack of Tillylodge (524063). Here, with the Queen's View signposted left and 'heritage trail' right, at the forestry gate of a track up Craiglich is advertised a woodland walk.

Here a right turn onto the B9119 leads in under a mile to Tillylodge and a left turn north, via rural back lanes through wooded hills and the Howe of Cushnie, to Donside. Two miles further east the B9119 intersects the Lumphanan-Craigievar A980 (**25**).

Turning west on the B9119, on the right a lay-by serves the Queen's View over Deeside to the hills beyond. On a clear day the view runs south to the cone of Mount Keen (3077ft; 939m), southwest to Lochnagar (3786ft; 1155m; **34**), and west to the long ridge running from Culblean Hill (1983ft; 604m) to the elegantly bald dome of Morven (2862ft; 871m).

In another mile, on a long bend by a steading is Culsh Souterrain or Earth House (504054; signposted). Penetrating a bank under the road, this Iron Age store-house was discovered *c*.1850 when a roofing-slab slipped. A stone-lintelled entry barely three feet high gives access to a narrow curving passage which, some 40 yards long, gets higher and broader towards the back. Built by the folk later called

Picts, and one of many in Scotland, Culsh typifies the Northeast type (those in Angus and Perthshire tend to be larger and multichambered, suggesting greater wealth). Used to store perishables and surplus food, the curved passage of this Iron Age fridge keeps out sunlight; the final chamber being wholly dark. With dry-stone walls roofed by heavy slabs, it is not hidden and so unlikely to have been used as a refuge. Folklore suggests that such odd subterranean passages were the *raths* of the fairies, the *daoine shi'ich* or 'men of peace'.

Just past Culsh a track on the right leads to Alamein, one of several farms once used by the MacRobert Trust to train young farmers. Sir Alexander MacRobert (1854–1922) was an Aberdeen businessman who bought land here. By his second marriage he had three sons, all killed flying, two during World War II as RAF officers. After the death of her sons his widow and co-trustees turned the House of Cromar by Tarland into Alastrean House, where RAF officers can rest and recover.

Two miles further west amid fertile, well-farmed land is wooded Tarland (pop. 576). With its roofless 1762 church and its more recent 1870 parish kirk dedicated to St. Moluag of Lismore (6th century), this pleasant village lies amid ancient hut circles, cairns and field systems, with a Pictish symbol stone west of the village by Corrachree, and the 4500-year-old stone circle of Tomnaverie to the south. Yet, though this upland has long been blessed with fertility, it hasn't always been so peaceful. In 1644 Argyll's Royalists sacked the area, and in 1335 a brutal battle (see **30**) was fought below the Hill of Culblean, three miles southwest of Tarland near Loch Kinord.

29.   Round Loch Kinord   *(Route, History, Walk)*

Leaving Tarland past a right turn (Logie Coldstone 3) then a left to Aboyne (B9094), in two miles at Milton of Logie (449021: **31**) the B9119 crosses the A97 running north to Donside from Dinnet (**32**) on the A93. Continue southwest on the B9119 (Braemar 24) a mile to the Muir of Dinnet National Nature Reserve. Under Culblean Hill past reed-fringed Loch Davan the wooded road bends south another mile to a visitor centre (429996) east of Loch Kinord and near the 1335 battlesite.

Loch Davan lies in a clay hollow left by ancient glacier-grind, while Loch Kinord occupies a depression where once a plug of old ice resisted a meltwater channel from the Ballater basin to the west. This forced the water to carve the Burn o' Vat gorge (425997) between Culblean Hill and Cnoc Dubh (1067ft) to the south. A short mile up the Vat Burn a path from the visitor centre reaches the Vat Cavern, alias Rob Roy's Cave. There is no evidence that the outlaw ever hid here, but again (see **12**) why spoil a good story?

The five-mile circuit of Loch Kinord is rewarding. From the carpark cross the road into the trees. At a cairn a few yards in, turn right (south) past a pole-gate. Parallel to the road, continue 400 yards to a second polegate by a minor carpark (433993). With Loch Kinord hidden, keep on south past another polegate through stunted silver birch under heather banks. At a Y-fork by a black ditch draining a reedy tarn, continue south up a heather bank. The track bends southeast towards the A93, traffic now audible. Past a gate (and the first view of Loch Kinord to the north) the path climbs from the wood to abandoned Meikle Kinord steading, the A93 skirting Muir of Dinnet a couple of hundred yards away. Here, by a gate and stile break left (east) over rough pasture to a lochside gate. Past an offshore islet and a promontory neck is a field, the A93 still nearby. With cattle in pasture by Clarack ahead, head up to the A93 then take the track north past Clarack (452987), or follow boggy lochside scrub before scrambling east to join this track north of Clarack.

Over a broad haugh east of the loch the track passes deserted Kinord Schoolhouse to New Kinord (448998), here meeting a lane from the A97 a half-mile east. Turn west past a gate to a track above the loch. Descend to the lochside past Castle Island (see **30**) and Crannog Island (441997) – wooded artificial Iron Age islets. Built on underwater piles, reached by sunken zigzag sunken causeways so only their inhabitants knew the safe way home, crannogs suggest dangerous times long ago. Or were they just a way to get away from the midges?

Immediately after Crannog Island, climb the bank on the right up and over rough pasture to rejoin the main track west. At a Y-fork between the two lochs (neither visible), follow the Burn o' Vat sign left, and left again after 30 yards. The path winds up and down through mixed woodland northwest then west of Loch Kinord, past reedbeds and up cobbled stone steps until, at last, it climbs open heather heath back to the cairn where you started.

The woodland road continues south a mile to the A93 (**32**).

30.   The Battle of Culblean   *(History)*

Defeated at Bannockburn in 1314, the English could hardly still claim Scotland. Via the 1320 Declaration of Arbroath and its French connection, the new Scots monarchy parlayed successfully with Rome, so that at Northampton in 1328 the new English king, Edward III, conceded Robert the Bruce's right to rule. But Bruce died in 1329, leaving his five-year-old son, David II, vulnerable to the Disinherited – sons of Scots nobles who, their fathers having been exiled to English estates, now clamoured for revenge and reconquest.

Persuading Edward Balliol to revive his dead father's claim, the Disinherited invaded via Kinghorn in Fife and soon took Perth and Edinburgh. Crowned at Scone in 1332, Balliol recognised England's Edward III as lord. When David's men expelled Balliol, Edward besieged Berwick and routed the Scots at Halidon Hill in 1333. With David soon in French exile and Balliol back on the throne, in 1335 by the Peace of Perth the two Edwards forced David's supporters to submit. Now declaring for Balliol and promised the office of Constable of Scotland, David of Strathbogie – son of the Earl of Atholl who'd died in English exile – marched northeast to drive out those who'd replaced the disinherited Strathbogies and Comyns. Devastating the land, he besieged Kildrummy Castle (**49**).

Rebuilt since its fall to the English and the beheading of its commander Nigel Bruce in 1306, now the 300-strong garrison under Sir John of the Craig held out. But Sir John had earlier been captured by Strathbogie then released, the ransom payable by 30 November. If not relieved by then, the rules of war said Kildrummy must be surrendered. So Kildrummy's *chatelaine*, Christian Bruce, sent for help to her husband, Sir Andrew Moray, Regent of Scotland during David II's exile. Mustering 800 men including Sir William Douglas, Moray rode north over the Firmounth into Glen Tanar (**27**).

Abandoning the siege, Strathbogie marched south, taking up a strong position on Culblean Hill above the Burn o' Vat. Fording the Dee at Mill of Dinnet to occupy a moated house east of Loch Davan where John of the Craig joined him,

51

Moray decided on stealth. On the night of 29 November he divided his forces and advanced. At dawn Douglas was seen approaching from the south, but held back as the Athollmen charged wildly down to the Burn o' Vat, where he engaged them. Amid the mayhem Moray, who had bypassed the enemy camp unseen, charged Strathbogie's flank and rear.

With his men in flight, Strathbogie fought to the death. Gordon lore claims that he was slain by Sir Alexander de Seton, the new lord of Strathbogie (see **80**). Sir Robert Menzies escaped to his tower on Castle Island in Loch Kinord, next day surrendering to Moray, though a Gordon tale is that Seton built rafts to storm the castle and slaughter the garrison. Much later, during the Civil War in 1646 Royalists restored the castle, but it was soon surrendered and demolished. Not a trace of it remains today.

The war went on. Aberdeen was torched in 1336, but Culblean was later seen as decisive. Scotland offered no easy pickings. France looked like a better bet to Edward III. In 1341, with Balliol and the Disinherited abandoned, David II came back to rule even as, over the Channel, the Hundred Years' War began.

31.   Morven & North to Donside   *(Route, Hill-Walk)*

From Milton of Logie crossroads (**29**: Huntly 32) the A97 climbs then descends eight miles north to Donside at Deskry (**46**). Just north of the crossroads is Balnastraid (*Baile na Sraide*, 'town of the street'). Now an experimental farm, once the community was dominated by Jacobite John Cattanach, who after the '45 returned to Balnastraid, defying warrants for his arrest. Sent from Aberdeen to take him dead or alive, a messenger-at-arms called Cuthbert stayed at an inn the night before the confrontation. Emerging next morning, he found Cattanach in his way. Producing a horse-pistol, Cuthbert aimed and fired, but got only a flash in the pan. Had Cattanach's friends sabotaged it as he slept? Cattanach brought up a musket and shot him dead then, in the belief that a murderer who saw daylight under his victim's body escaped justice, got a crony to lift the corpse. Next day the posse rode out from Aberdeen, but Cattanach was away, scot-free.

His comrade-at-arms had been Charles Gordon of Blelack, one of the 'red' Gordons of Blelack, anciently cursed for driving a fairy-clan '*...frae the Seely Howe/To the cauld Hill of Fare*' (**23**). With Blelack House reached by wooded avenues on the right, now under Morven the road climbs through the hamlet of Logie Coldstone, so named for the 1618 unification of the parishes of Logie-in-Mar and Coldstone, the kirk built to serve both being replaced in 1780 by the present steepled edifice. Next the A97 continues past right turns to the Migvie Stone (437069), a Pictish cross-slab with delicate Celtic-style interlacing, double-disc, Z-rod, crescent and V-rod, shears, and a knight on horseback. Here too are the remains of a 13th-century courtyard castle, and a 1770 kirk.

A mile further north amid wooded high ground to the right is Tillypronie House, once a Gordon seat (433078), in its grounds the Tomachar Stone, a Class I

Pictish symbol stone (**67**). With Z-rod and crescent and V-rod below, this came from Tomachar ('hillock of the stone') near Newkirk. Beyond this point the A97 descends past Boultenstone Hotel, over a rural crossroads (east up to hill-farms under Gallows Hill (1424ft; 434m) and Frosty Hill; 1352ft; 412m), and down to Deskry, there taking up the Donside A944.

This stretch is dominated by the grassy dome of Morven (377040; 2862 ft; 871m). Of several approaches, from the east the most direct is from Bridgefoot (414039) on the Coinlach Burn, reached from the A97 by lanes and tracks breaking west from and about Logie Coldstone. Beyond Bridgefoot, cross the burn on the track up Roar Hill to a junction (397024) with the path west to Morven Lodge (338029) above Glen Fenzie. *En route* this path is also met by paths north from Tullich and Ballater (see below). From Tullich the path starts just east of Bridge of Tullich (**32**) on the A93 and follows the east side of Crannach Hill (1857ft; 566m) north. From Ballater, follow the cinder lane east of Craigendarroch (**33**) past Monaltrie House (373967) to the Pass of Ballater. Turn east a few yards along the B972 to the start of a forested track opposite up Creagan Riabhach (1749ft; 533m). Where this swings west (380988) continue north up the glen of the Tullich Burn past a ruined lodge to the Morven Lodge path. There is no specific track to the top of Morven. I haven't done this walk myself, so please seek local advice.

32.   To Ballater   *(Routes, History)*

Two miles south of Milton of Logie the A97 meets the A93 at Dinnet, the steep-banked Dee here bridged to the B976. Just east of this hamlet, by Mill of Dinnet on the A93 (468989) a roadside stone declares that: YOU ARE NOW IN THE HIGH-LANDS. Others, however, consider the Pass of Ballater to be the true boundary.

Continuing west above the old railway track, the A93 crosses Muir of Dinnet's wooded heathland south of Loch Kinord (**29**). Met by the B9119, it rejoins the Dee by a gorge where the river bends north under Cambus o' May's ethereal 1905 suspension footbridge (421976). A mile on, with Craigendarroch prominent ahead above Ballater, the road crosses a haugh past Tullich old kirk (391976). With 16 cross-marked slabs in the circular kirkyard, an enclosure by the roofless shell contains a Pictish symbol stone with double disc, Z-rod, 'beast' and mirror. Dated *c.*1400, the kirk is on the site of a 7th-century chapel. It's said that, in penance for a 'great sin', its founder St. Nathalan (d.678) locked himself in irons and threw the key into the Key Pool of the Dee nearby. Seeking absolution in Rome, he bought some fish, and in the belly of one he found…you guessed it!

Is Tullich the source of the famed 'Reel of Tullochgorum'? Deeside folk say so, but Speysiders beg to differ. The lyric, by John Skinner (**105**), tells of a cold winter morn at Tullich when a congregation, shut out by a tardy minister, dance an ever-wilder reel. As for the reel itself, Speyside has a Tulloch, by Nethybridge; and a *Tullochgorum*, by Boat of Garten – plus a sad tale of the reel's origin. The Laird of Tullochgorum's raven-haired daughter Isobel loved Iain Dubh Gear ('short dark

Iain') of the outlaw Macgregors, but her folk disapproved. With his henchmen her brother Alan ambushed Iain who fought them off, shot Alan dead, then composed and danced the reel. Slain crossing the Spey, his head was shown to the pregnant Isobel. Dying of heartbreak, she was buried at Kincardine by the Spey. A plain slab marks her grave.

Just before Ballater the road forks, the B972 breaking right through the dark Pass of Ballater, a narrow gorge under Creagan Riabhach and Craigendarroch, claimed by some as the true gate to the Highlands. Over a haugh with high hills ahead the A93 enters Ballater by the broad, shingled Dee and the triple-arched Royal Bridge. Named and opened in 1885 by Victoria and the fourth on the site, it crosses the river to the B976.

We left the B976 at Bridge o' Ess by Glen Tanar (**27**), nine miles east. The scenic route between mostly follows the river, but cuts over several haughs, the first just north of Bridge o' Ess. Two miles on by the Dee's next northward meander is the ruined kirk of Glen Tanar (478983), burial-place of James Robertson of Ballaterach, his wife, and their daughter Mary. Aged 14, this lass inspired the 8-year-old Byron (**4, 77**) to write 'When I Roved a Young Highlander'; this when in 1796 he stayed at Ballaterach, so plaguing the Deecastle carpenter that the man locked up whenever he came near. Yet Deeside's grand hills impressed the boy as much as Mary, and today they still impress.

Below steep wooded slopes where the Dee foams under Bridge of Dinnet by a roadside well commemorating Victoria's reign, the road runs on three miles past Ballaterach then climbs the wooded lower slopes of Pannanich Hill (394943; 1972ft; 601m), *en route* passing the site of a vanished hamlet, Cobbletown of Dalmuchie. Here *c*.1760 an old woman allegedly cured herself of scrofula, a skin

54

disease once said to be cured by the royal touch and so called the 'King's Evil', by bathing in a bog to which dreams had led her. The growing fame of this 'miracle' led Col. Francis Farquharson (1710–90) of Monaltrie to develop the spa and wells at Pannanich Lodge by Cobbletown.

Ex-commander of the Jacobite Aboyne Battalion, he survived the '45 by the skin of his neck – literally. About to hang in London in 1746, it's said his last-minute reprieve was won by the appeal of rich Margaret Eyre of Essop, who fell for the fair-haired 'Baron Ban' at first sight – though maybe his father, a JP and government supporter, had a hand in it. Back from a 20-year exile, he set up Pannanich Lodge. It soon became fashionable. A major factor in Deeside's growth as a tourist destination, today the Pannanich Wells Hotel (395967) remains open, with fine views high above the river.

Beyond it, under the Craigs of Pannanich and neighbouring Craig Coillich ('Hill of the Old Woman; 1250ft; 397m) the B976 descends two miles to the Royal Bridge and so into Ballater via Bridge Street, the main thoroughfare.

33.   Ballater & Craigendarroch   *(Visit, Walk)*

Occupying a curve in the Dee under Craigendarroch's rocky wooded slopes and 700 feet above sea-level, this neat village (*baile challater*, 'town of the wooded stream'; or *bealaidh tìr*, 'broom country'; pop. 1536) is built round broad, airy Church Square, intersected south to north by Bridge Street, and dominated by the soaring spire of Glenmuick Church (see next page). 42 miles from Aberdeen and once the railhead – Victoria objected to the line being continued past Balmoral (**36**) to Braemar (**37**) – the station was once thronged by folk waiting to see the royal party disembarking here *en route* to their hielan' holiday home. Now the old railway is a walkway running east to Cambus o' May, while the Old Line (the section completed before the Queen declared herself unamused by railways past her front door) follows the Dee northwest through a rocky gorge to Invergairn.

With its royal connections, an information centre (Station Square; 013397-55306; April–Nov.), many recreation facilities, restaurants and hotels, and Bridge Street shops to supply every need, Ballater makes a fine centre from which to explore the region.

It wasn't always so. Just 200 years old, Ballater exists due not only to Pannanich, but also from need of a focus for the united parishes of Glenmuick, Tullich and Glengairn. In 1800, with the 'centrical kirk on the moor' built, William Farquharson, nephew of the 'Baron Ban', began laying out the new village. Built to a grid typical of planned communities of the time, growth came later, when Victoria and Albert bought Balmoral (seven miles further west) in 1852. The opening of the Deeside Railway encouraged tourism; Victoria's 1868 *Journal of our Life in the Highlands* turned it into a flood With hotels and villas sprouting, long straight streets soon ran west to the golf course, caravan site and campsite now on the flood-plain opposite the confluence of Muick and Dee.

Each August Ballatar's Highland Games are held in Monaltrie Park, their highlight a race to the summit of wooded Craig Coillich south of the town, its main track entered by a gate almost opposite the Royal Bridge. Tracks break left and right; to the left is the easier, diagonal climb. Yet the more popular walk is up Craigendarroch (*Hill of the Oaks*), perhaps because of the path circling it halfway up and its finer views.

For the start of the 700-foot climb up this forested granite outcrop, from Ballater walk north up the A93 towards Braemar to the signposted start of 'Craigendarroch Walk' between houses on the right southwest of the hill (361965). Various paths ascend the wooded slopes to a level path round the hill. From it a rough signposted track climbs to the open summit with its fine views south and southwest. The cone of Mount Keen peeks over ridges to the south, but Lochnagar hides behind the Coyles of Muick (1956ft; 601m) and Conachcraig (2827ft; 850m), both above Glen Muick.

34.   Lochnagar & Loch Muick   (*Routes, Hill-Walk, Loch-Walk*)

A week after reaching Balmoral, on ponyback on 7 September 1848 Victoria climbed Lochnagar (244862; 3786ft; 1155m). Named 'Loch of the Goats' after the lochan at the foot of its vast northern corrie, a precipice of over 1000 feet, this hill is so popular that some days walkers queue to gain the summit indicator erected by the Cairngorm Club in 1924.

Victoria approached from the Old Bridge of Invercauld (**37**) past Ballochbuie Forest. Today, some folk choose the seven-mile route from Loch Callater (**39**) south of Braemar, but most start from Spittal of Glen Muick.

From Ballater cross the Royal Bridge. Turn west on the B976 half-a-mile to Bridge of Muick. Here, by a cairn marking Victoria's 1897 visit, a narrow road turns southwest up Glen Muick (*Glen of the Pigs*). Climbing the glen's wooded east bank, soon to the west appear two peaks, Meall Dubh (1847ft; 563m) and the Coyles of Muick, the latter with a distinct cairn. After four miles the glen narrows to the Linn of Muick (332895), the river falling 30 feet to a deep pool which, noted Thomas Pennant in 1767, 'is supposed by the vulgar to be bottomless'. Beyond it bare moor opens up, Lochnagar dominant as, after eight miles, the road reaches a carpark.

Over a rocky broad burn, past the information centre and ranger post the continuing track forks. Facing glacial flats over which the River Muick winds from the loch ahead, the right turn northwest crosses the river to Allt-ha-Guibhsaich (298858), once royal lodge of Victoria and Albert. Here tracks diverge north, west and south to Loch Muick.

Lochnagar is climbed via the track rising west. Above a burn it ascends a heathery glen, after two miles swinging north by a cairn on the left. Here (274863) a rough path breaks southwest, climbing to a saddle between Meikle Pap on the right (270860; 3211ft; 980m) and Lochnagar. Continue west, not far, for a dizzy view down to the lochan past the corrie's sheer plunge, then bear left up a slope called the Ladder to a plateau by Cuidhe Crom (3553ft; 1083m). Continue west over stony ground round the top of the corrie past Cac Carn Mor, then north to the summit, Cac Carn Beag. Return as you came or, (two miles longer) from Cac Carn Mor bear southeast under Cuidhe Crom and down the glen of the Glas Allt to the 150-foot waterfall (271830) that Albert loved. Keeping to the right (south) bank, below it with care descend steeply to the loch at Glas-allt-Shiel where, after Albert died, Victoria had a cottage built, Allt-na-Guibhsaich retaining too many painful memories. Here, turn northeast up the lochside (see below).

Especially in winter, Lochnagar can be extremely hazardous. It demands fitness and full mountain gear. OS map and a compass are essential.

For the eight-mile circuit of Loch Muick, where the track first diverges past the ranger post, continue straight (south) over rocky heath, red deer grazing the peat-topped glacial flats below. At the next fork (304846), the signposted left turn climbs south via the Capel Mounth track five miles over the hills to Glen Clova (284762). Beyond it, still on the main track to the lochside, a path breaks right over the flats, a footbridge crossing the river to the loch's west bank track under the steep bare scarp of An t-Sròn (2329ft; 710m). The continuing east bank track now starts climbing above the hill-hemmed loch, itself at *c*.1300 feet, and in parts over 250 feet deep. With Lochnagar hidden, after two miles the track curls away from the loch down to and over the tumbling Black Burn to another fork (288923).

Here the left turn zigzags steeply southwest up under Sandy Hillock (266804; 2520ft; 768m) to meet another path from Loch Muick (starting at 273818) to Glen Clova. To the right, a signposted path descends to the loch and round it, over

two forks of Allt an Dubh, to its west bank. Just south of the old royal lodge at Glas-allt-Shiel, a track breaks two miles west up to crag-surrounded Dubh Loch which, at 2100 feet, was once icebound well into spring. Past the lodge, the track follows the loch two miles to its northwest verge. Here turn right over the flats to the east bank track, then left, or (slightly longer) continue north to Allt-na-Guibhsaich and turn right, and so back to the carpark.

35.   Ballater to Balmoral   *(Routes, History)*

Amid increasingly fine scenery, from Ballater the A93 runs six miles west to Balmoral, 16 to Braemar. Past a turn onto the Pass of Ballater B972, the road crosses the Gairn near its junction with the Dee, the A939 here departing north up Glen Gairn to Donside (**43**). Beyond the old coaching inn at Coilacreich, the A93 courses mature riverside woodland under steep slopes, the green hills south of the Dee here and there opening to brief views of Lochnagar's great corrie. With the Prince Albert Cairn prominent atop Craig Lowrigan above Balmoral, the road loops under Crathie Church and by the carpark meets the B976, here crossing the Dee from Balmoral Castle's Gate Lodge.

From Ballater and Bridge of Muick the B976 runs west past ruined Knock Castle (353952), scene of another bloody Forbes-Gordon feud (below, also **44**).

Over a wooded brae to fresh views the road crosses the Girnock Burn by Littlemill at the mouth of Glen Girnock and, under steep Creag Ghiubhais (1594ft; 486m) continues over a broad haugh to Mains of Abergeldie. Here, with Lochnagar prominent, Abergeldie Castle (287953) occupies wooded riverbank policies owned by the same Gordon branch since 1481.

A rectangular four-storey house with corbelled angle turret, it was built c.1550 by 'Black Alister' – Alexander Gordon. Supporting Huntly at Corrichie (**23**) in 1562; jailed then pardoned by Mary Queen of Scots, thereafter the Forbes feud consumed his life. In 1592 the castle held off Mackintoshes who, killing three local Gordon lairds, pointedly spared Arthur Forbes ('Black Airtir') of Strathgirnock. With his house torched by vengeful Gordons, Forbes came to terms but, falling for his daughter, Francis Gordon of Knock came asking for a 'thigging' (betrothal gift). Enraged, Forbes struck out with a scabbarded sword, but the scabbard flew off, and so did the young man's head. Forbes fled and Francis' father seized Strathgirnock, driving out its tenants. Returning with a warband, Forbes surprised Gordon of Knock's seven sons cutting peat on his land. Beheading them, he stuck their spades in the peat and impaled their heads on the spade-shafts. Receiving the terrible news at the top of his stairs, the shocked old man fell over the banisters to his own death. Another happy Highland love-tale...

Almost razed by the Covenanters, in 1689 Abergeldie Castle was garrisoned by General Mackay and besieged by John Farquharson of Inverey, the 'Black Colonel' (**37, 40**). Lifting the siege, Mackay then burned: 'at least twelve or fourteen hundred houses' in the area. Later, leased to the royal family as a dower house in 1848, Abergeldie was occupied by the future Edward VII, and thereafter became a residence for Balmoral guests. Now back in Gordon hands, it is linked with the Dee's north bank by an 1885 suspension footbridge, which replaced a rope-and-cradle bridge. In the cradle, you let gravity do half the work, then pulled hand-over-hand the rest of the way. Not a few folk perished amid the crossing.

Rich in natural woodland, this pretty reach inspired 'The Birks of Abergeldie', which Burns turned into the better-known 'Birks of Aberfeldy'. Dorothy Wordsworth asserted that, while at the time there was birch-aplenty on Deeside, Tayside had none.

From Mains of Abergeldie a back road climbs from the B976 then descends past Royal Lochnagar Distillery (266938; 013397-42273; open Easter–Oct.). Under a mile from Balmoral, it was built in 1825 by John Robertson of Crathie, an old smuggler who'd gone straight. Supplied to his royal neighbours, who permitted the use of the prefix 'Royal', this was once Scotland's most expensive whisky.

Continuing under the huge pyramidical Prince Albert Cairn on Craig Lowrigan – one of several royal memorials nearby – the lane rejoins the B976 which, bending past Balmoral's Gate Lodge, crosses the Dee to meet the A93 by the carpark under Crathie Church.

36.   Balmoral & Crathie   *(Visit, History)*

Today Balmoral and Deeside are so associated with royalty that it's hard to see either otherwise. Yet it wasn't always so. Sited under steep slopes on meadowland in a loop of the Dee 50 miles west of Aberdeen, the original 16th-century towerhouse occupied land once part of the old Earldom of Mar. With the estate first mentioned in 1452 as 'Bouchmorale', in 1539 the Exchequer Rolls cite Alexander and John Gordon as 'tenants of Balmurrell'. By marriage passing to the Farquharsons of Inverey (**40**), it became associated with Jacobitism, Charles Farquharson being wounded at Killiecrankie in 1689, and his nephew, 'Balmoral the Brave', joining both the 1715 and 1745 uprisings. Forfeited after the '45, in 1798 the Duffs Earls of Fife (**89**) acquired castle and estate in debt settlement; and it was their lessee, retired diplomat Sir Robert Gordon (brother of the 4th Earl of Aberdeen, Prime Minister 1852–55; see **76**), who first invited royal guests, having extended the old castle and established the Balmoral deer forest.

As mentioned (**17**), in 1847 Victoria and Albert were busy being soaked at Ardverikie by Loch Laggan. The queen's doctor Sir James Clark, his son currently Sir Robert's guest at sunny Balmoral, persuaded them to try Deeside. When news came that Sir Robert had dropped dead at breakfast, Albert began negotiating with the Fife trustees to take up the unexpired lease. Landing at Aberdeen on 7 September 1848, next day they were fêted all the way up the Dee to the 'pretty little castle'. It was love at first sight ('...All seemed to breathe freedom and peace, and to make one forget the world and its sad turmoils'), and in 1852 the royal couple bought the estate for £31,500. The present 1855 pile, built by William Smith of Aberdeen under Albert's supervision, replaced the old castle. Built to accommodate over 100 guests and entourage, it is more *schloss* than Scots.

On 14 December 1861, Albert died of typhoid. He was just 42. Inconsolable, Victoria retreated from public view, spending months at Balmoral or on the Isle of Wight, confiding only in her 'upper servant and permanent personal attendant', John Brown (1826–83), a farmer's son who'd become Albert's ghillie in 1849. Lately dramatised as a film starring Judi Dench and Billy Connolly (now with his own Donside castle: see **46**), Victoria's relationship with her 'Beloved Friend' caused a furore, upper-crust resentment being fueled by Brown's officiousness, blunt refusal to kowtow to his 'betters', and taste for whisky. When he died Victoria, dissuaded from writing his memoir, commissioned the Poet Laureate to pen an inscription for his memorial statue in the Balmoral grounds.

With the royal family holidaying annually at Balmoral, the grounds, gardens and exhibitions are open to the public (013397-42334; mid-April – July). Save for exhibitions in the Ballroom, the castle is closed and, hidden behind carefully-planted screens of trees, is hard to see from the public roads, save at a distance – from near Inver on the A93 a mile or so west, or from a point almost a mile north up the B976 (**43**).

Crathie Church nearby was designed in 1895 by A. Marshall Mackenzie, architect of Marischal College's massive front and tower (2, 41, 49). With a private royal entrance and transept, its many busts and memorials commemorate past royalty. It replaced the 1804 kirk on the same site, where Victoria worshipped in public view until, in 1893, she could no longer bear the gawking. That kirk had succeeded a medieval kirk, its ruin by the Dee two miles further west. Marked by a standing stone on a slope another mile west, the first Crathie foundation was established by St. Manire, said to have been buried there c.824.

37. To Braemar   *(Route, History)*

Immediately west of Crathie shedding the old military road (B976 continued) north-east to Gairnshiel Lodge (43), the A93 continues towards Braemar through Farquharson land. After a mile, between road and river in a circle of larch is the Carn na Cuimhnein (*cairn of remembrance*; 244944). Here, when summoned, Farquharson clansmen each brought and laid down a stone on a pile nearby. On returning from raid or war, each survivor removed a stone. Numbering the dead, the stones left were added to the cairn.

Past little Inver the rocky Dee runs under pine and silver birch another mile under a conical wooded hill, atop it the Princess Royal's Cairn. Past another white suspension footbridge (197908) and just before Invercauld Bridge, an estate gateway on the right leads to Invercauld House (174924).

Set above pine-dotted riverside meadows, the central keep of this Farquharson seat is 16th-century, the wings being added later. Descended from the Shaw Mackintoshes of Rothiemurchus (see *Round Moray...*), in the 14th century a son of this clan, Farquhar, settled in the Braes of Mar. Later marrying the daughter of Donald Stewart of Mar, Donald Farquharson gained the estate, his son Findla Mor (Big Findlay) being considered the first Farquharson of Invercauld. The current laird, 16th in direct line, owns the estate, Aberdeenshire's largest – almost 90,000 acres of mostly deer-stalking high ground.

Over Caulfeild's 1753 Invercauld Bridge (see 45) the road crosses to the Dee's south bank. the view suddenly expanding northwest to the Cairngorms. The eastern corries of Beinn a' Bhuird ('Table Mountain'; 093006; 3924ft; 1196m; 41) appear as, under the Lion's Face cliff of Creag Choinnich above Braemar, the road passes a carpark by the entry to Braemar Castle (155925; 013397-41219; open Easter–Oct., and as shown on the next page).

Built in 1628 as a hunting seat (and to check Farquharson ambition) by John Erskine, 7th Earl of Mar, this five-storey L-plan towerhouse was the scene of a rout when in 1689 John Graham of Claverhouse, alias 'Bonny Dundee', rebelled against the Scottish Convention's acceptance of William of Orange as king. With Farquharson of Inverey (35, 40) running wild, the Convention ordered Donside's Master of Forbes to arrest the 'Black Colonel'. Reaching Inverey too late, Forbes and his men camped for the night by Braemar Castle, to be rudely awakened when

Farquharson's band opened fire from Creag Choinnich above. Gun-shocked and scattered, the terrified horses took hours to recapture and calm, whereupon the garrison: 'forsook the house and galloped all their best down the country', Farquharson meanwhile firing the castle.

In 1715 the fate of the Earldom of Mar was sealed when the 11th Earl, called 'Bobbin' John' because he kept changing sides, raised the Old Pretender's standard at the Castleton of Braemar. Losing the Battle of Sheriffmuir, and the cause, his forfeited estates were sold to the Farquharsons of Invercauld who, after the '45, leased Braemar Castle to the British War Office. It was rebuilt and, as at Corgarff (**44**), surrounded by a star-shaped eight-pointed curtain wall, so to enfilade with fire any attack by rebellious Highlanders. Jacobitism was soon dead, but as late as 1831 the castle was garrisoned to patrol against whisky smuggling. Today, in addition to the iron-grilled Old Laird's Pit (the castle prison), here you can see the world's largest cairngorm – a semi-precious stone weighing 52lbs – plus a piece of tartan plaid allegedly worn by Bonnie Prince Charlie.

Bending south, in another half-mile the A93 enters Braemar.

38.   Braemar: Morrone & Creag Choinnich   *(Visit, Walks)*

Sited 1100 feet high amid magnificent scenery where the Water of Clunie runs north out of Glen Clunie to join the Dee, Braemar (pop. 528) was once two villages, Auchendryne on the Clunie's west bank under the Birkwood of Morrone and, on the other bank, Castleton under Creag Choinnich. The latter hill is named after King

Kenneth II (971–95). With a hunting-seat here, he inaugurated the original Braemar Gathering long before the famed annual event which, dating from 1817 and held the first Saturday in September, attracts vast crowds. Castleton is named after the Castle of Kindrochit, begun by Macbeth's nemesis Malcolm Canmore (1057–93), the later 14th century building in ruins by 1620.

Quiet in winter, in summer Braemar's two hotels – the vast Invercauld Arms and almost-as-vast Fife Arms – and boarding houses cater for many folk; some passing through, others here to ski, pony-trek, fish, walk the hills, or simply to enjoy the scenery. With gift shops galore, the information centre in The Mews on Mar Road is open all year (013397-41600; afternoons only Oct.–May).

Of the two hills above Braemar, Creag Choinneach (161918; 1764ft; 538m) is the easier climb. From central Braemar follow the A93 south, turning left at a signpost to the walk then, at the forest edge, left again through a gate to Scots pine and larch. Taking either of two paths left (all routes colour-coded), climb through forestry to the hill's steep upper moor, reaching the summit via a rough heather path. The view runs southeast to Lochnagar (**34**), east over Invercauld House, north over Braemar Castle to Ben Avon and Beinn à Bhuird, and west over Braemar to Morrone. There and back is about two miles.

A piebald ridge southwest of Braemar, Morrone (*Mor Shron*, 'Big Nose'; 133986; 2819ft; 859m) means a steady three-mile climb. From central Braemar turn west on the Inverey dead-end road, over the plunging Linn o' Clunie past the Fife Arms. Where the Inverey road curves right towards the Dee, turn left up Chapel Brae past the games arena to a carpark atop the road. Climb the track beyond to a crossing where a sign indicates the nature reserve. Keep left through birch and juniper some 450 yards to a viewpoint and indicator (142905) near a second fork. Keep left, not far. Near the ruin at Tomintoul, a cairn on the right marks the start of a faint path southwest up a grassy slope, the route marked by further cairns. With views unfolding the path grows more obvious, climbing over heathery peat and bog to the quartzite summit plateau and its radio mast.

Here Morrone is revealed as the final height in a ridge separating Glen Clunie from Glen Ey below to the west. Besides splendid Cairngorm views, below to the east the A93, *en route* to the Cairnwell, can be seen crossing the Callater Burn from Loch Callater – our next destination. From the top return as you came or, for a longer circuit, descend the continuing track first southwest, then southeast, then northeast to a lane running north along the Clunie's west bank, through Balintuim back to Braemar. This adds a mile to the walk, which from Braemar involves a climb of 1700 feet.

39.   Loch Callater & Beyond   *(Route, Walks)*

Two miles south of Braemar the Callater Burn joins the Clunie by Auchallater (166884) and the A93 bridge. To the left over the bridge a small carpark marks the start of a three-mile estate track (closed to traffic) south up Glen Callater to a glacial loch under a vast corrie. This simple six-mile there-and-back walk leads to Jock's Road, the most westerly hill-track between Deeside and the glens of Angus.

Past a gate above Auchallater the track flanks the birch-fringed Linn o' Callater under the dogleg glen's bare scree slopes, then descends to follow the cascading burn 1.5 miles to a broad plank-bridge. Continuing up the east bank with the vast corrie ahead and the loch hid under it, a right fork (167854) recrosses the burn to climb Bealach Buidhe. In another mile the main track, climbing gently, reaches a Y-fork by Lochcallater Lodge at the loch's northwest end. The left turn climbs east towards Lochnagar (**34**), in 1.5 miles rounding Carn an t-Sagairt Mor (208844; 3430ft; 1047m), the remains of a crashed Lancaster bomber scattered about. For the loch, fork right past the lodge to mini-beaches of red sand – a fine spot under a wild hilly amphitheatre leading south to the great corrie.

Jock's Road climbs 2200 feet, in seven miles descending to the carpark (284762) at Acharn in Glen Doll. From deserted Lochcallater Lodge a rough path follows the loch's east bank then climbs the corrie's shallowest, but still severe, slope. West of the track and a mile south of the loch, over the corrie's headwall near Loch Kander plunge the Breakneck Falls (197812), the finest of several that hurtle over these precipices.

On a clear day the return from Loch Callater offers fine views north to the tors of Ben Avon and, much closer, of Morrone's long high summit plateau.

Continuing south from Auchallater, the A93 climbs the old military road up Glen Clunie. Atop the pass, at over 2000 feet and ten miles from Braemar, the

Cairnwell carpark (139782) offers access to chair-lifts and ski-tows southwest up The Cairnwell (134774; 3059ft; 933m) and, just to its north, up Carn Aosda (135793; 3003ft; 917m). The climb is steep but short (750 feet), making these two bald Munros the land's easiest. From the ski centre a path climbs the Cairnwell Burn to a col between the summits then forks; left 500 feet up The Cairnwell, right 450 feet up Carn Aosda. To the top of the first and back is about four miles; the circuit of both, about six. Don't wander into the wilds beyond unless well equipped: though near the road, this is high, empty ground.

More demanding is a six-mile there-and-back trek up Glas Maol (167766; 3504ft; 1068m). From the carpark a faint path southeast climbs, falls, then above ski-slopes ascends Meall Odhar (156774; 3025ft; 922m). Follow the ridge southeast, descend between two corries to a saddle, then walk up broad Glas Maol.

Beyond this high point the A93 enters Perth and Kinross, descending rapidly past the once-notorious zigzags of the Devil's Elbow to the Spittal of Glenshee, and on to the strange and remote lands that lie beyond Blairgowrie, 34 miles south of Braemar...

40. To the Linn of Dee *(Route, History, Walks)*

From Braemar the Inverey road runs six miles west through beautiful land to the Linn of Dee, then doubles back east, north of the Dee past Mar Lodge, to end at Allanaquoich.

On a rising heathery bank above the Dee and under the Morrone Birkwood Nature Reserve, the road starts west two miles to a viewpoint above the confluence of Quoich and Dee. With red-roofed Mar Lodge visible ahead over broad green riverside flats, and the high hills beyond, this is a sublime spot, with better to come. Cresting, the road descends over the Linn of Corriemulzie, then continues past tall pines above a lodge by the white cast-iron 1848 Victoria Bridge. With a sign welcoming walkers, this crosses the Dee to Mar Lodge Estate. Here, under Creag an Fhithich ('Raven Crag'), just beyond the bridge by the road once stood the Gallows Tree of Mar. Riverside haughs open up as the road curves south through the hamlet of Inverey, once lair of Jacobite John Farquharson, alias the Black Colonel (35, 37).

Outlawed for killing the Laird of Braickley, then besieging Abergeldie and firing Braemar Castle, in 1689 this reprobate fought at Killiecrankie, then returned to Inverey. Here, after General Mackay slaughtered Jacobite Highlanders at Cromdale by the Spey on 1 May 1690, he was hunted. With his castle blown up (only fragments survive), he fled up the Ey Burn to hide at The Colonel's Bed (087871), a ledge in the burn's rocky gorge. Brought food by Annie Bhan, 'Fair Annie', he escaped, somehow managing to die in his bed in 1698. End of story? Not quite. Desiring burial beside Annie in the Chapel of the Seven Maidens at Inverey, instead he was 'planted' at St. Andrew's in Braemar. On three successive days his coffin was found disinterred. Towed on a boat up the Dee by a horse-hair tether, his remains were finally laid to rest beside Annie Bhan.

'Leave it!' his son Patrick told those untying the tether as he was laid to rest, 'My father may wish to rise again.'

To Inverey from Corriemulzie a six-mile circuit can be walked, the track south from Corriemulzie Bridge bearing southwest from the burn up a tributary in a side valley called the Glack. It crosses soft ground to a path which, above the Ey and The Colonel's Bed, reaches a prominent track north to Inverey. I haven't walked it; so please seek local advice.

Via the humpbacked bridge over the Ey Burn the road enters mature woodland. Amid it and after a mile, the Water of Lui from Glen Derry and Glen Luibeg high in the hills flows into the Dee, this just east of the Linn of Dee (062896).

Here, 1213 feet high and 65 miles west of Aberdeen, at the carpark north of the pine-hemmed 1857 bridge in summer the coach parties decant. Under the bridge the Dee boils through a three-foot gap in the schistose rock to dark pools below. Here the young Lord Byron, deeply affected by such places (see **4**, **77**), was saved from a fatal fall by a smart companion. Here too, under north bank trees, begin long-range hill-walking paths. These include: (a) the route to Coylumbridge and Aviemore via Glen Dee and the Lairig Ghru (20m; 32km); (b) to Kingussie and Kincraig via Glen Geldie and Glen Feshie (27m; 42km: an east-west route touted as a main road ever since Wade (**45**) proposed it 270 years ago, but still, mercifully, unbuilt); and (c) to Blair Atholl via Glen Tilt (22m; 35km). A Scottish Rights of Way Society sign warns: *Take care. You are entering dangerous and potentially demanding country.*

Every year, mostly in winter, unprepared folk *die* on the hills ahead, typically by exposure or fall due to loss of bearings in mist or storm. Please, don't be one of them.

41. Towards Beinn à Bhuird: Up Glen Quoich   *(Walk)*

From the Linn of Dee the road turns east, soon crossing the energetic Lui Water, as shown overleaf. Here a riverside walkers' track breaks north three miles to Derry Lodge (041934) southeast of Carn Crom (024954; 2920ft; 890m) and Derry Cairngorm (017981; 3788ft; 1155m). From it one high trail turns north up Glen Derry over the Lairig an Laoigh (*Pass of the Calves*) to Fords of Avon, east of Cairngorm and west of Glen Avon (**44**). The other follows Glen Luibeg west to the Lairig Ghru (**17**). These long treks demand proper planning.

On over heather heathland under a steep open slope the road passes two entries to Mar Lodge (National Trust; 096901). Here, by the riverside flat of Dalmore, ground held by the Mackenzies since the 15th century was, due to their Jacobitism, forfeited in the 18th century and bought by the Duff Earls of Fife who also bought Balmoral (**36**). In 1889 the 6th Earl married Princess Louise and so got the Dukedom of Fife. With New Mar Lodge (*c.*1850) by Corriemulzie destroyed by fire in 1895, the Princess Royal sketched out the present building which, with A. Marshall Mackenzie (also **2**, **36**, **49**) as architect, was completed in 1898. Past its gardens and riverside walks, continue east two miles over the tumbling Quoich to the carpark near Allanaquoich (119903).

Here a public footpath, long fought for, departs east along the north bank of the Dee via Invercauld, and another, more demanding, northwest up Beinn à Bhuird. The latter track starts by following the tumbling Quoich's well-wooded east bank past the Punch Bowl, a rocky hollow from which in 1715 Bobbin' John's Jacobites (**37**) drank whisky toasts to the success of their rebellion, to the Linn of Quoich (111912). Here, by a boarded-up cottage and a footbridge to the pine-rich west bank, the Quoich storms over rocky schistose ledges. Beyond, the path climbs to a main northwest track. Through Old Scots Pine under bare Creag Bhaig (2159ft; 658m), this gains open moor, Beinn à Bhuird ahead. For another two miles the track follows

the Quoich northwest towards this bulky mountain. Leaving forestry, but with a planted ridge to the left, it swings north, now directly towards then up Beinn à Bhuird's southwestern flank.

Here (079937), amid bare moor with forestry to the left, a heathery track breaks left to the plantation's northeast apex. Overgrown, it's easily missed. More obvious, just beyond and over a burn, a left turn up a grassy path past a gate leads to a pass, Clais Fhearnaig. Climbing west between low bare brows past two artificial lochans created early in the 20th century, in two miles this path descends to join (058924) the Glen Lui track southeast from Derry Lodge. A left turn southeast on this track leads two miles to the road a mile east of Linn of Dee, so creating a final circuit two miles longer.

For the shorter, higher circuit; if at first you miss the track and reach the burn, cut back and right to a gate at the forestry edge (079936: the current OS map misrepresents the forestry due to recent felling). Climb the forest track southeast nearly a mile to open moor and a shallow crest (077919) with exhilarating, panoramic Cairngorm views. Beyond it, the track curls southeast down past Old Scots Pine to a high stile by an estate deer-fence then, with evocative views over the Dee to the hills beyond, descends a rough slope over a track-crossing, and so down to the road by Mar Lodge.

Follow the road east two miles back to the carpark, or explore the Mar Lodge riverside trail as a longer, alternative way back. This 10-mile walk takes four hours, and may be extended in many directions.

Now we travel north, to Donside.

The Lui near the Linn of Dee

Section 3

Strathdon

42.   Introduction: 'So Quiet Flows the Don'

Rising at Well of Don (196067) on an open slope a mile southeast of and above Inchrory in Glen Avon, Scotland's sixth longest river (after the Tay, Spey, Clyde, Tweed and Dee) runs 83 miles east, reaching the North Sea at Aberdeen two miles north of its sister Dee.

Comparisons between the Don and the Dee are inevitable. Both rise in the Central Highlands and flow east; are of similar length (the Dee is two miles longer); and reach the sea close by. The Dee is named after an ancient fertility-goddess, Deva: likewise the Don, after Danu (who also gave her name to the Danube, Dnieper, Dniester and the Russian Don celebrated in Mikhail Sholokov's famous novel, 'So Quiet Flows the Don'). Yet there are as many contrasts as similarities between the two rivers.

Where for the last century Deeside has had the tourists and attention, Donside has been largely ignored, especially its upper reaches, until the development of the Lecht ski-slopes brought welcome new life. Where from Glen Dee onwards the Dee runs almost straight to the east, the Don has many changes of direction, and the broader haughs of its lower reaches are more fertile, as in: *River Dee for fish and tree/But Don for ham and corn*, or: *Ae mile o' Don's worth twa o' Dee/Except for salmon, stone and tree*. And where the Dee is rocky and urgent, mostly the Don is placid, which may explain a third old saw, also derived from the old belief that water divinities demand human sacrifice: *Bloodthirsty Dee, each year needs three/But bonny Don, she needs none.*

From the start picking up feeder burns, over bare moors under the Lecht (**43**) and past Corgarff (**44**) the Don winds northeast up a narrow glen past Strathdon (**46**), *en route* swelled by intersecting streams – Deskry, Nochty, Carvie, Ernan and Comrie. By Glenbuchat it turns east past Glenkindie, then north past Kildrummy (**49**), then east again past Bridge of Alford (**54**). Now winding gently over the broad Howe of Alford, south of Castle Forbes it enters the picturesque gorge of My Lord's Throat (**57**). Leaving the hills at Monymusk (**58**), it turns northeast past Kemnay (**59**) to Inverurie (**62**). There taking up the Urie, it loops past Kintore (**8**) and Hatton of Fintray (**7**), turns southeast past Dyce with enough fall to power paper mills, and enters a final gorge under the Brig o' Balgownie (**4**) in Old Aberdeen before running under Bridge of Don and over the sands to the sea.

So, now we travel north from Deeside to the Lecht and Tomintoul, then follow the Don east to Inverurie with, *en route*, a loop north to Rhynie and the Cabrach, thence south over the Correen Hills back to the Don at Alford.

43.   Glen Gairn to Tomintoul   *(Route)*

Despite many proposals over the years to link Deeside and Speyside by a road through Glen Feshie, the most direct route from Deeside to Speyside remains via Donside, the Lecht and Tomintoul.

The most westerly route from Deeside to Donside starts either via the A939 from Invergairn (**35**) or the B976 from Crathie (**37**); these meeting after six miles at Gairnshiel Lodge. Initially the A939 follows the Gairn through a winding glen under craggy slopes; while the B976, an old military road, climbs a steep brae with fine views back over Balmoral to Lochnagar (**34**). Crossing a wide heather moor, it descends to join the A939 by the broad, shallow Gairn. Turning past Gairnshiel Lodge and over the 1751 military bridge (**45**), the continuing A939 climbs steeply to glacier-scrubbed moor dotted with lone wind-bent pine. Cresting in three miles at 1738 feet and shedding the old military road (296064; now a public footpath to Cockbridge), it descends through forestry to Colnabaichin and crosses the Don to a junction. Here the A944 breaks right, following the Don eastward (see **46**).

Turning west, the A939 enters the upland Donside parish of Corgarff, passing the riverside cemetery where in 1938 was buried James McHardy, Queen Victoria's piper and valet, and a rival to John Brown (**36**) for her affections. Often travelling abroad with her, when he left the royal service Brown's curt testimonial read: 'James McHardy left. Gave no offence. Signed: John Brown'.

Crossing the Don via Luib Bridge (1830), past grim Corgarff Castle (**44**) the road recrosses the river by the Allargue Arms Hotel at Cockbridge. A mile or so west of this point up the Burn of Loinherry is Tobar Fuar, the Cold Well, Scotland's second largest spring, its waters alleged to cure the lame, the blind and the deaf.

Abruptly, just past the hotel the road starts steeply up Allargue Hill to a bleak high moor. With Ben Avon's tors to the west, and as bare as the moon, this leads to the Lecht Pass (2090ft; *leacht*, 'stony'), usually Scotland's first stretch of road to be blocked by winter snow. From the ski-slopes at its summit and here entering Moray, the A939 begins a long descent down an empty glen. Levelling out at the bottom over the Bridge of Leachd and the Conglass Water, it turns west past Well of Lecht (235152) and a carved memorial to the 33rd Regiment, which in 1754 built this road. The restored square two-storey building nearby is the old Iron Mine, erected in 1730 by the York Buildings Company (see **15**).

A mile on by riverside flats is the ruined cottage where in 1920 Percy Toplis, the notorious 'Monocled Mutineer', hid out. Shooting and wounding a farmer and policeman investigating the fire he'd lit, he fled by bike over the Lecht. A few days later, Britain's most wanted man was ambushed and shot dead by police near Penrith. He was just 23 years old.

Passing Blairnamarrow ('Field of the Dead': 210154), the A939 meets the B9008 from Dufftown and Glenlivet. Taking it up, the A939 enters Tomintoul, turning up the single main street to its wide Square (museum/information centre: 01807-580225; Easter–Oct.). Here folk have fond memories of their benefactor, 'Lord Williams of Tomintoul', the accountant who defrauded Scotland Yard of £5 million before being jailed in 1995.

Leaving Tomintoul and crossing the Avon, the A939 continues west over high moor to meet the A9 near Grantown-on-Spey (see *Round Moray...*).

71

44. The Sack of Corgarff *(History, Walk)*

Stark on a bare slope under the Lecht, restored with star-shaped curtain walls (see **37**), Corgarff Castle (255086: Historic Scotland, 01975-651460; open daily April–Sept., winter weekends) has a fiery history. Built in 1537 as a hunting lodge of the Earl of Mar, in November 1571 it suffered: 'the most atrocious deed in the

history of Mar' (Simpson), when Adam Gordon of Auchindoun (**532**), or his lieutenant, incinerated Margaret Campbell, wife of the absent Forbes of Towie, and their children and servants. In all, 27 died. This outrageous act led an unknown bard to pen the ballad, 'Edom O'Gordon'. It's said Adam – *'It fell about the Martinmas/When the wind blew shrill and cauld'* – attacked Corgarff with lustful intent, but Margaret would not surrender. Infuriated, the villain bellowed:

> *'Gie up your house, ye fair lady*
> *Gie up your house to me,*
> *Or I will burn yoursel therein,*
> *Bot and your babies three.'*

Margaret still refused, so Adam carried out his threat. Corgarff burned. All within died but, ballad claims, for Margaret's 'dochter dear'. The child was lowered from the burning castle in a pair of sheets, but Edom speared her to death. Only on turning over her body with his spear did he regret his deed, crying: *'You are the first/that e'er I wist alive again'*.

Whether as in the ballad or not, the atrocity occurred during the civil war triggered by Queen Mary. Forced to abdicate after her marriage to Bothwell and the murder of Darnley, in 1568 she'd escaped Loch Leven and fled to England, leaving Scotland 'ruled' by regents during the minority of her son, James VI. With Gordons among her last supporters (ironic, given their opposition in 1562: see **23**), in 1571 the Forbes-Gordon feud erupted into open war.

Dating from the 1520s when a Forbes gang murdered Alexander Seton, cousin of George Gordon 4th Earl of Huntly, the feud had deep roots. Traditionally descended from a Dark Age Irish prince, O'Conchar Forbhasach ('the man of courage') and settled in Mar for many centuries, the Celtic Forbeses were among the few great Northeast families not of Norman descent or recent arrival. Not so the Gordons. Fecund johnny-come-latelies (see **80**), they'd expanded so rapidly that after barely a century they were supreme in the North, pressing hard on the lands of older residents like the Forbeses. And while they remained defiantly Catholic, the Forbeses were as fervently Protestant.

In October 1571 Adam of Auchindoun clashed with Lord Forbes at Tillyangus near Clatt (**53**). Routed, with his brother Black Arthur of Putachie slain and many men captured, the Master of Forbes escaped to Edinburgh, where Regent Mar equipped him with a royal army. Meanwhile Adam sent forces to occupy Forbes houses. A Captain Ker came to Corgarff, though whether he or Adam fired the castle is unclear. The Master marched north, but on 20 November at Aberdeen's Craibstane (**2**) the Gordons again triumphed. With the Master jailed at Spynie near Elgin, their victory seemed complete. Yet at the Pacification of Perth in 1573 they had to accept that their cause was lost. As for Adam, he died in bed at Auchindoun in 1580. So who says crime doesn't pay?

Restored by the Earl of Mar and in 1645 occupied by Montrose, in 1689 Corgarff was again burned, this time by Jacobites. Later (after another torching) converted for use as a barracks for Hanoverian troops after the '45, in the early 19th century it became a base to control whisky smuggling. Today it shows no sign of its bloody past.

From Corgarff a 13-mile track runs to Tomintoul, first south then west by the Don past the ruined lodge at Delnadamph (227085) to open moors. Continuing past a right fork (210082; see below), in two more miles it crosses the fledgling Don (189082) north of Well of Don, then descends under Ben Avon to Inchrory (179081), at the junction of tracks north to Tomintoul, east to Corgarff, south up Glen Builg, and west to Loch Avon. The Inchrory estate road follows the Avon six miles north up Glen Avon to Tomintoul. To loop back to Corgarff, two miles north of Inchrory and just past Dalestie (163110) break right (164114) up the Burn of Little Fergie and over The Eag before descending southeast to a track down to the main fork (210082) bypassed earlier.

45. Wade's Military Roads *(History)*

Hereabouts it's hard to avoid the roads built by General George Wade (1673–1748) and his successors, notably Major William Caulfeild (d.1767) – yes, Caulf*ei*ld is how it's spelled. Throughout the Central Highlands these roads and bridges were built to link Hanoverian military outposts established after the first two Jacobite uprisings (1689, 1715). Made to aid the movement of troops, baggage and gun-trains through wild, formerly roadless terrain, they are named after Wade. In fact he oversaw about 250 miles of road and 40 bridges; his successor Caulfeild 1000 miles of road and 800 bridges.

Inspector of Roads from 1740 until 1767, Caulfeild delegated widely, as to Lord Charles Hay, builder of the Lecht road – part of the route, built between 1748 and 1757, from Coupar Angus via Glenshee and Braemar to Fort George by Inverness. In the same period he oversaw the routes from Corgarff to Aberdeen; and from Fettercairn to Fochabers via Cairn o' Mount (**22**)

Yet Wade developed the network, and created the major routes, including those from Inverness to Dunkeld, Inverness to Fort Augustus, and the spectacular traverse of the Corrieyairick Pass (2519ft). Traversing the Monadhliaths from Upper Speyside to the south end of Loch Ness at Fort Augustus, this 28-mile route is his masterpiece, with 13 (some say only 11) hair-raising hairpin-bends cresting the pass. A phantom piper and other fearsome spectres are said to haunt the route which, with 18 stone bridges, was completed between April and November 1731. 500 soldiers worked a 10-hour day with no days off. When this huge task was fin-ished, Wade gave: 'each detachment an ox-feast and liquor; six oxen were roasted whole; one at the head of each party. The joy was great…' – is *that* a surprise!

Planning and surveying these routes himself, Wade preferred fords to costly bridges (though not stinting when it came to the Tay Bridge at Aberfeldy; designed by William Adam), and where possible drove straight. The road-builders got dou-ble-time, save when bad weather made work impossible, and they went unpaid. The required work-rate was one-and-a-half to two yards per man per day. Every ten miles camps and forges were set up; some becoming Kingshouses (inns). Bridges were built by contracted civil labour. These methods remained standard after Wade retired in 1740.

Grandson of a man whose Irish lands had in Cromwell's time been granted in lieu of pay, Wade had risen steadily through the ranks of the army. A proven sol-dier, later an MP and intelligence agent, his time came when in 1724 George I sent Wade north to: 'conduce to the quiet of his Majesty's faithful subjects'. Now Commander-in-Chief North Britain, he arrived in Inverness in 1725, first trying to drive a road south via Essich, but finding it too circuitous. In 1732, he tried again, getting as far as Foyers along Loch Ness-side before the geography defeated him. At one section by Inverfarigaig over 2000 yards of conglomerate precipice dropping sheer into the loch had to be blasted, the miners dangling by ropes from the top while drilling charge-holes!

Leaving Scotland in 1740 he became a privy councillor in 1742 and a year later was promoted to field-marshal. Dying in London with a fortune of £100,000 (he held shares in the lead and strontium mines at Strontian), he was buried in Westminster Abbey. Yet he lived to see his work aid the final crushing of Highland society after the 1745 revolt. In the 'British' National Anthem (in a verse now diplomatically ignored), the hope is expressed that Wade will: 'like a torrent rush, rebellious Scots to crush', and: 'confound their politics, frustrate their knavish tricks'.

Yet, as the old saw has it: *'If you had seen these roads before they were made/You would hold up your hands and bless General Wade'.*

46.   Upper Strathdon *(Route)*

From the riverside junction at Colnabaichin (**43**) the A944 starts east through Strathdon, a parish 20 miles long and hardly a *strath*, there being few haughs or flats as the river winds under forested hills hugging close on either side. Intersected by the glens of the Deskry, Nochty, Carvie, Ernan and Comrie, the valley supports few folk save at Strathdon, three miles east of the junction. Once the area's populace was thought 'rough and uncivilised' – in the 17th century a local laird beheaded a minister, Mr Baxter, with a Lochaber axe – but no such events have been reported lately. Illicit whisky distilling and smuggling were rife too, especially in Glen Nochty, where famously once the gaugers (see **99**) under a man called M'Bain were given short shrift in a clash with the smugglers. One of these bold reprobates was a man named Sandy Davidson, a crack shot who later turned to poaching, and who in time was found dead in the hills, his dog keeping watch over him.

Twisting and turning along the north bank, the road passes the drive to Skellater House, once home to John Forbes of Skellater who, marrying a Portuguese princess, became a Field Marshal in the Portuguese army before dying in Brazil in 1800. Round a long bend past Lonach and opposite the drive to Inverernan House – once home of 'Black Jock' Forbes, a stalwart of the 1715 uprising – the Culfork road breaks south over the Don (see photo on previous page) to a fork under Gallows Hill. The left turn loops north to Strathdon, the right climbs south alongside the Conrie Water to tracks up and about the bald Socach (325074).

Past the Culfork road and the gated drive to Edinglassie House, the A944 enters dense forest above Candacraig House. Built in 1835, reconstructed after a fire in 1955 and currently owned by a Scottish show-biz celebrity (see **36**), it stands near Candacraig Gardens. With a small roadside carpark, this three-acre walled nursery garden is open to the public (May–Sept.; 019756-51226), while a gallery featuring local artists is found in the Victorian Gothic summerhouse built into the garden wall.

Beyond Candacraig and the tiny hamlet of Roughpark the road winds through the wooded village of Strathdon, where an old humpbacked bridge over the Don allows access to lanes climbing steep wooded slopes on the valley's south side. This straggling, pretty village merges with Bellabeg, where the Nochty joins the Don near the Doune of Invernochty, a huge 12th-century motte-and-bailey which the Earls of Mar used as their castle before Kildrummy Castle (**49**) was built. The soaring 1853 Kirk of Invernochty nearby also impresses, while the kirkyard contains a two-storey red granite Egyptian-style mausoleum dating from 1829.

On a field by Bellabeg the Lonach Gathering is held annually, the Lonach Highlanders marching to it from Inverernan. In 1999 this quintessential Highland event made the news when attended by the current laird of Candacraig and his celebrity guests, all kilted. What local folk made of Hollywood actor Robin Williams puffing his way up a nearby hill when taking part in the traditional annual run is anyone's guess.

47. Glen Nochty & Auchternach *(Route, Walk)*

By Bellabeg's minimart a narrow road breaks north to Glen Nochty and Glenbuchat, then loops southwest to join the A97 by Glenbuchat Castle (**48**).

From Bellabeg this lane climbs above the Water of Nochty towards bare round heathery hills, and in two miles near Torrancroy reaches a Y-fork (337158). With a sign for the oddly-named Lost Gallery (see below), the left turn soon passes a forestry track breaking left. Park here, 200 yards short of two unusual lodges with tall Tudor-style chimneys. These flank the drive to the ruin of Auchternach Garden (also below).

About four miles long with possible extensions, this circuit involves some up-and-down, but nothing steep. Entering the forest, the track soon reaches a three-way junction by Auchternach Bridge, a double-arched span over the Nochty, its parapets ending in piered curves; the west face inscribed: ERECTED/BY/GEN. N.

FORBES/1832. Without crossing it, turn right on a track west up Glen Nochty by the river's north bank. Crossing a wooden-bridged burn, it runs straight through thick forestry for a mile until the glen opens out. Past a plank-bridge just before the forestry ends it curls right over open ground to a guard-railed bridge (317154), this side of which a gated track bears north up a forested slope (see below).

Cross the bridge over the Nochty to a track climbing away from the river above the Quillichan Burn. Over pasture and heath this track leads to a derelict steading at Tolduquhill. Under a bare ridge to the south running from Green Hill (1867ft; 569m) to Knapps (1798ft; 548m), continue up the narrowing glen over the burn past a metal gate to pasture where the track peters out. With birchwood cloaking Dubh Breac ('speckled black') Hill to the right, the way ahead is via a narrow pass. The OS map shows a track just beyond the top of the pass (297141) and immediately west of the Knapps; also a path running east-west along the ridge-top – but here, pressed for time, I turned back to the bridge (317154) and the gate beside it.

Beyond this gate a rutted, grassy track climbs steadily northeast through the forest to a Y-fork, both forks rising to a main east-west track (321158). Turning right and right again, follow this main track east to a junction. Here, where a left turn breaks north towards Moss Hill (2159ft; 658m), another Lost Gallery sign points west. The name sounds very mysterious, but probably began life as Losset, perhaps meaning 'a small meeting place'. Either way, Lost or Losset lies near Belnabodach, 'town of the ghost', or 'town of the old men' – both appropriate, given the glen's depopulation over the last century or so.

Continue straight on over the junction, east, soon descending past a whitewashed cottage. Views now open up as the track mutates into a chestnut-lined avenue emerging from the wood by a bizarre, derelict walled garden. Four-square with battlemented towers, its wall allegedly modelled on an Indian fort, Auchternach Garden (1809) has survived Auchternach House, demolished in 1945 and: 'long reputed the best in the district'. The continuing track descends past another oddity – Firs Cottage, also 1809 and probably built by the same Forbes laird. With an outside stair at the gable, a two-storey timbered porch, and standing stones and a saltire in the garden, it has an art deco look. From it, follow the drive past the lodges back to your car.

To continue north to the head of Glenbuchat, bear right past the lodges to rejoin the road north, in two miles passing Glenbuchat Lodge (1840) above the Coulins Burn, over which the road loops before bending south, as described next.

48.   Above Glenbuchat: Creag an Sgor *(Route, History, Hill-Walk)*

From Bellabeg the continuing A944 passes Colquhonnie Hotel and a left turn (370123) north past forest walks at Mill of Newe (*Neyouw*) to Glenbuchat, then crosses the Don at Bridge of Newe, a charmless 1993 span replacing the barrel-vaulted 1858 original by engineer John Willet. In another mile the A97 from Muir of Dinnet (**31**) takes up the A944, crosses Deskry Bridge (Willet 1858) then recrosses the Don via the two-arched Buchaam Bridge (Willet 1856). Past a sign advertising Ben Newe Forest Walks and by a narrow strath under steep slopes – wooded on Ben Newe (1854ft; 565m) to the north, and bare to the south – the road follows the Don northeast to two turns left into Glenbuchat.

The first climbs a short brae to a carpark by Glenbuchat Castle (397148: Historic Scotland; all year), a Z-plan towerhouse above the Water of Buchat. Built in 1590 by John Gordon of Cairnburrow and still substantial with the first two storeys well-preserved, here lived Glenbuchat's last Gordon laird, 'Old Glenbucket of the '45'. A veteran of Killiecrankie and the 1715 rising, 68 when the '45 began, he raised a local army and fought so fiercely that, it's said, during the march south to Derby, he gave George II nightmares. Fleeing from Culloden to Norway in 1746 with £1000 on his head, in 1750 he died destitute in Boulogne.

Devastated by Clearance, Glenbuchat's beauty is stark. With the lane north from the castle ending short of the bridge at Milton (384158), return to the A97, on it turn left over the burn, then turn left northwest up the glen on the east bank lane. After a mile a left turn over the burn at Milton leads to Kirkton of Glenbuchat (376152), its early 18th-century kirk preserved as an ancient monument. The lane then bends right to a fork (374156).

From this fork the left turn climbs south to forest walks at Deochry then descends past Mill of Newe to join the A944 east of Bellabeg (370123: above). Also from this fork, the right turn recrosses the burn to the north bank lanes. The highest of these climbs northwest past a belt of forestry to open ground and a junction at Smithyford (175172). Here, under the bare ridge of Creag an Sgor, for a nine-mile hill-walk park by the roadside above the burn.

Start west along the road past Upperton and above what may be one of Glenbuchat's old lime-kilns (another is shown opposite); a semi-chamber with stepped internal recess. Follow the burn a mile northwest under wooded Stony Hill, deserted crofts all about, to Dulax. Here, between one derelict and the next (on a steep motte), a *private no entry* track turns north to Peatfold and Creag an Sgor. With Glenbuchat Lodge a mile ahead to the left, continue 600 yards to a track by a stand of pine, and follow it to Newseat (344494), a newly-painted farmhouse.

Here turn hard right (east) up a grassy track towards a rocky saddle, its slopes striated by heather-burns. Where the track fades, swing left through a ruined dyke, a glen opening to the north. The track up it shown on the OS map isn't obvious: continue east past a derelict (349199) down to a fence, over a burn, and diagonally right round the southern flank of stony Creag na Gamhna. Descending over boggy ground then up to the Peatfold track, turn left on it half-a-mile northeast to a junction under Creag an Sgor (375197; 2076ft; 633m).

Here turn right then, in a few yards, left, climbing past grouse-butts. Cresting under summit crags, the track swings east (right) then northeast. Several paths rise to the rocky summit tor, with its splendid views south to Lochnagar (**34**), west to Ben Rinnes, north to the Knock (**86**) past the Buck (2366ft; 721m; **52**) nearby, and northeast to Bennachie (**68**).

Continue southeast over the summit plateau to a junction (380194). Follow the east-bound track past Creag an Eunan onto Meikle Firbriggs Hill (1922ft; 588m) where, near the top, at 388180 another track breaks southwest down to the road. For

a shorter route, 100 yards after the junction turn right onto a path down a gully. At, first, between blaeberry banks, this resembles an old drove trail. Lower down, it's more like the bed of an old burn. With views still broad, descend to a red-roofed steading (378172). Rejoining the main track by a gate, bear right past the steading and another lime-kiln down to the road, and turn right back to Smithyford.

49.   Kildrummy Castle   *(Route, Visit, History)*

With the strath now broadening, a mile east of the Glenbuchat entry the A97 passes the columned gateway of Glenkindie House (424144), a U-plan 16th-century château-style riot of towers. At the eastern edge of Glenkindie hamlet a right turn south over the Don to Towie leads to a network of lanes running west under Frosty Hill to Boultenstone (**31**) and east through the hilly backland between Alford (**54**) and Craigievar (**55**). Not far on, river and road part company, the A97 bending north under steep grass slopes before descending into a dark wood above the Den of Kildrummy. Soon a sign on the left indicates Kildrummy Castle (456164; Scottish Heritage; 01975-571331; open daily April–Sept., winter weekends).

On a green slope under wooded hills, this vast stronghold of the Earls of Mar (illustrated at the start of this section) is the region's oldest surviving courtyard castle. Begun *c*.1230 to the orders of Alexander II and modelled on the Château de

79

Coucy near Lyons (home of Alexander's second wife, Marie), it was built to command the Donside-Moray route. Soon the lancet-windowed chapel arose and, by 1300, four round angle towers and two great gatehouse towers, the latter added by England's Edward I in imitation of those at Harlech Castle in Wales. Later a barbican was built and, in the 16th century, the Elphinstone Tower.

Here in 1306 Sir Nigel Bruce, brother of Robert I, was besieged by the future Edward II. Bribed by the English with the promise of as much gold as he could carry, the treacherous Osbarn the Smith fired the castle with a red-hot plough-blade. Forced to surrender, Sir Nigel was beheaded at Berwick, and the traitor got his promised gold – molten, it was poured down his throat.

Partly destroyed, Kildrummy was rebuilt after Bannockburn in 1314 and in 1335, during the Second War of Independence, was again besieged, David of Strathbogie being driven off then defeated at Culblean (**30**). Returning from French exile, David II guested here in 1342 and in 1362 requisitioned the castle. Several times the Earls of Mar lost it then won it back before in 1435 James I seized both earldom and castle, so destabilising the entire Northeast by removing the former centre of local authority (see **53**).

This followed the seizure of Kildrummy and its heiress, Isabel Countess of Mar, by Alexander Stewart, bastard son of the infamous Wolf of Badenoch. With the Wolf barely cold in a royal Dunkeld grave, his son's thugs seized Isabel's husband, Sir Malcolm Drummond, who soon died in a dungeon. Taking Kildrummy in 1404 and forcing Isabel to marry him, Stewart gained the Earldom of Mar and Lordship of the Garioch. Accepted by Aberdeen's cowed burghers as their protector, untroubled by the heartbroken death of his 'wife', in 1411 the new Earl of Mar redeemed himself at Harlaw (**65**), beating back Donald, Lord of the Isles. Now like his father before him virtually ruling the North, his threat to Scone led to the stronger southern power's inevitable response.

Fired in 1530 by John Strachan of Linturk, captured by Cromwell in 1654, again fired in 1690, it was at Kildrummy that John Erskine, 11th Earl of Mar ('Bobbin' John': see **37**), planned the 1715 uprising. After that, this last survivor of the region's courtyard castles was dismantled, being out of date and supplanted by the Northeast's many later towers and fortified houses.

Near the ruin is Kildrummy Castle Hotel (1900) a fine Jacobean pile designed by A. Marshall Mackenzie (**2**, **36**, **41**) for James Ogsdon, an Aberdeen soap-merchant who, buying the castle in 1898, tried to live in Warden's Tower, once the jail. Told by his wife to choose between the ruin or her, he built what is now the hotel, its terraced gardens in the Back Den open daily, April–October. There is also a woodland walk.

50.   To Rhynie & The Cabrach   *(Route, History)*

A mile north of Kildrummy a right turn leads up to the prominent 1805 parish kirk, by it a Bronze Age burial mound. In another mile, just past Mossat Antiques, is a junction (478195). Here the A944 breaks east (Alford 7, Aberdeen 33) via the Don's wooded north bank and under Lord Arthur's Hill (**53**) six miles to Bridge of Alford (**54**).

The continuing A97 runs north from Donside past Rhynie in Strathbogie to Huntly (**80**). Now we visit Rhynie, Tap o' Noth and the Cabrach, loop east to Clatt, then return south over the Correen Hills to Bridge of Alford.

ₐA mile or so north of the junction, the A97 reaches the airy moorland village of Lumsden. Founded *c*.1825 by Keith Lumsden of Clova House (1760; 445225) a mile to the west under the moors, this remote place hosts the Scottish Sculpture Workshop and the Sculpture Walk, both advertised at the village's southern edge by a huge steel-plate sculpture resembling a circular saw blade. Continuing, the road climbs over the watershed then descends to the Burn of Craig, headwater of the Bogie. Here (485245) the B9002 turns left (west) past a roofless 13th-century ruin, St. Mary's Auchindoir, its beech-hedged kirkyard by an old castle motte above the deep Den of Craig. From it the lane climbs to a steading (473249) opposite the entry to Craig Castle (471249; private). Here, a right turn runs three miles north past Wheedlemont to Rhynie, *en route* passing, left of the road where it continues east past a fork, remnants of a megalithic circle (483269).

Hidden in woodland, Craig Castle (*c*.1548) is a castellated, pink-harled L-plan château, among Scotland's finest, and in World War I victim of a Zeppelin raid, maybe due to its unshielded electric lighting. The first Gordon here was a grandson of Jock of Scurdargue (**51**, **80**), one of the Northeast's two main Gordon progeni-

81

tors. This grandson died at Flodden in 1513; *his* grandson fell at Pinkie in 1547; the next laird was involved in the murder of the Bonny Earl of Moray in 1592 (**23**) – and so on. 16th-century Scotland was rarely less than turbulent.

From Craig the B9002 climbs west over the bare Cabrach moor to meet, under the elegant north slope of the Buck (**48**), the Rhynie- Dufftown A941 (**52**).

Past the B9002 turn the A97 follows the Bogie two steep miles down to Rhynie, a draughty crossroads village under Tap o'Noth's bare dome (*'When Tap o' Noth puts on her cap/Rhynie folk will get a drap'*). The heart of an upland parish which Forbeses and Gordons both claim as their original Northeast home, today Rhynie is quiet. Yet, with a broad Square and pretty green, its spired 1823 parish church and 1920 war memorial stand out. The granite infantryman on the memorial's tall square plinth was sculpted by Robert Morrison (1890–1945). Lured back from the USA by the post-1918 demand for such memorials, he is called by some the finest granite craftsman of his era.

As talented was the ancient sculptor of the Rhynie Man – a bearded, tonsured man in a belted knee-length tunic, slender axe over right shoulder. Carved on a gabbro boulder and dated *c.*AD700–850, he may have been a Pictish (**67**) leader in a time when Christianity gained ground. The boulder, ploughed up in 1978 at Barflat nearby, is one of several local symbol stones. Unusually depicting a single figure, this – Grampian's first known figure carving – is to be found in Woodhill House, the Regional Council's Aberdeen HQ.

Near the cemetery just south of Rhynie and west of the Bogie is the Crawstane (497264) – another Pictish symbol stone. And if it's ancient mystery you're after…

51.   Tap o' Noth: Vitrified Mystery   *(History, Hill-Walk)*

Above Rhynie looms Tap o' Noth (484294; 1848ft; 563m; shown opposite)), maybe named after the Brittonic God of the Underworld, Gwyn ap Nudd. A bleak dome prominent for miles about, its steep slopes are crowned by the vitrified slag walls of one of Scotland's most spectacular, and second highest, Iron Age forts.

The way up starts at Scurdargue (484283; hereabouts in the 14th century lived Jock of that ilk: **80**) two miles west of Rhynie on the Cabrach-Dufftown A941. From a carpark by the red-roofed steading climb a track to a copse of beech and fir. At its top left edge, bear left on a grassy track skirting cattle-pasture and following a fence parallel to the base of the hill. Stick to this track. The direct climb through thick gorse then steeply up is hard. Nearing forestry, turn right up to a track climbing the hill's heathery south flank. Near its start, a path climbs steeply right – an option easier for descent. With views widening, the track traverses the south slope to the fort's main eastern entry.

The size of a football pitch, with an old well near the east end, the grassy interior lies under huge walls of tumbled slag, on the south and east sides vitrified – fused by vast heat into runs of lumpy, glassy stone. Tap o' Noth haunts the imagination. Who built the fort? What caused the vitrification? Nobody knows, but the earliest such forts (*c*.700BC) match the arrival in the land of iron-working, horse-riding continental Celts, possibly Q-Celtic-speaking Gaels, followed later by Brittonic P-Celtic-speakers who may have driven the Gaels on into Ireland, at least for the following millennium or so. Their purpose seems plain: defence against marauders. So, again, what caused the vitrification?

One theory is that huts were built against wooden palisades atop wood-interlaced slag walls, and firewood laid up against them. By accident amid gale (thrown sparks), or by enemy design, the lighting of this wood fired huts, palisades and walls, causing such heat as to achieve vitrification in hours, not weeks. But many find 'vitrification within hours' unlikely while, given up to 50 such sites from Bennachie (**68**) to the Inverness area, it assumes failure to learn from experience; or that conquerors destroyed such sites rather than take them over. And where did the wood come from? How was it dragged up such a steep slope? Tap o' Noth is well above the nearest trees. Though in the warm, wet early Neolithic (*c*.4000BC), the treeline was over 3000 feet, after 1500BC the climate was bitter. For centuries Scotland was almost empty. Folk returned or immigrated as the weather improved – but were Tap o' Noth and the adjoining Hill o' Noth forested *c*.500BC?

Tap o' Noth is dreich, especially in wild weather, yet in sunshine the view is splendid – north to Huntly (**80**), west over forested hills to Ben Rinnes, south over Rhynie to the Correen Hills, and east past Dunnideer (**69**) to Bennachie (**68**).

For a longer, circular seven-mile walk via Tap o' Noth, start at Scurdargue or park by the A97 at Oldnoth (522309) three miles north of Rhynie, and under wooded slopes follow a track west up the Glen of Noth. Entering forestry at the head of the glen, the track curls south to the edge of the wood (476292) a mile northwest of Scurdargue. Turn left up the forest fringe to the Tap o' Noth track. On leaving the fort, bear northeast over the saddle between Tap o' Noth and the rounded Hill o' Noth, then follow the latter's southeast flank two miles to Old Noth, staying high until gaps open in the gorse below, the going trackless but easy.

Just beyond Oldnoth the A97 sheds a right turn east over the Bogie to the B9002. Here a right turn through Kennethmont leads seven miles to Insch (**69**); the left turn in yards to Leith Hall (**70**). The A97 continues past Gartly (**82**) five miles to Huntly (**80**).

52. West of Tap o' Noth: The Cabrach *(Routes)*

A mile past Scurdargue the A941 passes a right turn at Mains of Lesmoir (471282). This north-bound lane leads to a forested upland cut through by ravine-bound burns and tracks weaving for miles on end. Flanking the forest, the continuing A941 climbs the lonely Cabrach ('stony pass') – the moorland parish by the Deveron's source under the Buck (**48**). Soon the district boundary – it runs north from the Buck through the junction with the moorland road from Craig Castle (**50**) – is crossed. At Cabrach joining the fledgling Deveron, the A941 follows the now-wooded river north and winds down past the Grouse Inn (379305) to the confluence of Deveron and Black Water by Bridgend. The Cabrach was once a whisky-smuggling trail; and appropriately the Grouse Inn is famed for the number of its malts on optic.

At Bridgend a minor road breaks north (374317) up the Deveron. Winding seven miles north past Haugh of Glass to the Huntly-Dufftown A900, it repays exploration. Past Lower Cabrach church and a primary school it climbs the open glen's west flank, the Deveron below, the bare opposite ridges of the Daugh of Corinacy (402312) impressive. With many of the scattered hill-farms derelict, from the crest a gradual descent passes Mill of Lynabain, pink-harled Beldorney Castle (423370), and a stone circle left of the road (425378). Reaching the river at Haugh of Glass, by a war memorial (424394) the road forks: left to a lane up the Markie water; right along the wooded riverbank past Blairmore School to the Huntly-Dufftown A920; or straight on a mile to the A920.

From Bridgend the continuing Cabrach route squeezes through a narrow pass before descending to Glen Fiddich. Crossing the river it climbs past the stark hilltop ruin of Auchindoun Castle (347376). Built on Pictish earthworks in the 15th century by Thomas Cochrane, the Earl of Mar hanged by the barons in 1482, later it was the lair of Adam Gordon who sacked Corgarff (**44**). In 1592 it was torched by the Mackintoshes, who that year also raided Deeside (**35**) to avenge the murder of the Bonnie Earl of Moray: **23**, **80**). A crumbling three-storey tower – its loose masonry unsafe – surrounded by curtain walls, it's reached by a stony track (Historic Scotland marker) climbing half-a-mile east from the A941, which itself in another half-mile descends to the A920 by Dufftown (see *Round Moray…*).

Now it's time to return to Strathdon via Clatt and Suie Hill.

53.   Druminnor to Lord Arthur's Hill   *(Route, Walk)*

From Rhynie Square, Bogie Road (to Druminnor, Clatt and Leslie) departs east up over a staggered crossing. Further up the brae, keep right at the next fork (Clatt 3) and up past a wooded lodge on the left, serving Druminnor Castle (515265).

In origin an L-plan towerhouse built by Alexander 1st Lord Forbes in 1440, Druminnor's construction marked the rise of Forbes power in Mar and throughout the Northeast, but their long feud with the formidable Gordons (**80**) taxed them hard. In October 1571, a Forbes-Gordon battle at nearby Tillyangus (**44**) led to the partial sack of the castle; but Lady Margaret Gordon, wife of the jailed Master of Forbes, stayed on with her lover Patrick Hepburn, bastard son of the Bishop of Moray. Divorcing her on release in 1573, in 1577 the Master of Forbes restored Druminnor, which in 1660 was converted into a mansion, with later remodellings. Meanwhile the Forbes seat had gone over the hills to Putachie by Keig (**57**).

In Druminnor's Great Hall, it's said, 15 Gordons were slain by their Forbes hosts at a dinner held to end the feud, which simmered on thereafter. Still Forbes-owned, Druminnor is private, but may be visited by written request.

On the right just past the Druminnor lodge a lane (513263) climbs south. For a triangular eight-mile moorland trek south over the Correen ridge, west up Lord Arthur's Hill, and back north over Brux Hill, take this lane. In a mile, having passed right turns to Barflat and Bankhead, at a fork above Bankhead bear right up to a second fork by a belt of forestry (504251). Parking, start up a grassy track east of the forestry, wide views all about. With Clova Hill ahead the track bisects gorse-hemmed pasture and reaches a gate, cattle-pasture and a small pine-wood beyond. Flank the wood to the top of the trees, where a fence runs right to a wooden gate (506240). Over it, start up heathery Clova Hill, the faint rising track soon more obvious. Ignoring turns, past grouse butts and a little burial cross (a dog?) climb just east of south (160°) to a bare saddle under a low crest (1598ft; 487m) to the left.

By now the rutted track has passed what the OS map shows as a track breaking right (507236), southwest over Brux Hill. This exists, save for the final section, and may be joined a half-mile south of the map-given junction, at approx. 512228. The short connecting track is south of a little lochan amid boggy ground.

Past it continue southeast on the clear main track under the wooded Hill of Millmedden (1444ft; 440m), Lord Arthur's Hill prominent beyond boggy Limer Shank below. Past an old quarry the track curves east then steeply down towards derelict Hillock of Terpersie. With Manahattock Hill (1375ft; 419m) ahead, descend over a burn to an east-west track (534204) from Dubston by Terpersie Castle – also a possible starting-point for this walk.

Climb this track west up the Fouchie Shank ridge leading to Lord Arthur's Hill (514198; 1699ft; 518m – the photo next page looks east from this ridge. Where the track curls under the hill to a crossing, continue straight over and up past the grouse butts to the rock shelter atop the hill – the easy summit track isn't shown on

the map. With grand views of Donside below, continue west over the heather and off the hill, the Buck, Tap o' Noth and Ben Rinnes all prominent. Descending to a moorland junction (506202) continue west a mile past native pinewood up bare Edinbanchory Hill (1532ft; 467m). At a Y-fork (a lone tree just ahead), keep right to a point where, above Strathbogie with the track ahead fading, an old track breaks right (505205; north) over Brux Hill (500210; 1558ft; 475m).

Though faint, this track's line is plain, the heather moor easy, and orientation simple. With Bennachie to the east and Tap o' Noth ahead, as the track improves the quarry and outward track may be seen over the sink of Limer Shank. Now nearing the outward track, the only problem is that, as mentioned, the map misleads. Curving round Badingair Hill (507225; 1568ft; 478m) the track fades then (by an electric fence) vanishes. But, just south of a lochan, a path breaks right, not far, to join the outward track at approx. 512228. Return as you came, perhaps detouring to Cairnmore (504260), an overgrown Iron Age fort on the southern edge of the forestry by which you parked.

54. Over Suie Hill to Alford *(Route, Visit)*

From Druminnor, the lane from Rhynie continues two miles up the brae and above the Gadie Burn to Clatt (*cleith*, 'hidden'), an upland hamlet made a burgh of barony in 1501. Here (left two miles north to Kennethmont: **70**), turn right (east) towards Leslie and Auchleven then, in under a mile and by the old village hall, right again (547254). Soon passing the drive to Knockespock House Hotel (544242), the road, another old military route, climbs to a forested saddle between the Hill of Milmedden and Suie Hill. Here lay-bys offer fine views north over Strathbogie and the Garioch; also an information board showing places to visit. A carpark east of the road (548232) serves the western end of the Gordon Way, which runs 12 miles east over Suie Hill, Knock Saul, the Brindy and Bennachie to the Bennachie Centre (**68**). This is one starting-point for a circular walk round Suie Hill and Knock Saul (**56**).

Now descending to the green Donside haughs of the Howe of Alford, the road enters Tullynessle and Forbes, parishes united in 1808. By Tullynessle's 1876 Gothic kirk (558196), a lane breaks northwest a mile to Terpersie Castle (546202: private); a miniature Z-plan 1561 Gordon mansion, restored 1983–9. Just before its drive, a track breaks left over a burn to Dubston and west up Lord Arthur's Hill.

At a junction (567178) a mile south of Tullynessle turn left for Montgarrie, Keig, and the route through My Lord's Throat to Monymusk (**58**). From this junction a right turn down the brae joins the Donside A944 at Bridge of Alford, once Boat of Forbes, with its welcome pub. Here the triple-arched 1811 Forbes Bridge crosses the Don. On the south bank the A944 takes up the A980 from Banchory (**21**) via Craigievar (**55**), then turns east into Alford (*Aa-ford*; pop. 1972).

Ringed by hills 25 miles west of Aberdeen, this small town (or large village?) developed rapidly when the Vale of Alford railway, now long closed, opened in 1859. The old station houses the Railway Museum and an information centre (019755-62052; April–Sept.), and a narrow-gauge line runs from the village north to Haughton House Country Park. Here too is the Grampian Transport Museum (019755-62906; April–Oct.), and the Alford Heritage Centre (019755-62906), housed in the old Auction Mart which closed in 1986 – it was on these lush haughs that the famous Aberdeen-Angus breed of beef cattle was first bred. Alford is also the birthplace of Charles Murray (1864–1941), author of *Hamewith* and among the finest poets to write in Doric (**107**).

A mile southeast of the village, white-harled Balfluig Castle (1556; 586151) is an old Forbes house sold to the Farquharsons in 1753. Deserted, it was restored in 1966. Another local Farquharson seat is Haughton House (1790), now amid the Country Park which, with visitor centre and waymarked trail, was opened to the public in 1975. Two miles west of Alford is the ruin of Asloun Castle (542148), where Montrose (**2**, **15**, **78**) spent the night of 2 July 1645 before at Bridge of Alford luring Covenanters under General Baillie onto boggy ground. Routing them, his victory was spoiled by the death of Lord George Gordon, killed pursuing Baillie.

55.   South of Alford: Craigievar   (*Route, Visit, History*)

Under a mile west of Alford, where the A944 bends north over the Don, the A980 climbs south under rolling hills three miles past Muir of Fowlis and Ladymill. From these hamlets lanes depart west above the Howe of Cushnie in the hill-parish of Leochel-Cushnie where, in woodland southwest of the present kirk, lies the overgrown ruin of St. Bride's Church (1637). Beyond this backland, lanes and tracks run northwest towards the Don at Kildrummy (**49**), *en route* skirting the southern flank of Coilliebhar (1747ft; 573m). On it in 1887 Donside folk built the region's biggest bonfire to celebrate Victoria's Jubilee. Other lanes weave south to the Midmar-Tarland B9119 (**28**)

Five miles south of Alford a signposted right turn off the A980 rises a mile to wooded lawns round Craigievar Castle (566095; National Trust; 013398-83635). Built between 1620 and 1626, this fairytale extravaganza is widely considered the Bell family (**24**) masterpiece.

Pink-harled amid its grounds, with views east over the vale below to Corrennie Moor and northeast to Bennachie, Craigievar impresses because it was never fudged by the later extensions spoiling so many other buildings of the same era. A 'consummation of Scottish châteaux, perfect both in mass and detail'; the 'epitome of the Jacobean renaissance in Scotland' it's basically an L-plan tower-house, on the ground floor sober, but increasingly inventive as, rocket-like, it ascends. From the first floor two corbelled stair-turrets jut from the walls; three storeys higher angle turrets erupt. With no one profile like any of the others, and unmarred by surrounding walls and out-houses, this exquisite tower was built for

'Danzig Willie' – William Forbes, brother of the Bishop of Aberdeen and a rich merchant trading with Danzig in the Baltic, thus his nickname.

Yet Craigievar is still a stronghold, with gun-slits at ground level, narrow windows above, and only one entry – an arched doorway protected by a thick iron-studded outer door and by a yett (gate) of interwoven iron bars. The two spiral stair-cases climbing the castle are so narrow it's said that, though generations of the Forbeses who lived here might enter by the door, they all left by the window, it being as hard to get coffins down the stairs as it was for raiders to get up them. None ever did, though until the mid-18th century many a malefactor was tried by the barony court under the decorative pendants and rich relief work of the groined vault of Craigievar's great hall.

South of Craigievar the A980 winds on through wooded hills over a staggered crossing of the B9119, in six miles reaching Lumphanan (**25**).

56.   North of Alford: Round Suie Hill & Knock Saul   *(Walk)*

Starting from Suie Hill carpark (548232; **54**), or from Tullynessle Glen north of Alford, this six-mile circuit follows the Gordon Way over Suie Hill and Knock Saul, and returns west via forestry tracks. The route from the carpark described here involves an extra mile. The Tullynessle approach is described when reached.

At the forested crest of the road from Clatt, from the carpark the Gordon Way starts east by a noticeboard. Past a 'march stone' marking an old estate boundary and through a new plantation it rises gently a half-mile east to heather moor atop Suie Hill (557232; 1362ft; 415m). Enjoying the fine views, keep on past an old fenceline and the return path (below) to swing left under Black Hillock down to the treeline, following a spruce-needled path east into mature forestry. Over a logged area the track levels and narrows, a short further descent east leading to a way-marked left turn to a main track at the forest edge.

Turn right 50 yards then, with the track curling south, break diagonally left (107°) over scrappy newly-planted ground, then zigzag down a bank via wooden steps to a main track in Den of Drumgown. With Knock Saul's dense-wooded slopes opposite, turn left (north) 30 yards to a fork (575234). Turn right then, in a few feet, right again on a narrow waymarked path. Over a footbridge this zigzags steeply up through gloomy wood to a level, rutted, russet-carpeted track bearing southeast. Where this vanishes, bear left 20 yards past tree-stumps to the next waymarker and continue right (128°) up to a north-south forest road. Over it climb a grassy, slippery firecut steeply up to Knock Saul's heather dome (580231; 1353ft; 412m).

With a cairn giving shelter from the wind, the views are fine – Bennachie and the Garioch ahead, Deeside hills to the south, Ben Avon faraway, and Tap o' Noth with Ben Rinnes beyond to the northwest.

Descend east over a forest road (583229) then over a cleared area to a second road (587230). Leaving the Gordon Way (it descends southeast past Priests' Wood via Brindy Hill, crossing the B992 before climbing the Bennachie ridge), turn right. Curl southwest above fields, briefly back into forestry. At a T-junction beyond a pole-gate at the edge of the wood, turn left to a second junction, above Knockhill (578225) in Tullynessle Glen.

(Here, atop the public road with room to park, is the alternative start. From Alford, drive north through Montgarrie on the Redhouse road and, at a junction two miles further north, keep left past Muckleton to Knockhill.)

With fine views over the Don, from Knockhill continue northwest on a track curling left under the forest and through south-facing fields to Millburn (573228). Here turn right up a broad track 30 yards to a Y-fork. Keep left uphill to a junction.

Turn left (west) along the slope above Coldwells, entering mature forestry. At a turning circle, continue northwest up the cut beyond on a rough, horse-churned path. This leads to a broad heathery gap running north up Suie Hill. Amid this gap turn left up a faint path. At the open top by the fenceline this path intersects the Gordon Way. For Suie Hill carpark turn left (west), back as you came. This varied, stimulating walk should take three hours.

Note: initially I continued west beyond Millburn to Coldwell (564226), seeking a path shown on the OS map as running from west of Coldwell northwest to the carpark; but at Coldwell angry dogs, fences, a steep gully and devastated slopes discouraged me...

57. East of Alford: To My Lord's Throat & Monymusk   *(Routes)*

From Alford the A944 runs east past the B992 junction at Whitehouse, in three miles starting up wooded slopes to a crest where, at Tillyfourie, the B993 breaks northeast to Monymusk, Kemnay and Inverurie (**62**). Just before this, a bridge (635131) over the old railway line marks the start of a there-and-back four-mile forest walk up to the Green Hill (644146; 1305ft; 398m). Near the summit is Luath's Stone, where allegedly Macbeth's son, also known as Lulach the Fatuous, was slain after his father's death (**25**). *En route* is a remnant of Whitehill stone circle, with only two megaliths still standing (644135). Past this point the A944 descends towards Aberdeen via Dunecht and Westhill (see **11**).

North of Alford and the Don, reached from Alford or Bridge of Alford, with its huge Victorian meal-mill Montgarrie is a pleasant backwater. Through it the road from Bridge of Alford continues three miles over broad farmland to Keig, a hamlet above road and river. With a fine Gothic parish kirk (1834–5), Keig is also entered by a lane which, looping north from Montgarrie (the Redhouse road; above) descends under the wooded, fort-topped Barmkyn (599201) past the recumbent stone circle (596194) at Old Keig. At 53 tons, the recumbent is Scotland's largest, and is thought to have been carried eleven miles. The circle, in a strip of wood below the road, is immediately northwest of the 17th century Old Church of Keig, a roofless rectangular ruin, its kirkyard now used for Forbes family burials.

At the east end of Keig these routes meet at a junction with the B992, which from this point runs south over Telford's single-arch 1817 Bridge of Keig three miles to the A944; and north six miles through Auchleven to Insch (**69**). Opposite the junction a tree-lined drive leads to Castle Forbes (620194; 1815–21; private), originally called Putachie. Of this vast block the contemporary Lord Cockburn sneered that: 'Lord Forbes...has lately built a new house, in as bad taste as possible.' Was he paid to say this by Gordons pursuing the futile ancient feud...?

Turning north on the B992, at a second junction (615195; signposted Donview & Forest Walks: 4 miles), the right turn follows the north bank of the Don through the richly-wooded gorge of My Lord's Throat towards Monymusk. Named after My Lord Forbes, once Scotland's premier baron, this scenic route winds under

Black Hill (1411ft; 430m) past a dyke of massive stones before descending to the river. Under Millstone Hill and just past Mains of Tilliefoure, a wooded riverbank avenue breaks west through large gates to the Place of Tilliefoure (659195); a 17th-century Leslie tower restored 1884–5, and so among the first 'modern' restorations of an older ruin. Not far beyond, the roadside Donview carpark (672191) marks the start of forest walks up Millstone Hill (1340ft; 408m) and on to Bennachie (**68**). Continuing under steep wooded slopes where the green-banked Don surges past midstream boulders, the road soon leaves gorge and river and now, amid fertile haughs, reaches a junction (686171).

From this point, in a mile the left turn north to Chapel of Garioch (**66**) reaches another junction at Blairdaff, where the right turn soon forks; left to Inverurie, right to Kemnay (**59**). Continuing north under the Mither Tap of Bennachie, over a broad-viewed ridge in two more miles the Chapel of Garioch road passes a turn (700218) to the Bennachie Centre and carpark: this at the start of forest walks, the Gordon Way, and the ascent of Bennachie (**68**).

For Monymusk, at 686171 turn right, then right again over the Don to a crossing. Here a dead-end right turn west passes Pitfichie Castle (677176: c.1560–70): a pink-harled tower which, roofless after 1769 and a ruin by 1936, was rebuilt in 1977. With wooded Pitfichie Hill above, the lane beyond runs to Old Paradise Wood by the Don; a popular beauty spot favoured by many.

From the crossing, turn left along a tree-lined avenue a mile into Monymusk.

58.   Monymusk & Castle Fraser *(Route, Visit, Walks)*

With its leafy main street ringed by low hills amid rich Donside haughs, this 'secret heart of the North-East' (McKean) is magical, its Square (c.1830–40) almost too pretty. Neat black railings pen a wooded green once used by Banffshire drovers as a cattle-pound; and red cast-iron lamp-posts flank granite ashlar cottages, each with diamond-paned windows and canopied wooden gables. Laid out in 1716 by Sir

Archibald Grant, the original heather-thatched stone houses, mostly rebuilt in the 1860s, were tudorised between 1889 and 1902 by Sir Arthur Grant.

Like Old Deer (**103**) in Buchan, Monymusk's chief magic lies in its antiquity as a site of worship. The Square is dominated by the square tower of St. Mary's Parish Church, Aberdeenshire's only Norman kirk (see previous page). Established as an Augustinian Priory by Gilchrist, Earl of Mar in 1170, from which era date the chancel arch and red granite tower, its dressed sandstone masonry came from Kildrummy (**49**). There are two Pictish symbol stones (**67**) built into the nave, and a third, the Monymusk Stone, (*c*.800) in the entrance. These attest to even earlier worship here, for long before St. Mary's was built Monymusk was the home of culdees (*celi dei*), christianised druids who practised the new religion in its early, Celtic monastic form. And just as Old Deer was the home of the 9th–10th century *Book of Deer*, the earliest-known surviving text in Scots Gaelic, so in St. Mary's long lay the Monymusk Reliquary or Brecbannoch.

Containing relics of St. Columba, early Scots kings carried this casket into battle to aid their cause. Removed to the House of Monymusk during the Reformation, it's now in the Scottish National Museum. As for the House of Monymusk, this vast Forbes courtyard palace on the north bank of the Don incorporated some of the priory buildings when built *c*.1584, and in 1712 was sold to the Grants, who remain the owners.

From Monymusk Square the road continues south through the village to meet the B993 to Kemnay. Here a left turn east, past a lane south to Cluny Castle (688127: **11**) and the A944, leads towards Castle Fraser (723125; National Trust; 01330-833463; open daily May–Sept and October weekends; grounds all year). To visit this huge pile, after two miles turn either first or second right off the B993, south through Craigearn. Half-a-mile on, fork left on a lane signposted to Dunecht, Castle Fraser also indicated. Climbing above Donside haughs, turn left onto the castle driveway. Between broad lawns this descends a fine oak avenue past the John Bell Memorial Stone; a standing stone in a wooden paddock by a dead tree, commemorating one of the architects.

Begun in 1575 for Michael Fraser, the 6th laird, by Thomas Leiper (**72**) and completed 1617–18 by Bell, this grandly elaborate Z-plan castle was originally called Muchalls-in-Mar. Renamed in 1695, '*Fraser's glorious pile...whose structure is by none excelled*' (as the 18th-century poem 'Don' puts it), it remained in Fraser hands until the 20th century. Above two low wings, the six-storey main block with its corbelled corner turrets culminates in elaborate upperworks and excellent views over the grounds. There is a huge heraldic frontispiece on the north wall of this block, within which the Great Hall, its fireplace almost three yards wide, occupies the entire first floor. With a square walled garden, a tearoom and adventure playground, estate trails winding through the 350 acres of parkland and well-wooded policies are open to walkers.

59.   Kemnay & Fetternear to Inverurie   *(Routes, Walk)*

From Castle Fraser returning north, at Craigearn keep straight on through the hamlet past the 12-foot high Lang Stane of Craigearn (724149) to the B993, and turn right (northeast) a mile into Kemnay (pop.3450). To the left at the southern edge of the village roads break northwest and north. Crossing the Don, the first leads towards Fetternear (see below); while, slanting through Kemnay, the second loops round the quarries on Paradise Hill before returning to the Inverurie-bound B993.

Named after the 'kame' or 'kem', the gravel ridge on which it stands, in the 19th century Kemnay's population increased fivefold due to the arrival of the railway and quarrying of the silver-grey Kemnay granite, exported over the world and used in at least seven bridges over the Thames. The first Paradise Hill quarry was opened by John Burnett to make alterations at Kemnay House (17th century); but it was after Aberdonian John Fyfe founded his firm (nowadays producing the synthetic Fyfestone) in 1846 that business really boomed. With other quarries nearby at Leschangie and Whitestones, what had been 'a paltry hamlet' prospered, but later declined until the region's recent oil boom brought a new demand for housing. With lovely views over broad Donside haughs to Bennachie, Kemnay's population is again expanding.

From this now-largely residential village the B994 breaks east three miles to the A96 south of Kintore (**8**); while the B993 climbs northeast above the Don, in three miles passing Bruce's Camp near Crichie. With an Iron Age fort atop the hill, here Robert I is said to have lain sick before defeating the Comyns at Barra (**64**). Past Crichie the road descends to Port Elphinstone on the A96 Inverurie bypass.

93

For a roundabout route to Inverurie via Fetternear, take the road northwest from Kemnay's south end (see above). Over the Don bending left, after a mile it reaches, on the right by a high stone wall, a lane signposted to Fetternear and Netherton Business Centre. In under half-a-mile turn right onto a speed-bumped driveway past the business centre. Parking, walk on to a wooded right turn then, on the left, cross a bridge with the sign CAUTION WEAK BRIDGE. Beyond it (DANGEROUS RUINS NO ENTRY) is the roofless but impressive ruin of the House of Fetternear (see previous page). With the footings of the palace begun in 1226 by Bishop Ramsay of Aberdeen and extended in 1330 by Bishop Kyninmond nearby, this huge, elongated mansion was added to the Old House by Count Patrick Leslie in 1691–3. The Old House itself had been built after the bishops leased then gifted the land to John Leslie, 8th Earl Balquhain, in 1550. With a fine 1693 armorial panel over the main door displaying the coronet of a Count of the Holy Roman Empire, and also boasting 19th-century crenellated parapets and corner towers, this unusual mansion burned down in 1919. With its pleasant woods and timeless air, Fetternear is worth a visit.

From Netherton continuing north, in half-a-mile turn right two miles to the lovely wooded den at Burnhervie, after which the road follows the Don's north bank past a fork (see below) before crossing the A96 into Inverurie.

First, though, a trip through time…

60.   Megalithic Mystery: Easter Aquhorthies   *(Route, Prehistory, Walk)*

Of the stone circles already met on this tour (Cullerlie, Clune, the Nine Stanes, Sunhoney, Midmar, etc.), and those still to be met (Loanhead of Daviot, Rothiemay, Strichen and others) perhaps the region's best-known is sited on a hillside a mile north of the Don and two miles west of Inverurie, at Easter Aquhorthies (733208).

Dated *c.*3000BC and signposted from Inverurie's north, Blackhall roundabout, the site can also be reached from the north bank Donside road. A mile northeast of Burnhervie the road bends left to a fork, the right turn continuing a mile to Inverurie. Turn left half-a-mile to a second fork, and left again a mile to a carpark by the track to Easter Aquhorthies. About 200 yards up it turn right to the fenced-in circle. 64 feet (19.5m) in diameter, it consists of nine stones set in a low bank, a huge recumbent (12.5ft; 3.8m), and two flankers which, over seven feet high, are noticeably taller than the other stones. The impression of a gunsight or sighting device fixed on the southwest horizon is strengthened by the presence amid the grassy circle of a small flat stone, suggesting a sighting-position. In addition, in front of the recumbent two large blocks of stone define an area implicitly enclosed, perhaps for ceremonial purposes. The recumbent is of smoothed reddish granite from Bennachie; the flankers are of grey granite, and the circle stones are rough pink porphyry. The site has not been excavated, but an early reference to a cist suggests that there may have been a central cairn.

94

So to the big question: what were these circles *for?* Lunar observatories and calendrical calculators? Sites of healing and ceremonial? Maybe. But accumulators set up to tap and store fertilising geomagnetic energy? Navigational beacons erected by extraterrestrials? Such notions are no more bizarre than the older beliefs of folklore; that the stones are 'false men' or 'dancers'. In Lewis, the Callanish stones were men allegedly petrified by a wizard. Oxfordshire's Rollright Stones (a king and his men likewise petrified) go down to the river to drink, moving about so confusingly that it's said they can't be counted. Of the 'Giants' Dance', Stonehenge, it's said the magician Merlin 'flew' or 'sang' the stones from Ireland. The Irish druid Mog Ruith flew about in a vessel made of stone. Stones like the Lia Fail (Stone of Destiny), and the stone from which Arthur drew Excalibur, were said to recognise or confer true kingship, as if somehow alive.

Odd lights and will-o'-the-wisps (geomagnetic anomalies?) were seen at such sites, from which the Church found it hard to draw folk away. Saints trying to found a church elsewhere might find the 'Devil' nightly removing the stones back to the old mound or circle, so that many churches, especially in Wales, ended up within stone circles, on old earthworks, or on alignments between megalithic sites.

Their sophisticated geometry only deepens the mystery. Surveying Callanish and many other surviving circles, in every case the engineer Alexander Thom found a ground-plan derived from a 'megalithic yard' of 2.72 feet and basic right-angle triangles – Pythagorean geometry 2000 years before Pythagoras! Thom also showed how megalithic geometry derives from the extreme positions of sun, moon and stars as they cross the horizon. Alignments of 'sighting' stones may have been set up to indicate which heavenly points would determine the shape of each design. With each ground-plan thus astronomically prefigured, the architects generated circles and ellipses with an accuracy close to one part in a thousand. Abstracting celestial motions into a system of geometry and math demonstrating the later hermetic epigram 'As above, so below', they left their stone textbooks of natural science and law for us to try to read, 5000 years later.

As for Easter Aquhorthies, recent research suggests that it may have been used as an 'echo chamber', amplifying sound during ceremonial. The distribution of sound may somehow be controlled by the distribution and shaping of the stones. Impossible? Maybe not so, given that its name may be derived from the Gaelic for 'field of prayer', suggesting that the circle's purpose was remembered long after it had been abandoned. But one thing *is* sure – the mystery of the circles will never be settled finally or in full...

Section 4:

The Garioch, Formartine & Ythanside

61. Introduction: North of Bennachie

East and north of Bennachie and the Correen Hills and south of the River Ythan the land varies from coastal plain and undulating farmland to bare upland. It consists of the Garioch ('Geerie', from the Gaelic *garbhthach*, 'rough ground'), the old thanedom of Formartine, and the backlands north of the Glens of Foudland (**71**) between Fyvie (**78**) and Huntly (**80**).

A medieval earldom that runs from Kemnay, Kintore and Inverurie northwest past Insch (**69**), much of the Garioch is as its name suggests – rough ground, but also ground long inhabited. Rich in megalithic circles, as at Broomend of Crichie (**62**), Loanhead of Daviot (**66**) and Easter Aquhorthies (**60**), its steadings and stone-dyked pastures are haunted by the ghosts of folk who were here at least five millennia ago. Later, Iron Age tribes fortified the hill-tops, as at Crichie (**59**), Barra Hill (**64**), Dunnideer (**69**), and the Mither Tap of Bennachie (**68**); and *c*.AD83 the Romans came marching through, camping at Kintore (**8**), Durno (**66**) and Ythanwells (**71**), and perhaps fighting Calgacus on the slopes of Bennachie (**16, 66**). Later still, leaving only their symbol stones (**67, 69**), the Picts 'vanished' and the Scots prevailed, until feudalising Canmore kings introduced Norman barons to the region, which thereafter witnessed much bloody mayhem, as at Barra (**64**), Harlaw (**65**) and Inverurie – until, after the '45, the centuries of violence ended.

East and northeast of the Garioch, and occupying the fertile eastern lowland end of Gordon District, Formartine embraces the coastal plain from north of Aberdeen to the Ythan estuary (**73**), then bears west past Ellon (**75**), Pitmedden (**72**) and Oldmeldrum (**64**) to Haddo (**76**), Methlick, and the Braes of Gight (**77**). Beyond Gight, save for brief fertility in the pleasant, Ythan-watered Vale of Fyvie (the old boundary between Formartine and Buchan: see **78**), there opens up gaunt, raw high ground which, bisected by the Oldmeldrum-Turriff A947, and by the Inverurie-Forgue B9001, has little in common with gentler Formartine's broad fields, gardens and great houses.

Starting with Inverurie and the area about, this section explores Bennachie, continues northwest through the Garioch; then returns east to journey through Formartine and Ythanside, from the coastal Sands of Forvie inland past Ellon to Fyvie.

62. Inverurie: Ancient & Modern   *(Visit, History)*

Made a royal burgh by Robert the Bruce after its folk helped him defeat the Comyns at nearby Barra in 1308, in 1663 appointed 'heid burgh for the regality of the Gareoch', today Inverurie (pop. 10,603) is Gordon District's administrative centre. Sited between the Aberdeen-Inverness railway and the A96 trunk route in the neck of the flood-plain at the confluence of Urie and Don, snug under hills dominated by Bennachie, the town's ancient remains indicate how important the site was to the Garioch's first farmers.

Of the early settlement at the Stanners by the twin alluvial mounds of the Bass (782206), it's said that on seeing it a Roman centurion sneered, 'Urbs in Rure' (*'city in the country'*) – today the motto on Inverurie's coat of arms. *C.*500 the Picts (**67**) established a centre here, amid the old ford of the Don placing a stone, on it carved a salmon – if you could see the salmon, the river was safe to cross. From the palisaded fort round the Bass this crossing led to ancient burial grounds and the start, at the Druidsfield (Broomend of Crichie), of a processional causeway running three miles southeast to Kintore's Castle Hill (**8**). Of 72 stones once lining the route only three survive, one, in the Druidsfield circle, being later carved by the Picts. From another carved stone – the Brandsbutt Stone, now standing amid an Inverurie housing estate – after *c.*700 Pictish Christian missionaries preached and converted, as they did also from a kirk by the Bass.

After 1057 Malcolm Canmore and his descendants, notably David I (1124–53), encouraged Norman settlement. The Bass became the motte of David of Huntingdon, the Bruce's great-great-grandfather; the Norman royal burgh of Nrurin or Enrowi being built about it. But this site, *whaur creepin Urie greets its mountain cousin Don*, as the 'weaver poet' William Thom (1798–1848) put it, so often flooded that in time folk moved to higher ground round about the main Aberdeen-Inverness turnpike.

With Barra and Harlaw (**65**) the area's main medieval battles, during the 17th century Civil War both the Covenanters and Montrose's Royalists occupied Inverurie. A century later in 1745 the Jacobites drove government forces out of the town and away from the fords over Urie and Don but, *en route* to Culloden in 1746, two regiments of Cumberland's infantry were billeted in the town, during their stay torching the Castle of Balquhain two miles northwest of the burgh (732237: **66**).

Modern prosperity began with the opening in 1807 of the Aberdeenshire Canal, which ended at nearby Port Elphinstone (thus the name). With the triangular market place dominated after 1862 by the baroque granite 1862 Town Hall, the railway's arrival in 1852 led to the growth of the Railway Works which, until their closure in 1969, provided mass employment. Tate's Paper Mills also aided Inverurie's growth, but the many private slaughterhouses caused problems until the end of the 19th century, the: *water in some parts* [of the burgh] *being so polluted as to be unfit to give an animal to drink.*

13 miles from Aberdeen, today oil-related work and housing-demand ensure that Inverurie remains vigorous. With the information centre in Inverurie Bookshop (18 High St., 01467-625800) open all year, there is plenty to do hereabouts – angling, golfing, the walks up Bennachie, visits to ancient sites and to the popular Thainstone Sunday Market with its stalls and car boot sales…plus local walks like the one described next…

63.   The Bass to Keith Hall   *(Walk)*

This easy, varied three-mile circuit can be started from central Inverurie by the Town Hall or, more evocatively, from the Bass. From central Inverurie, drive south down High Street. Where it swings right (St. James's Place), continue via Keithhall Road (B993; signposted to Keith Hall and Whiterashes). Pass under the railway bridge and park on the left by the cemetery wall, being sure not to block access. Here, amid headstones and by the banks of the Urie, the green flat-topped mound of the Bass is prominent, a path winding diagonally up it inviting closer inspection.

   Start north up a short lane between cemetery and railway embankment. Bear right to the riverbank, then left (north) over a stile. Follow the riverside path 250 yards to a second stile. Here, where the Urie bends east, continue up a wooded bank parallel to the railway, pasture to the right. Bear right round the house ahead, over a rise, left past the house towards Inverurie, and right onto a lane (Old Port Road). With hedged fields to the right and the railway and town to the left, follow this straight lane nearly a mile towards the railway station. Before reaching it, the lane bends right, up to Souterford Road (Oldmeldrum B9170) at the town limit. (If starting from the town centre, take this road.)

   Via pavement then roadside path follow this road northeast past industrial works, and after 600 yards (fields now either side) cross the Urie at Souterford. At a junction (Kingoodie 4) by the bend a few yards on, turn right uphill 50 yards, and right again onto a drive past the North Lodge of Keithhall, noting the request to keep your dog on a lead. Continue southeast along a beech and silver birch-fringed avenue past a left turn to Keithhall Nurseries, and on past banks of rhododendron under tall wellingtonias.

At a crossing (787214) just past an equestrian field turn left (east) on the continuing main avenue through stone gateposts to the Home Farm steading. Opposite it and before a second set of gateposts, turn right (south) on a track through reedy parkland. Soon, with a green slope climbing left, through trees on the right appears pink-harled Keith Hall (788213; private) – *Keithhall* refers to the parish.

Originally Caskieben (the name of an earthwork castle, its remains still visible nearby), this Renaissance mansion began life as a 16th-century Z-plan tower-house, in it born Arthur Johnston of Caskieben (1587–1641), known as 'the Scottish Ovid' due to his skill in Latin. With a large, four-panel heraldic shield over the main door, the four-storey south front was added in 1690 by Sir John Keith, 1st Earl of Kintore. Credited with saving the Honours of Scotland during the 1651–2 siege of Dunnottar (**15**), he'd bought the estate from the Johnstons in 1662 and gained his earldom in 1677.

Past the mansion the driveway curls southwest above a wooded, reed-rich pond, then descends to the B993. Turn right downhill past South Lodge (*c*.1810), its eye-catching turreted central white octagon colonnade-linked to mini-projections. Below it, carefully cross the narrow 1809 Urie Bridge – there is no pavement and oncoming traffic is hard to see. Immediately beyond it are the cemetery and the Bass, where we started.

64.   Kinkell, Barra & Oldmeldrum   *(Routes, History)*

Besides the bypassing A96, various other routes depart from Inverurie. To the east, over Urie Bridge and above South Lodge the B993 bends right then, further up the brae and atop the bank below which Don and Ugie meet, left at a fork, continuing five miles over undulating open land to the A947 at Whiterashes, between Newmachar (**7**) and Oldmeldrum.

From the fork a road signposted to Balbithan and Fintray, also Kinkell Church, continues straight on. At a second fork after half-a-mile, the dead-end lane ahead soon reaches Kinkell and the roofless 16th-century kirk on its Donside haugh. By its ruined walls stands the evocative graveslab of Sir Gilbert de Greenlaw, who fell at Harlaw (**65**). The carving on it shows him in full plate armour; sword belted at left hip, dagger at right, chain-mail under the plate, helm conical, and his hands joined in prayer.

From the Kinkell fork the Balbithan road climbs east two miles to a crossing: left to Balbithan House; right to Kintore (**8**). Cresting amid forestry that conceals ancient hut-circles, it descends another two miles to the Kintore-Hatton of Fintray B977 (also **8**), this above Mill of Fintray.

North from Inverurie, the Oldmeldrum B9170 (**63**) crosses the Urie then runs through open land, in four miles passing Barra Castle (793257: private). Surrounding three sides of a cobbled courtyard, a screen wall containing the fourth, the present building began life as an L-plan tower, which in 1592 was forfeited by the Blackhalls to George Seton, Chancellor of the Diocese of Aberdeen. He built most of what survives, further changes being made by new owners. Used as a farm-house after 1766, it was restored in 1910–11.

Opposite it, a track starts up grassy Barra Hill (803257; 633ft; 193m). To gain the Iron Age fort at the top, leave the track where it bends right and continue up. Nearby, probably between the hill and the Lochter Burn, and probably (accounts vary) on Ascension Day 1308, Robert the Bruce routed John Comyn, Earl of Buchan. Up from his sickbed after a long campaign (they'd clashed at Slioch near Huntly on Christmas Day 1307: see **71**), and propped up in his saddle by men on either side, it's said his appearance so terrified the 'small folk', who'd been told he was too ill to fight, that the mere sight of him led them to flee. Soon Buchan's own men took to their heels, followed by Buchan and his knights. With the battle fol-lowed by Bruce's violent 'Harrowing of Buchan', so ended the century-long rule of the Comyns in the Northeast.

Five miles north of Inverurie and at the junction of a web of roads, Oldmeldrum (Gaelic *meall-droma*, 'hill of the ridge'; known as *Meldrum*; pop. 2115), became a burgh of barony in 1672 and by 1690 had 16 merchants to Inverurie's four. Superseded in the early 19th century by the arrival at Inverurie of canal and turnpike, and now home of Glengarioch Distillery (01651-873450), its narrow climbing streets, tight-packed old houses and Bennachie views lend it an air of slightly decayed but timeless charm.

Just north of the village the A947 from Dyce (**7**) sheds the B9170 to New Deer (**101**), this by the decorated white gateway of Meldrum House Hotel (814291), a baronialised mansion with round flanking towers capped by conical turrets. Climbing north over a broad open land the A947 continues to Fyvie (**78**), Turriff (**87**) and Banff (**88**).

Also running east to Ellon (**75**), from Oldmeldrum the A920 departs west through farmland past Mounie Castle Hotel (766287; a 1641 rectangle built by Robert Farquhar, Provost of Aberdeen) then, bypassing Daviot (**66**), crosses the B9001; a useful road bound northwest from Inverurie through remote Rothienorman to Forgue (**85**) and the Huntly-Banff A97. Next, under the bare Hill of Rothmaise, the B920 sheds the B992. This follows the infant Ythan north through bleak Kirkton of Auchterless – birthplace of Lewis Grassic Gibbon (**3**), it boasts a soaring Gothic parish church but little else – and then via the barren Howe of Auchterless meets the A947 by Towie Barclay Castle (**78**).

Finally, 11 miles west of Oldmeldrum the A920 joins the A96 trunk route at Kirkton of Cusalmond, this at the start of the climb to the Glens of Foudland (**71**)

65. 'Reid Harlaw'   *(Route, History)*

From central Inverurie the B9001 (above) is reached via Harlaw Road, or North Street parallel to it. Bear right over the Urie for half a mile, then left past

Bathalgardy a mile up to the Harlaw Monument (752241). Commanding broad views, this bulky granite tower was erected in 1911, 500th anniversary of 'Reid Harlaw', or the 'Sair Field o' Harlaw'.

Fought on the Pley Fauld, the open high ground nearby, the battle was between Highland Gaels and Northeast men. With the young King James I imprisoned in England, the opportunistic Donald Lord of the Isles and his caterans had marched west, seizing Dingwall and torching Inverness before advancing on Aberdeen. His stated purpose was to secure the Earldom of Ross against the ambitions of the Stewarts and Scotland's Governor, Albany, but doubtless Aberdeen's rich pickings also drew him on.

By 23 July 1411 Donald's men were camped on Harlaw's stony plateau. Three miles away by the Bass of Inverurie, and planning a dawn attack, the Earl of Mar marshalled his forces – Forbeses, Irvines, Keiths, Leslies and Setons; men from Angus and the Mearns; and Aberdeen burgesses led by Provost Davidson. Mar was Alexander Stewart, the Wolf of Badenoch's upstart son who'd seized Kildrummy (**49**), its heiress Isobel, and the earldom itself. Yet, more capable and less vicious than his father, on grabbing the prize he'd kept the peace and won the loyalty of those who, levied to defend Aberdeen and the Northeast, now followed him into this crucial, insanely brutal battle.

Lack of reliable sources plus balladry's claims and counter-claims make the course of the struggle unclear, save that it was exceptionally bloody. With each side several thousand strong, and no horse or archers involved, the day-long slaughter led to heavy losses on both sides. Mar's men were better-armoured but the heavy 'lang swords' of the clansmen 'laid on us fu' sair', so that 'the bludy battel lasted lang'. About 900 clansmen died, and maybe 600 of Mar's force, with many more wounded on both sides. Among the dead were Maclean of Duart; Provost Davidson of Aberdeen; and Sir Alexander Irvine, Laird of Drum (**18**); also Sir Gilbert de Greenlaw (see **64**).

The day ended in stalemate, the invaders withdrawing, though later the historian Hector Boece (*c*.1465–1536) suggests that both sides thought they'd lost and retired simultaneously under cover of night. Yet Aberdeen was spared and, though indecisive, Harlaw encouraged the growing two-nation view of Scotland – civilised Lowlanders versus savage Highlanders; a view highlighted by the exemption from feudal dues of the heirs of those slain – a privilege usually granted only in the event of foreign war. In addition, the scale of the slaughter deterred both sides from similar future adventures. Save for later Jacobite excursions, the Gaels never again tried to extend their lands outside the Highlands.

Past the monument the road reaches a junction by the parapets of Harlaw House's narrow four-storey tower. For the A96 turn left downhill, over the railway. For the continuing B9001 to Daviot and the fine stone circle nearby, turn right then right again, then left onto the B9001.

66.   Loanhead of Daviot to the Maiden Stone   *(Route, History)*

Three miles northwest of Inverurie, with views south to Bennachie and north to harsher lands, Daviot (*davoch*, an old measure or portion of land) is a ridge-top village today consisting largely of neat new bungalows. West of it and prominent from the bypassing B9001 is House of Daviot; now a hospital, built in 1876 for Mackenzie of Glack who, after one night in it, went right back to the friendlier Old House of Glack (1723) nearby.

Past two right turns to the village the B9001 continues a mile northwest to a third (737293), signposted to the circle. At a junction after half-a-mile again turn right, to Loanhead, just north of Daviot. From the small roadside carpark pass through scrubwood to the circle (747298). (Or take the first right into Daviot, and in the village bear left.)

Dated *c*.3000BC, this circle (67ft; 20.5m wide) consists of eight uprights about a 12-ton recumbent and its flankers, oddly set just inside the perimeter. Oriented southwest, as at Easter Aquhorthies (**60**), the recumbent and flankers may have been used to follow the moon: 12 cupmarks on the inner face of the stone by the east flanker may mark the rising moon's position at different seasons. Charcoal, broken pottery and traces of children's cremated bones were found under a low cairn in the circle; and beside it is a later (*c*.2500BC) circular cremation site, its rubble concealing a rectangular pit, in and about which were found fragments of at least 31 people, several of them children.

Two miles south of Daviot, and four miles northwest of Inverurie, the A96 hamlet of Pitcaple (Brittonic *pet capuill*, 'place of the horse') hugs the Urie's south bank. Over the river stands Pitcaple Castle (726263; private), a 15th-century Leslie tower rebuilt in the 17th century as a four-storeyed Z-plan château. A mile further west, also north of the Urie, old Logie Durno kirkyard (704265) lies near the site of the 144-acre Roman camp (699274) by Westerton. Interrupting the normal spacing of marching camps, it's claimed as evidence by those who believe that the battle of Mons Graupius (**16**) was fought on Bennachie's slopes.

Above Pitcaple and under Bennachie's Mither Tap stands the mysterious Maiden Stone. From Inverurie's north roundabout, follow the A96 a mile north to Drimmies. Here turn left past ruined Balquhain Castle, a 15ᵗʰ-century Leslie seat torched in 1746 (**62**), and climb two miles to Chapel of Garioch, a tiny hamlet on a broad ridge. Or, continuing to Pitcaple, turn south over the railway up to Chapel of Garioch. Either way, at the hamlet continue west past a left turn south to the Bennachie Centre (**68**), then past another left turn, to Pittodrie House Hotel (696240). Hugging the craggy Mither Tap's wooded slopes, this 1841 neo-Jacobean mansion was developed out of a 1675 foundation, Montrose (**2**, **15**, **54**, **78**) having sacked the earlier 1480 house, from which the ancient wheel stair survives.

Half-a-mile past the Pittodrie turn, the Maiden Stone (704247) stands by the road, with parking in a layby not far on.

67.   The Picts & Their Symbol Stones   *(Route, History)*

A pink granite column 10 feet tall (3.2m) with relief carvings both sides, this fine Class II Pictish symbol stone gets its name from the comb and mirror carved at the foot of its east face. Above, in separate compartments, are (see photo) the 'swimming elephant', a notched rectangle and Z-rod and, in the top panel, four fabulous beasts including a 'centaur'. On the west face, above a complex roundel, an elaborate cross underlies the image of a man (Jonah?) between two fish monsters. The narrow north face contains flowing knotwork; the corresponding south face, interlacing patterns. It's a work of genius – but who carved it, and what do the symbols mean?

After the old culture declined *c*.1500BC (due to eruption by Iceland's Hekla B volcano?) there is little sign of human activity in Scotland until, c.700BC, stone *duns* and timber-laced stone hill-forts begin to appear, maybe due to invasion or steady infiltration by iron-working horse-riding warriors – perhaps originally north European Gaels later displaced to Ireland (before in time returning via Argyll) by P-Celtic Brythons. Crossing the North Sea, these mew arrivals overwhelmed or assimilated the remaining indigenous folk, so creating a tribal society that in time became the warlike, artistic Pictish culture.

With Celtic Britain wholly subdued by the Romans only as far as Anglesea and Carlisle, the Irish Scotti ('pirates') and Caledonia's tribes remained free. Agricola's expedition to the Northeast (**16**) was a one-off. This remote poor land just wasn't worth the effort, and so Rome withdrew behind the Hadrian and Antonine Walls. The latter soon fell, but the former provoked the tribes to persistent sea-raids as far as the Humber, and in AD297 the chronicler Eumenius calls them *Picti*, 'painted people' – the first known use of the term, and similar to the Gaelic Scots name for them: *Cruithni*, 'people of the designs'.

With the Romans gone, by AD500 the Picts were supreme in the north. In 664 the Kingdom of Fortriu was born; other kingdoms rising and falling as North and South Pictland competed; and at Nechtansmere in 685 a Pictish army defeated invading Anglo-Saxons. But since c.450 the Scots, Ulster Gaels, had been infiltrating the land via Argyll (*oirer Gaidheal*, 'coast of the Gael'), and c.790 the Norse attacks began. So, beset by both, by the mid-9th century the Picts 'vanish', leaving no written records save late king-lists in Latin. Their legacies are place-names (*pit*, 'piece of land'; as in *Pit*todrie and *Pit*caple), and the enigmatic symbol stones, found only in north Scotland.

In the earliest (Class 1) abstract symbols and zoomorphs (birds, beasts, etc.) are cut into rough-hewn boulders. 'Dressed' Class 2 stones show symbols in low relief joined by human figures, a Christian cross on the obverse. Class 3 stones (c.800) portray only human figures and a cross. Yet, early or late, there is no sure interpretation. Antiquarian Kenneth Jackson suggests that specific symbols in varying combinations depict dynastic alliances between local kingdoms. Or they may have been territorial notice-boards, or memorials, or statements of land-charter. Nobody knows for sure.

At Forres in Moray a 23-foot-high monolith, Sueno's Stone, is the last and greatest Pictish symbol stone. Or is it? In carved bands it depicts a bloody battle, with fleeing and beheaded warriors. Long thought to celebrate a Pictish triumph over the Norse, it may instead (Jackson again) have been erected by the first Scots king Cináed (Kenneth) mac Alpin (d.858) to remind the beaten Picts who now ruled the roost.

Of the Maiden Stone, folklore says it recalls a daughter of the Laird of Balquhain, slain here after eloping with her lover. Another tale is of Janet Maitland, daughter of a local farmer. With her family out digging peat, a warlock got her to agree to marry him if he built a path through the peat-hag so her folk could return safely. She agreed, believing it impossible. To her horror, he did it then claimed her, so she turned to stone rather than embrace him. Or the Devil bet her he could build a road up Bennachie faster than she could bake bread. Doing so (thus the 'Maiden's Causeway', the Iron Age track up the Mither Tap), his demand led to the same result. The 'elephant' symbol on the Maiden Stone is allegedly the Devil or warlock; the mirror and comb represent the deceived girl.

68. Bennachie (Walks)

'To hell with your Alps, Rockies and Himalaya,' declared Lord Aberdeen of Haddo (**76**), 'Bennachie's the hill for me.' Many still agree. 20 miles northwest of Aberdeen, the granite tors of Bennachie (*beinn achadh*, 'mountain field') dominate the land about. A long, high, forest-skirted ridge, this eastern outrider of the Grampians is small fry height-wise: its summit at Oxen Craig is just 1733ft, 528m high. Yet size isn't everything. East of Oxen Craig and utterly distinctive, the sharp, craggy prow of the Mither Tap (1698ft, 518m) is visible from Buchan to the Bin of Cullen (**94**). Described by W. Douglas Simpson as 'the sphinx of the Garioch', Bennachie symbolises the Northeast.

Almost as important, its miles of heathery ridgetop offer endless hours of fresh air and exercise to those escaping city streets for a day out under the sky.

Besides the Donview carpark (672191) by My Lord's Throat under Milestone Hill (**57**), three carparks serve Bennachie's trails: (**a**) Esson's at the Bennachie Centre (698217) two miles south of Chapel of Garioch; (**b**) Rowan Tree (693244): from the Maiden Stone (**67**) descend a wooded brae past a back drive to Pittodrie and turn left, (or, from the A96, climb this lane from a point (695256) 200 yards east of the A96 junction with the B9002 to Oyne); or (**c**) Back O' Bennachie (662245): from the A96 take the B9002 two miles west through Oyne, and just past Archaeolink Prehistory Park (**69**) turn left.

Taking each starting-point in turn:

(**a**) The Bennachie Centre (open daily except Monday) marks the start of way-marked trails including the 12-mile Gordon Way west to Suie Hill (**56**). A map of this and other routes south over Milestone Hill and northwest over Bennachie is available at the Centre, also from Forest Enterprise (01466-794161).

To climb the Mither Tap, start west along the Gordon Way to a junction by a bench (693216) and turn right, up past the ruined remains of The Colony, a 19th-century crofting community. At the next junction, keep right over the forest road and up a path opposite. Where trees to the right shape a V, follow green/orange way-markers up to open heath for the final rocky clamber. It may make you puff, but it's worth it – and not just for the views. At the tor's northern base, a narrow path between tumbled boulders marks the gate of an Iron Age fort.

Marking surrounding heights and landscape features, the summit indicator was erected by the Bailies of Bennachie, a group formed in 1973 to fight litter and vandalism on this popular but hard-trod height. Views run north over the Garioch and Formartine; east to Aberdeen and the sea; south to Clachnaben (**22**) and Lochnagar (**34**); and west, via the gentler Correen Hills, to Tap o' Noth (**51**). Nearby to the south is Milestone Hill and, west over the ridge, Craigshannoch and Oxen Craig (see **c**). Also at the summit is found the Thieves mark, a square cut in the rock with the letters 'P', 'LE', 'B' and the date 1858. This refers to the 'Theft of Bennachie', when the Commonty (common land) of Bennachie was seized and split between local landowners.

From here return as you came or explore further:

(**b**) From Rowan Tree carpark, climb steadily up a rocky path between gorse-banks. Ignoring intersecting tracks, continue up through forestry to heather moor. Breasting huge granite slabs below the Mither Tap, the broad, ancient Maiden Causeway (see **67**) rises past isolated wind-torn groves to Hosie's Well, a clear pool brimming from the bog (681232). Soon after, a path branches right to Craigshannoch (below). For the Mither Tap, keep straight on over a boggy burn to clamber up the final stretch, entering the old fort from the north, as above. Again, return as you came, or explore further, as in:

(**c**) The Back O' Bennachie carpark makes a fine start for a circuit of Craigshannoch, the Mither Tap, Oxen Craig (shown below), part of the Gordon Way, and back via Watch Craig.

Follow a burn up through the wood to a main forest road (661243). Turn right over it then immediately left up a steep path (now the other side of the burn) to a fork. Bear left 100 yards up to another fork and continue straight up (right) through the forest to open slope under Little Oxen Craig (664233). Follow the main track (gravelled, stepped, and lined by white stones from the Lintel Quarry above). Passing east under the quarry to a fork (right up to Little Oxen Craig), the track continues 200 yards to a crossing (664232) under Oxen Craig (664226). For Oxen Craig keep straight on.

Turning left (east) on the broad path under the ridge, keep left up the southwest flank of Craigshannoch (672232). Under tumbled slabs the rocky path crosses a heather shoulder to broad views north and east. At a fork (left to the top of the crag), continue east over the moor past two paths rising southwest from Hosie's Well (b). By a bog pool, the second path (677227: yellow waymarker signposted 'Via Oxen Craig') rises west along the ridgetop. Note this turn before continuing up the Mither Tap. On returning from the Mither Tap, at this junction turn left up a stony path between heather banks and over a saddle. Where it bears right towards Craigshannoch, at a signposted Y-fork keep left, climbing past a junction with a path (665226; below) to the serrated slabs of Bennachie's highest point (1733ft, 528m).

From Oxen Craig return north past Little Oxen Craig and so back as you came or, for a wider circuit, descend east 250 yards to the junction at 665226. Turn right (south) 100 yards to a Y-fork, then right again, Donside below, and so down the rocky path to the Gordon Way (666223). Now bear west round Oxen Craig to fine views up Donside to Morven (31), then northwest above wooded slopes and My Lord's Throat (57) to Watch Craig (654224; 1617ft, 493m). At a second waymarker under Watch Craig, break right on a rough path up over the crag's east shoulder, continuing over open moortop then, with Insch ahead and below, down to the forestry edge (651232).

At the forest line a waymarked path, hard to spot, descends right through dense wood over a logged clearing to a main forest road (651242). Turning right, keep right at the next Y-fork, due east to (661243) the burn and path climbing from the carpark.

If this splendid 9-mile walk doesn't refresh the soul, what will?

69. Insch & Dunnideer   *(Routes, History, Cycle/Walk)*

Two miles west of Pitcaple the A96 bends northwest towards the Glens of Foudland (71) and Huntly (80). Here the B9002 breaks left through open land. Cutting under the railway past the compact Z-plan château of Harthill (686252; *c.*1600) then, a mile on, Westhall (677258; also Z-plan, begun in the 16th century), it bisects sleepy Oyne, then passes the entry to Archaeolink Prehistory Park (01464-851500; April–Oct.) – an educational theme park that aims to bring the past to life. Currently it offers reconstructions of an Iron Age farm and a Roman camp, with a medieval fort in preparation.

Passing the turn to Back O' Bennachie, in two more miles the B9002 sheds the road west to Auchleven, Clatt (**54**) and Rhynie (**50**) then, crossing the railway, continues west towards Kennethmont (**70**) past right turns to Insch (pop. 1644).

With its random street pattern and pretty Victorian cottages, and almost unique locally in retaining its railway link, Insch (*innis*, 'island') is just that, an island of local business and housing amid this backland of hill and dale. Once the site of monthly cattle fairs, this old burgh of barony is dominated by a ruined tower atop the bare, conical hill of Dunnideer (613282; 879ft, 268m) a mile to the west.

Pierced by a sky-gaping lancet window and visible for miles about, this ruin consists of the remaining wall of a great hall above the rectangular base of a castle built *c*.1260, and so one of Scotland's earliest towerhouses (**18**). To explore it, from Insch walk (or drive) out on Western Road. Where under the hill the road bends right at a copse of trees (the Belts), a short steep path climbs to the top. The castle was built partly from the rubble of the previous Iron Age vitrified fort, this of a type known as 'unfinished'. Other examples are found a mile to the south atop Hill of Christ's Kirk (602275; 1020ft, 311m), and atop Durn Hill (**86**) near Portsoy (**91**).

About Insch and Dunnideer a treasure-trove of Neolithic and Pictish remains may in turn be visited via an eight-mile road-circuit. There is a single stone east of the road 300 yards north of the Belts by Dunnydeer Farm (616286); 500 yards further west a recumbent and two flankers occupy a field south of the road (608285); then, just south of a Y-junction half-a-mile on at Stonehead, there is a huge recumbent with flankers (601288). Here turn right (north) a mile past Candle Hill. The nearly-complete circle atop it (599299) stands next to a quarry used as a rubbish dump. In another half-mile, and now under the Skirts of Foudland, again turn right, to Netherton. In just over a mile, the road here a fine wooded avenue, in a field south of the road is the Picardy Stone (610303; *c*.AD600).

Guard-railed, this tall pillar of grey whinstone is carved with double disc and Z-rod, a serpent and Z-rod, and a mirror. Set in a low circular cairn with a rectangular grave below it, it can also be reached via Ancient Monuments signs off the B992 from Insch. Finally, continuing east and turning right (southeast) to Insch at the next junction, west of the road in another mile is a dilapidated circle by Inschfield (610287)

Returning to Insch (this circuit ideal for cyclists, less so for walkers), the road joins the B992 by the village. From it, the B992 runs north two miles to the A96. South of Insch the B992 climbs then descends two miles to Auchleven. To the west, the B9002 follows the railway through a wooded, steep-sided glen, five miles to Kennethmont.

70.   Backlands: Auchleven to Leith Hall   *(Routes, History, Visit)*

Leaving the B9002 west of Oyne, after two miles the back road (see **69**) to Clatt and Rhynie reaches Auchleven, a crossroads hamlet with an inn (Premnay Arms Hotel) and little else. Here intersecting the B992 from Insch south to Keig (**57**), the road runs on west through rural backland, soon passing Leslie Castle (599248; a private hotel). White-harled and L-plan, it was built in 1661 for William Forbes of Monymusk (**58**), whose father had gained the land by marrying the widow of his debtor, the last Leslie of Leslie.

The first Leslie was Bartholomew, or Bertolf, a Flemish adventurer promised by Malcolm Canmore all the land for a mile about wherever his north-ridden horse finally collapsed, which was here at Lesselyn, already an ancient estate. Later, also by marrying a widow, his descendant Sir Norman got the Earldom of Rothes in 1296 and held onto it by doing homage to England's Edward that same year. The Leslies clung onto Rothes Castle until a Covenanting zealot torched it, after which they moved to Glenrothes in Fife.

At a crossing (598247) west of Leslie's few houses, continue west to Clatt or turn right to Kennethmont. The Clatt road follows the Gadie Burn under Knock Saul and Suie Hill (**56**), soon passing the bizarre Tower Lodge (668249; 19th century, once the entry to Knockespock House: **54**). Basically a cottage overrun by a corbelled, crowstepped upper block flanked by a narrow high stair-tower, it looks like a stone rocket carrying a bulky Space Shuttle piggy-back over the cottage launching-pad. *Very* odd. Just after, with Tap o' Noth (**51**) ahead, at Ford of Clatt and the old village hall the road meets the Clatt-Bridge of Alford route (**54**). Turn left for the latter; right to Clatt and Rhynie (**50**).

From Leslie the right turn runs five miles over high old farmland, then gradually descends to Kennethmont (*ceann-moine*, 'moss-head') and the B9002 from Insch. With its 1812 parish kirk and kirkyard dedicated to St. Rule or Regulas, under wooded Knockandy Hill (1424ft; 434m) this long village is the home of Ardmore Distillery, founded in 1899 by Adam Teacher (open May-Sept.; 01464-831213).

Close by are, or were, two great houses, one still intact, the other not – Leith Hall and Wardhouse (563307; *Wardis*). The latter stood two miles east of Kennethmont and north of the B9002. Begun in 1757 by Arthur Gordon, in 1763 this vast Palladian rival to Haddo (**76**) was inherited by his nephew

Alexander who, in 1769, was beheaded (among the last so executed) as a spy. Alexander's brother Charles Edward (1750–1832), finished the building then gave it to his eldest son, who emigrated to Spain. His grandson, Pedor Carlos (*The Mad Laird*) built the Spanish-influenced Home Farm with its vast bull-yard (1835–42). In 1906 the King of Spain honeymooned here but, when in 1931 the Spanish monarchy fell and Franco gained power, Rafael Carlos Gordon fled back to Scotland, destitute. In 1952 the house was sold, then gutted. This is a Gordon tale as exotic and self-destructive as that of Mad Jack and Lord Byron at Gight (**77**).

For Leith Hall (National Trust; 01464-831216; open Easter–1 Oct.; grounds all year), continue west through Kennethmont past left turns to Clatt and the Rhynie-Huntly A97 to the wooded drive (542298). With 286 acres of parkland, gardens, wildlife trails and exhibitions this elegant semi-castelled château is absorbing. Begun in 1650 and later extended, it was Hay or Leith-Hay land for 300 years, until in 1939 a motorbike accident ended the line. With a guidebook to the architecture, paintings and memorabilia, the wooded grounds offer many walks. The walled garden holds two Pictish symbol stones, one the Wolf Stone from Percylieu; the paddock contains highland cattle and Soay sheep – Europe's oldest breed, from stock once on St. Kilda, far west of Lewis.

North of Leith Hall, in another mile the B9002 crosses the railway to join the A97 to Huntly, this three miles north of Rhynie (**50**) by Gartly (**82**).

71.   Through the Glens of Foudland

Beyond Pitcaple and the B9002 turn the A96 follows the Urie northwest past Old Rayne, site of the old St. Laurence Fair, or Lourin Fare, once a vital horse and cattle market. Next, shedding the B992 south to Insch, the road continues past Colpy where, under the bare Skirts of Foudland, lanes break west under Gartly Moor's bleak braes. Here there was once a distillery called Jericho, fed by the waters of Jordan, a feeder-burn of the Urie, its product vital to the Foudland quarriers. Later it was renamed Benachie [sic].

Taking up the A920 from Oldmeldrum (**64**) at Kirkton of Culsalmond, the A96 climbs north through a narrow pass between the slate-quarried Hills of Skares (1079ft; 329m) and Tillymorgan (1250ft; 381m), by the east flank of which the old Cadgers' Road descends to Culsalmond. Once it brought drovers, pedlars and balladeers south to a fair held here, St. Serf's or St. Sair's, where 'many a bloody racket' occurred. From St. Cadger's Road and above the hamlet a second track forks round the hill's west side and, with linking tracks to the north, could make for an interesting six-mile circular walk.

From a bend atop the pass at the start of the Glens of Foudland a back road breaks north six miles over bare land past Ythanwells to the B9001 in Glendronach, southeast of Forgue (**85**). A mile east of the Ythanwells crossroads amid this desolate land of decayed hill-farms, in AD83 the Romans established a 33-acre marching camp. It's safe to say that the legionnaires had no fun here.

Though less severe than the Lecht (**43**), the stretch of road through the bare Glens of Foudland can be treacherous in winter. Along it 200 years ago Alexander Scorgie began a passenger 'Caravan' – a two-wheeled cart covered with painted canvas. Drawn by one horse with four passengers inside, and a fifth seated outside by the driver, the Scorgie Caravan ran from Aberdeen's George Street to Huntly's West Wynd. Later he designed a bigger Caravan, with glass windows and space for six passengers, and capable of five miles an hour. He and his competitors would stop at Bainshole (611350), where the road bends. At nearby Newtongarry was another inn, allegedly haunted, and sited under the now-abandoned slate quarries of the Hill of Foudland (603333; 1532ft, 467m).

Gaping wide on the southern hillside above the A96, in the 19th century these quarries produced the light-blue slate used to roof Balmoral Castle (**36**). Paid a then-fortune of 12 to 16 shillings a week (the quarriers and splitters getting the highest wage), the 65 men working the Foudland quarries produced up to 900,000 slates a year, splitting the slate with wedges, but using gunpowder if it was especially hard. They were thankful for the *uisguebaugh*, the water of life that came their way from Jericho!

Past Whinbrae, Clinkstone and Broomhill the A96 (here briefly offering a third, climbing lane) rises to a crest by Bogside beyond which, with broad views of Strathbogie and the lands ahead opening up, it descends past Slioch (562383), where at Christmas 1307 Robert the Bruce fought a draw with the Comyn Earl of Buchan (**64**). Descending past the Banff A97 and between the wooded Ba' and Battle Hills, the road bypasses Huntly (**80**) in fertile Strathbogie, where the rivers Bogie and Deveron meet.

Huntly and Deveronside soon. First, from Formartine to Fyvie.

72. Pitmedden and Tolquhon *(Route, History)*

Under a mile east of Oldmeldrum (**64**) the A920 breaks left from the Dyce A947 towards Pitmedden and Ellon (**75**). In three more miles, and via a fine beech avenue, a right turn south leads to Udny Green, a pretty, peaceful olde-worlde hamlet by Udny Castle.

At Udny Green lived Jamie Fleeman (1713–78: see **105**), the Laird of Udny's fool, renowned for the speed of his wit. Remaining awake amid a long sermon with half the congregation nodding off, the minister pointed to him. 'My brethren,' cried the Man of God, 'you should take an example from that poor fool.' 'Na, na,' replied Jamie, quick as a flash, 'If I hidna been a feel, I would hae been sleepin' tae.'

Past this turn the A920 reaches a junction by the gates of Udny Castle (private), a 16th-century château with a baronial mansion added in 1875–6. The B9000 continuing ahead runs on past Pitmedden village to briefly join the B999, then breaks east over the coastal plain eight miles to Newburgh (**73**), while here by the castle gates the A920 turns sharp left past the entry to Pitmedden House and Great Garden (884278; National Trust; 01651-842352; open daily May–Sept.).

From Aberdeen (14 miles) reached via the Tarves B999 from the A90 roundabout opposite Balgownie Links (**7**), Pitmedden's Great Garden was begun in 1675 by Sir Alexander Seton. Son of 'Bonny John Seton' who fell at the Battle of the Bridge of Dee in 1639, this law lord lost the favour of the future James II/VII and decided to create a garden instead – a good choice! Divided into an upper and lower garden, this huge rectangular enclosure by Pitmedden House has, since the Trust bought it in 1952, been restored to its original classical tranquillity. Elaborate and formal, it's best enjoyed when in full bloom in August. There is a Visitor Centre and a Museum of Farming Life, complete with a dark, earthy bothy evoking the hardships of 19th-century farming (**104**).

Continuing, the A920 crosses the B999 and runs on through rich farmland past the ruined 15th-century L-plan Castle of Esslemont (934297; abandoned 1769) before after four miles descending to Ellon (**75**) by the Ythan.

Turning north on the B999, in a mile a lane on the left leads to one of the jewels in the Castle Trail – the roofless but exotic ruin of Tolquhon Castle (873286; Historic Scotland; 01651-851286; open daily summer; winter weekends). The datestone tells how ALL THIS WARKE EXCEP THE AULD TOWR WAS BEGUN BY WILLIAM FORBES 15 APRIL 1584 AND ENDIT BY HIM 20 OCTOBER 1589. There is no mention of the man who developed the earlier Preston Tower into a courtyard mansion; master-mason Thomas Leiper, who began the building of Castle Fraser (**58**). With its galleried gatehouse, enclosures, walled garden and great hall Tolquhon – like similar late-Renaissance castles at Huntly (**80**) and Boyne (**91**) near

Portsoy – is a cultural conceit, its thin walls and fancy gun-loops suggesting more interest in style and comfort than any fear of attack. Nearby, an award-winning gallery exhibits the work of local artists.

From Tolquhon the B999 continues north a mile through the bungalow village of Tarves (pop. 1016), *en route* passing a lane on the right to a carpark under the Prop of Ythsie (885315). Atop a low hill, with broad Buchan views, this red granite castellated tower dates from 1861–2. Erected by the tenants and 'grateful servants' of Haddo estate, it was designed by the 5th Earl of Aberdeen in memory of his father, George Hamilton Gordon (1784–1860), Prime Minister during the Crimean War. Better remembered for planting 14 million trees than for his dubious political skills, his seat was at Haddo House (**76**), two miles north of Tarves.

But before more ancient seats, and for the moment bypassing Ellon, now for two bracing coastal walks eight miles east of Pitmedden.

73.   Newburgh to Collieston & Old Slains   *(Route, Walk)*

Save for the climate, parts of the coast between Inverness and Aberdeen suggest the Sahara. There are impressive sand dune systems at Culbin between Nairn and Findhorn Bay; about Rattray Head and the Loch of Strathbeg (**109**) and from Collieston south past Newburgh and the Ythan estuary almost all the way to Aberdeen. Of those on the east coast, the largest is at Forvie, between Collieston and Newburgh.

Britain's fifth biggest dune system (at 3600 acres, Culbin is the biggest), Forvie's plant-rich heathland and thriving bird-colonies made it among the first of Scotland's National Nature Reserves, being so designated in January 1959. It also has what Culbin lacks; a fine cliff-top walk, from Collieston south two miles to Rockend. Beyond this, with views south to Aberdeen, the broad beach runs on another two miles to Newburgh Bar at the mouth of the Ythan. In between is space enough to get happily lost for a day.

To get there: if approaching from Aberdeen on the A90, three miles north of Balmedie (**7**) turn right on the Peterhead A975 into Newburgh (pop.1466), once Ellon's port and a place where sailors retired. In the village – separated from the Forvie Sands by the Ythan's broad tidal lagoon – the B9000 from Pitmedden joins the A975; this a mile or so east of its staggered crossing over the A90 amid the coastal plain.

With wildlife-rich mud-flats (also protected) extending another three miles north, the modest Ythan's lagoon is due to glacier melt. Once a torrent, the river dumped clays and gravels, building new land against a rising sea which, 12,000 years ago when the melt began, was 200 feet lower than today. An Ireland-Scotland land-bridge existed until *c.*7500BC, and until *c.*6500BC you could walk from the Humber to the Elbe. A later fall in sea-level, though slight in comparison, exposed glacial deposits which, blown inland, formed the Forvie Sands. Reaching Collieston by 1759, they later stabilised.

North of Newburgh the A975 crosses the estuary to the dune system's wooded western edge. Here a carpark (004271) serves tracks forking east and south over the dunes – one starting-point for a walk. Or, as here, continue north two miles and turn right to Collieston (B9003). After half-a-mile, the clifftop village visible ahead, a right turn climbs to the Forvie Centre – another starting-point (see below).

The continuing road descends past potholed Whinnyfold Road, which climbs left (north) a mile past the track to Mains of Slains and the ruin of Old Slains Castle (054299) on its coastal crag beyond. Past this turn and now by the village, a second left turn drops steeply to Cransdale, a clifftop viewpoint by the path north to Old Slains. From a stone step a wooden staircase climbs the cliff, then follows its edge north a mile to this old seat of the Hays of Erroll who, when it was sacked in 1594, moved north to Cruden Bay (**111**). Via clifftop path, careful scramble, the rough track past Mains of Slains, and the lane south back to Collieston, this worthwhile Old Slains circuit is three miles long.

As for Collieston, this steep-laned, dead-end little harbour village was already a holiday resort when, 80 years ago, Lawrence of Arabia came here. On leave from the RAF and in hiding from the world, he rented: 'the nearest hovel to the high-tide mark', and spent weeks walking what he called: 'the sand-tussocked desolation of Forvie.'

74.   The Sands of Forvie   *(Natural History, Walk)*

Desolate to Lawrence maybe, but with its wide range of habitats – mobile and fixed dunes up to 200 feet high, heathland, grassy cliffs, dune slacks and salt marsh – Forvie is rich in plant and birdlife. To date at least 348 species of flowering plant have been recorded here, and some 225 species of bird visit, with 43 breeding here regularly. Gulls wheel and cry; skylarks soar; in autumn pinkfoot and greylag geese descend by the thousand; from Iceland whooper swans visit the resident colony of mute swans; while waders, mallard, teal, goldeneye, long-haired duck and four species of tern are among other regular visitors or residents. So too are 5000 or so eider duck, the UK's largest breeding colony, that in summer arrive to breed and feed on the mussels found in the lower estuary, which at times is off-limits to reduce the pressure on these birds.

In addition the dunes cover many signs of ancient human occupation. As early as 9000 years ago (burned hazelnut shells found in 1996 at Crail in Fife have been carbon-dated to *c.*7600BC) Mesolithic hunter-gatherers probably visited the sheltered, food-rich estuary; later Neolithic farmers built large round communal houses, clearing ground for crops and grazing. Later still, near the salmon-fishing station at Rockend, a medieval settlement developed round the now-ruined 12th-century Forvie Kirk, built on the site of an earlier chapel dating possibly from AD704. But with the sand moving north, by the 15th century the fields, kirk and village were buried, this allegedly due to a storm caused by a curse uttered by three sisters set adrift in a leaky boat to deny them their inheritance.

All this and more is explained at the Forvie Centre, from which a rewarding six-mile triangular walk (with longer options) departs, as follows:

From the centre there are two obvious paths – to the village, or to the dunes. For the latter, bear right through a gate past a *Birds nesting please keep dogs on lead* sign, then fork right (south) on a waymarked path through grassy dunes and past scrub-cloaked heather heath. At the next Y-fork keep right over duckboards, meandering SSW amid the dunes (you're asked not to walk on them April-August due to nesting). Keeping left past a right fork (031181: see return below), bear east, then south past a reedy lochan, then east (this section of path not on the OS map) to the clifftop path south from Collieston.

In places stepped as it continues south above a rock-bound sandy cove, in a mile or so, and now above the broad, curving beach of cliff-hemmed Hackley Bay (shown here) with Forvie Ness beyond, the path forks – down to the beach or right through clifftop reed-fields. Round the headland south of the bay with Bennachie

visible, miles of beach to the south open up as the path drops to the shore at Rockend. At a fork bear left to the beach, or down to a track starting east past the salmon-fishing station (021265). Pausing at the rectangular base of Forvie kirk's remaining walls nearby, continue west a mile on this sandy track, past high scrub-colonised dunes and over a ridge to wide views west.

Just before a final crest beyond which the track descends to a gated lane west to the estuary carpark (**73**), on the right an overgrown track (012269; by it a sign: *Danger fire no stoves or fires*) breaks north then, after 100 yards, northeast. Though often faint, it can be followed, and offers space and wide views as, twin-rutted through the heather, in near a mile it reaches dunes, here forking. Keep straight on over a dune. Briefly the track vanishes but north of the dune continues clearly over an open crest to a Y-fork. Turn left 300 yards to a second Y-fork (031181; see outward route above). Turn left, then left again at a third Y-fork, and so back as you came to the Forvie Centre.

East of Newburgh the A90 continues north two miles to a roundabout, from which in a mile the A948 enters Ellon (pop. 9220).

75.   Ellon & the Ythan   *(Routes, Visit, Walk)*

Five miles inland and 17 miles north of Aberdeen, this Ythanside gateway to Buchan (once defined as the land north of Don and east of Deveron, now seen as starting north of the Ythan), gets its name from the Gaelic *eileann*, 'island', this after islets in the Ythan, itself maybe from *athan*, 'ford'; or *eithe-an*, 'boggy place'. Both fit – this shallow slow stream is easily forded, but as easily floods its low-lying banks, so creating 'boggy places'.

Once Buchan's main Pictish settlement, Ellon's medieval kirk was gifted by David I (1125–53) to the bibulous monks (they set up the first *brasinas* or brewery at Keith in Banffshire) of Kinloss Abbey in Moray. Later Comyn earls of Buchan held court at the Moot Hill – there's a memorial in Market Street – and so in 1308 Ellon was torched by Robert the Bruce, 'harrying' Buchan after routing the Comyns at Barra **(64)**. In the 16ᵗʰ century Ellon Old Castle was built and, though twice rebuilt (*c*.1706–15; 1781–5), was demolished in 1851. With Ellon Academy now occupying its approach, only the south wall remains, though the tale of a secret tunnel leading from it under the river to an old rectory survives (see **14**).

Today an Aberdeen commuter dormitory, Ellon's main streets hug the Ythan by the Old Bridge, built in 1793 with three main arches and a smaller, subsidiary fourth arch, perhaps to deal with floodwater. Beside it, the 1940 bridge carries the A948 south to the A90 and Aberdeen. Yet, with its riverside park and walks, Ellon remains rural. Sea-trout and salmon pass through to spawn further upriver; heron and dipper are seen and also, sometimes, otter and grey seal. The river, which until 1924 carried the 'Dispatch', a paddle steamer tug that delivered supplies, also hosts an annual Raft Race.

For an Ellon walk: from the north bank carpark by the Old Bridge start west under the two bridges and cross the reedy flood-plain to the old railway bridge. Over it runs the Formartine-Buchan Way; a walker's route following the old line from Dyce north 13 miles through Udny Station to Ellon; thence north 28 miles via Auchnagatt, Maud **(102)** and Strichen **(106)** to Fraserburgh **(100)**. Crossing the railway bridge over the Ythan, descend left to a tarmac path and follow the riverbank east under the new bridge, and cross the old bridge back to where you started.

Near Ellon was born General Patrick Gordon (1635–99), a mercenary soldier who, like James Keith of Inverugie **(109)**, had a spectacular continental career.

Fighting for both sides in the 1653–61 Swedish-Polish war, when it ended he joined the Russian army, which in time he commanded and reformed. Later Governor of Kiev and close friend of the memorable Czar Peter the Great, he was buried in Moscow.

North of Ellon, between the A92 to Mintlaw (**105**) and the A948 to Auchnagatt and New Deer (**101**), is a hilly backland linked by a maze of lanes. Save for Hatton, a village off the A957 two miles west of Cruden Bay (**111**), this entire area between Ythan and Ugie is rural, with hardly a hamlet to mention; yet with some grand views north to Mormond Hill (**106**), as from the top of the Hatton-Clola lane (001437).

From Ellon's Station Road the B9005 runs west. In a mile a back road breaks south over the Ythan and west four miles to the Haddo House entry (865325) north of Tarves (**72**). Continuing north of the Ythan, in three more miles the B9005 reaches Ythanbank where, crossing the river, it runs past Haddo to Methlick (**76**; Ellon 9). From Ythanbank the north bank lane continues two miles to a junction (888362). The left turn crosses the Ythan to the Methlick B9005; the right turn climbs north past the House of Schivas (896367; *c*.1585; private) a Leiper masterpiece similar to Tolquhon (**72**), but complete and restored. Beyond it, lanes twist up and down past lonely steadings to the A948 hamlet of Auchnagatt, past which the B9030 climbs then descends northeast four miles through neat Stuartfield to historic Old Deer (**103**).

76. Haddo House to Methlick *(Visit, History, Walks)*

From a crossroads north of Tarves, the drive to Haddo House runs north through wooded policies over chassis-scraping 'sleeping policemen' that make its one mile seem like five.

A celebrated Palladian mansion (866347; National Trust; 01651-851440; Country Park Ranger Service 01651-851489; open Easter; 1 May–3 Oct., gardens and grounds all year), it was designed by William Adam for the crabby 2nd Earl of Aberdeen and built 1731–35. Following 18th-century redesign, and since *c*.1950 famed for its choral and operatic society (Vaughan Williams, Benjamin Britten and Sir Michael Tippett have conducted here), this three-storey pile with flanking wings of granite ashlar is noted for its ground-floor colonnade and grand entry hall. With wide lawns and an early 19th-century wall garden, amid parkland designed to please the eye Haddo was Scotland's first great house opened to the public by advertisement (1883, in *The Scotsman*), and in 1979 passed to the National Trust for Scotland.

Remembered, if not as Prime Minister, by the Prop of Ythsie (**72**) two miles to the south, George Hamilton Gordon (4th Earl), did better by Haddo than Britain. Spending a 19th-century fortune of £60,000, by his death in 1860 he'd planted 14 million trees, built schools, improved farms and turned moor into fertile land. Here

entertaining Queen Victoria in 1857, it was he who dismissed 'your Alps, Rockies and Himalaya' in favour of Bennachie (**68**). Foreign Secretary for seven years and Prime Minister 1852–5; described by the louche Lord Palmerston as: 'a piece of antiquated imbecility', he was blamed for the disastrous Crimean War, and widely dismissed as an austere incompetent.

Yet, due to him, you can enjoy Haddo and its Country Park (you're asked to leave by dusk). With bird hides, a dog-play area, a shop and restaurant, park boundaries are marked by pheasant signs. Waymarked walks explore the woodland, fountained lawns lead north to the Avenue and to the 1847 Golden Gates by an ornamental lake.

Two miles northwest of Haddo is Methlick, a pretty hill-hemmed riverside village on a pleasant haugh. Here, so that no riverside view is blocked, it's illegal to site houses opposite each other along the single street running south then north of the Ythan. Into this peaceful place the B9170 (having taken up the B999), descends to the B9005 from Ellon, the roads meeting by the roofless 1780 parish kirk dedicated to St. Devenick, the legendary 5th-century saint who proselytised Deeside from Maryculter (**12**).

Turning west along the single main street, by the 1867 parish church is the burial enclosure of the Gordons of Haddo. Nearby is the Ythanview Hotel, built in 1876 for Haddo House workers. Here you may hear about the Hagberry Pot, a hole under the Ythan into which vanished a piper who, seeking the lost treasure of Gight, never returned.

With the Polesburn road continuing straight to the west end of the main street, the B9170 swings right over the 1844 girder bridge crossing the Ythan, then climbs north six miles to New Deer (**101**). From the lights just over the river, the B9005 breaks west to Fyvie, soon climbing above Gight Castle, where the poet George Gordon, Lord Byron (1788–1824), spent his unhappy early years...

77.   The Braes of Gight   *(History, Walk)*

Like Auchindoun (**52**) and Findlater (**93**), Gight (*Gecht*) Castle is dreich. Built *c*.1560 by the architect of Towie Barclay (**78**) and Delgatie (**87**), this fenced-off L-plan ruin lies in cow-churned pasture above the Ythan and amid the Braes of Gight two miles northwest of Methlick. No place to grow up, but it offers the focus for a fine six-mile circular walk.

In Methlick take the Polesburn road west to the end of the village. Where the road swings uphill, park, then continue straight past a builder's yard to a gate preventing access by car. Above the Ythan and under forested slopes, this mostly-wooded track continues northwest almost two miles to a fork (841393). Here turn right, over the Ythan by an old stone bridge. Briefly joining the Fyvie-bound B9005, turn left a few yards, then left again onto a westbound track (840396), this where the road climbs right.

At first by the river and under dense forestry, follow this grassy track west under Little Gight (recently the site of finds from the Mesolithic era), then past stone gateposts into Badiebath Wood. At a fork, bear left over a stone bridge and continue through the wood, swinging southwest. Past a second set of stone gateposts and a wooden gate, climb out of the wood to sloping pasture; amid it the fenced-off ruin of Gight Castle (827393). Haddo Estate notices warn that this crumbling wreck is dangerous. Its dark, barrel-vaulted ceilings certainly suggest a hard life.

The Gordons of Gight were famously wild long before Catherine, the 13th of the line, married 'Mad' Jack Byron, who gambled away the entire estate then fled abroad to die in 1791. Destitute, with her three-year-old son Catherine retreated to Gight, which had been bought by the Gordons of Haddo and from which the herons had fled, so fulfilling Thomas the Rhymer's ancient prophecy (see **78**):

> *When the herons leave the tree*
> *The lairds o' Gight shall landless be.*

Hating the place, Byron never returned once he'd left for London, notoriety, and his death, aged 36, in Greece. By then *Don Juan*'s author (**4, 32, 40**) was renowned as much for debauchery as for his satirical poetry. Dark Gight suggests why he chose as he did.

From the ruin's northwest corner a Scottish Wildlife Trust path descends a steep bank through Gight Wood to a wooden footbridge over the Ythan. On the south bank a track breaks right: I followed a faint path left (south) up under spindly spruce to a grassy east-west track (837397), which takes up the other track not far to the west.

Turn left (east) 30 yards over a stile by a gate to rising pasture. With the rough track ahead continuing east to the fork at 841593, bear diagonally right up rough pasture. With forestry to the right, aim for the triangular plantation above, so meeting a track. Zigzagging east with views over the gorge to Gight Castle, this approaches Haddo Farm steading (827383), soon visible to the right. Through three wooden gates the track curls southwest past a left fork and through the steading to a tarmac lane. Turn left then, at the bottom of the steading, right, under the farmhouse. Follow this lane south then east up to a broad plateau, and past Crofts of Haddo gradually descend a mile. At the left turn to Wardford keep right 100 yards to a junction, then turn left a mile down to Methlick.

For Fyvie, from Methlick follow the B9005 eight miles west, climbing above Gight past a lane north to Cuminestown (**101**), then over open land to a high rural crossroads from which lanes vanish north into lonely Buchan backlands. Here the B9005 strikes southwest through the bare hamlet of Woodhead, once a royal burgh, and down to Fyvie (pop. 492), meeting Main Street by the war memorial. Turn left past the Vale Hotel to the Oldmeldrum-Turriff A947, or right then immediately left onto the elegantly-wooded, mile-long driveway to Fyvie Castle. (Or, first, visit the village centre where, behind the Market Cross the Buchan Stone, a large quartz boulder, marks the ancient boundary between the Earldom of Buchan and the Thanage of Formartine.)

78.   Fyvie Castle & Beyond   (*Visit, History, Folklore*)

Sited amid fine woods, gardens and pools on a bluff above the Ythan, with its immense south front, battlemented façade and five tall towers, Fyvie Castle (764394; National Trust; 01651-891266; open May–3 Oct.) has been called the 'crowning glory of Scottish baronial architecture'. This is no exaggeration. Developed after 1400 out of the earlier royal fortress visited by William the Lion (1165–1214), Alexander III (1249–85) and, in 1296 by England's Edward, each of its five towers – Preston and Meldrum flanking the great south front, Seton forming the arched central entrance, Gordon (added in 1777) and Leith (1890) – commemorates each of the five families who have owned it.

As impressive within as without with its great wheel stair and cornucopia of tapestries, antiques and paintings by Raeburn, Reynolds and others, Fyvie is also rich in spooky lore. The Green Lady, Lillias Drummond, murdered by her husband Alexander Seton, still stalks the corridors; and there are two famous curses. The best-known claims that first sons will never inherit Fyvie until three hidden stones be found; their location cunningly half-revealed by the 13th century wizard, Thomas the Rhymer:

> *Ane in Preston's Tower,*
> *Ane in my lady's bower,*
> *And ane beneath the water-yett –*
> *And it ye shall never get.*

It's said this curse was laid when, during the tenancy of Richard le Cheyne, Baron of Inverugie (**109**), dread Thomas (born *c*.1220 at Earlston near Berwick) sought entry. With the gates long left open to him, when at last he came a storm slammed them shut, yet not a breath of wind stirred the grass at his feet. Enraged, he uttered the curse – and, time and again since, though not always, Fyvie's male succession *has* failed. Whether or not the curse preceded folk noticing such a frequent failure is moot.

The other curse warns that, should anyone ever enter the Secret Chamber under the Meldrum Tower: 'The Laird of that day would surely dee, and his leddy would go blind of her e'e.' The prophecy was allegedly fulfilled when, having married one of his servants, Isobel Black, General William Gordon tried to enter the room. Unsurprisingly (he was 80) he soon died but, oddly, Isobel *did* go blind. Now nobody enters that room.

With the general's son dying childless in 1847, in 1889 Fyvie passed to the Forbes-Leith family, from which later the National Trust obtained the castle.

Less supernatural but as tragic are two famous ballads associated with Fyvie 'The Bonnie Lass O' Fyvie' and 'Mill of Tifty's Annie'. The first tells how the Captain of a company of Irish dragoons quartered at Fyvie, where 'there's bonny lasses mony', fell in love with a lass called Peggy, who spurned him, so that, when the dragoons left:

> *Lang, lang ere they wan to Auld Meldrum toon,*
> *They got their captain to carry,*
> *And lang ere they wan to Bonnie Aberdeen,*
> *They got their captain to bury.*

'Mill of Tifty's Annie' tells how Andrew Lammie, Fyvie's trumpeter, fell in love with Annie Smith, daughter of the miller at nearby Tifty. The miller locked her up; Lammie was exiled after blowing one last sad call from the roof of Fyvie, and Annie died of a broken heart. Is there any such thing (outside of Burns) as a *happy* Scots love-song?

Returning to the village, from Main Street the unnumbered Cuminestown road climbs north past Montrose's Camp, this just above the castle. Here, a month after the sack of Aberdeen (**2**), on 27 October 1644 the brilliant Montrose camped the night before a bloody clash in which, over two days, and even though taken by surprise, his vastly-outnumbered Highland and Irish irregulars withstood a Covenanting army led by Argyll and Lothian. This road continues past Tifty to a bare backland of bankrupt hill-farms.

From the A947 at the bottom of Fyvie, lanes climb southwest to the bare lands round Rothienorman and Auchterless (**64**). The A947 itself climbs from the dell, following the Ythan four miles north past Towie Barclay, a fairy-tale pink-harled 1593 tower, lately restored. Here both Ythan and the B992 depart southwest; the latter through bleak Auchterless to the A920. The A947 continues north past a wooded right turn (746467) to Hatton Castle, an 1814 castellated mansion built by the Mowats round a 17th-century manor. Beyond it the B9170 breaks northeast to Cuminestown (**101**), and the A947 continues two miles to Turriff (**87**) on the Deveron.

So now to Huntly in Strathbogie, where the rivers Deveron and Bogie meet.

Section 5:

Deveronside & Old Banffshire

79. Introduction: The Hidden River

Rising under the Buck amid the moors of the Cabrach (**52**), the placid Deveron (*dubh eren*, 'black water', as it is in its upper reaches) seems unsure of its course and shy to be seen. Lacking the glamour or clear direction of Dee, Don or Spey, in its 60-mile run it zigzags north, east, north, east, then finally north again to the Moray Firth, weaving through hilly backlands like a drink-taken driver using rural lanes to avoid the law. Virtually unflanked by major routes and rarely visible from them, it passes only two towns of any size – Huntly (**80**) and Turriff (**87**) – and can boast few great houses along its banks before finally it slips into the sea between Banff (**88**) and Macduff (**96**).

Unsung and praised faintly, if at all, (it has been called 'a first-class, second-class salmon river', though in 1924 a salmon weighing 61 lbs (27.6kg) was hooked from it), the charms of this river and the land about it must be sought out deliberately – there is no 'Whisky Trail' or 'Castle Trail' to entice folk here. Yet its very anonymity makes Deveronside more interesting than its modest reputation suggests. Unlike Dee or Don it creates no prior expectation, and its many secluded glens, woods, and hidden hamlets repay the small effort involved in discovering them.

Taking up the Black Water at Bridgend in the Cabrach, the Deveron's hill-hemmed seven-mile course north to Haugh of Glass is a delight (see **52**). Turning east below the Huntly-Dufftown A920, it loops north round Dunbennan Hill then approaches Huntly. Crossed by the A96 and running briskly past Huntly Castle, it takes up the Bogie then winds north and east past Rothiemay – a lovely stretch. Now swelled by the Isla, it continues past Marnoch (**83**) and Inverkeithny (**85**: another fine stretch) almost to Turriff. Here taking up the Idoch, at last it makes a firm choice of direction, turning north for its final nine-mile run past aptly-named Eden (**88**), under the Bridge of Alvah, and past Duff House (**89**) into Banff Bay, so largely defining Buchan's western boundary.

Though rising in Gordon District, for much of its course the Deveron runs through the old county of Banffshire, since 1974 divided administratively between Banff and Buchan to the east, and Moray to the west. With the boundary running from the river at Rothiemay (**83**) and Marnoch north over the Knock (**86**) to the coast just east of Cullen (**93**), technically Banffshire no longer exists, but it retains its identity. Never as douce or well-off as Aberdeenshire or Moray, the old county was always rich in roguery, from coastal smuggling (**99**) and illicit distilling to the activities of outlaws like James Macpherson (**88**). Accordingly, this section also explores that part of the old county west of the Deveron about the Knock, and the coast from Banff to Cullen, where it ends atop the Bin (**94**).

80. Huntly & the Gordons   *(History, Visit)*

Northwest of the Glens of Foundland (**71**), the Aberdeen-Inverness A96 descends past the A97 north to Banff (**88**) then bypasses Huntly (pop. 4336), a pretty burgh sited where Deveron and Bogie meet under wooded hills in fertile Strathbogie.

Created a burgh of barony in 1545 and laid out round a spacious square by the Duke of Gordon after 1776, Huntly is several towns. First came the castle complex by the Deveron, then the old town above the Bogie, next the solid new burgh, and lately the inevitable industrial estate and housing schemes. East of the burgh under Battle Hill and above the Bogie the railway station serves the Aberdeen-Inverness line. Yet Huntly's real focus is reached by driving from the Square under the narrow Gatehouse arch of the elegant Gordon Schools (1839–41), and up a tree-lined avenue to ruined Huntly Castle (533407; Historic Scotland; 01466-793191; open all year) – perhaps Scotland's finest Renaissance palace, and long the chief power-base of the Gordon Earls of Huntly.

Leaving place-names like Gourdon in southern France and entering Britain with the Normans, this family gained Border lands from Malcolm Canmore (1057–93). Gifted Strathbogie (see **30**) by Robert I in 1319, Sir Adam Gordon's descendants on one side were Jock of Scurdargue (**51**) and his brother, Tam of Ruthven (**83**), the progenitors of most northern Gordon branches. On the other, Elizabeth Gordon's 14th century marriage to Alexander Seton birthed the Seton Gordons, Earls of Huntly (Old English *hunta leah*, 'huntsman's wood'; a Borders name), the earldom being created *c*.1450.

Covering the old Aberdeen-Moray trade-route, the riverbank site was fortified in the 12th century by the Celtic Earls of Fife, their earth and timber Peel of Strathbogie replaced *c*.1400 by a massive L-plan Gordon stone tower. Though torched by the Earl of Moray amid the war between James II (1437–60) and the Black Douglas, it and the pre-eminence of the Gordon Earls grew together. In 1496 James IV visited to celebrate the marriage of the English pretender Perkin Warbeck to Lady Catherine Gordon, 'the White Rose of Scotland'; and by 1556 George 4th Earl had built his *new wark*, a grand château-style palace-block. Then came civil war and feud. Opposing Mary Queen of Scots and in 1562 defeated at Corrichie (**23**) by her half-brother James Stewart, after the battle George dropped dead and Stewart, now Earl of Moray, sacked Huntly Castle. The Gordons led Catholic resistance to Reform, and feud escalated. With Moray assassinated in 1572, 20 years later his son ('The Bonnie Earl o' Moray') was murdered by Gordons led by George, 6th Earl, who in 1594 with Hay of Erroll (**111**) defeated the Protestant Argyll at the Battle of Glenlivet. Cornered (George was his favourite), James VI exiled him, then in 1597 restored him as 1st Marquis of Huntly. By 1606 George completed the new palace, his *full fayre house*, its ruin still impressive (see below).

The Civil War led to ruin. Starved into defeat, in 1647 the castle's royalist garrison was massacred and the castle thereafter neglected. Taken in December 1647, the 2nd Marquis was beheaded in Edinburgh. The Gordon power-base moved to Fochabers, where *c*.1480 the 2nd Earl had begun Castle Gordon on the Bog of Gight. His successors (the 'Gudemen o' the Bog') prospered, so that after 1769 Alexander, 4th Duke and 18th Gudeman, extended the castle into 'the most magnificent edifice north of the Forth', or, 'a tedious quarter-mile of two storeyed crenel-

lated regularity': take your pick. His wife, the lovely Duchess Jane, helped raise the Gordon Highlanders by offering recruits their sign-up shilling from between her lips – apparently an effective lure.

Yet Huntly remains the Gordon centre, and the castle its grandest sight, its south-side oriel windows inspired by the French Château of Blois, with a huge inscription (it runs the entire 17.7m length of the upper works) commemorating the marriage of the 6th Earl/1st Marquis to Lady Henrietta Stewart. Finer still is the great heraldic doorpiece, defaced by Convenanting vandals. Frame by frame depicting humanity's rise from the Garden of Eden, some call it Britain's finest carved crest. Within, over kitchens above earlier vaulted basements and a deep round prison-pit, the two main floors with their private chambers and carved fireplaces are reached by a ceremonial staircase; while a narrow spiral stair climbs the huge round tower to the topmost southwest gable with its wide strategic views over the land about – a land most walkable.

81.   Round Huntly & up Clashmach Hill   *(Walks)*

There are many walks in and about Huntly – via street and riverbank, or to wooded Battle Hill east of and above the station, or Ba' Hill a mile south of town, or the Clashmach to the southwest, or the Bin (**83**) two miles to the northwest.

One town walk, described in a leaflet at the information centre in the burgh's elegant Square (01466-792255; April–Oct.) as the 'George MacDonald Town Trail', refers to author George MacDonald (1824–1905). Born above what is now the Huntly Carpet Centre in Bogie Street and a friend of Ruskin and Morris, this man of the cloth wrote Doric (**107**) novels (*Alec Forbes of Howglen, Malcolm,* etc.), but is better-known for his 'fairy' tales (*Lilith, The Golden Key*). Influencing Lewis (*Narnia*) and Tolkein (*Lord of the Rings*), his work is subtle and enduring.

A two-mile circular walk exploring Huntly and its setting starts from the picnic area and carpark by the Castle. Follow the Deveronside path west through the fields, wooded Ordiquhill (816ft; 249m) and the Bin (1023ft; 312m) above to the north. In a mile, at a junction by the river-bridge onto the Portsoy B9022, turn left onto a tree-shaded pavement, and left again back to Huntly. Just before the cemetery a path descends through woodland to the edge of the fields. Via rustic bridges over deep ditches, cross a track and climb through the wood up to Gordon Primary School on Meadow Avenue. Bear south to the Square, then follow Castle Street north through the Gatehouse archway, and so back to the Castle.

For wider views, the four-mile climb up and about the Clashmach (1230ft; 375m) – the bare gorse-fringed ridge a mile southwest of Huntly – is a must.

From the Square drive to the bypass roundabout, turn right on the A96 a few yards, then left past Huntly Mart up the Tullochbeg lane to a bungalow (514390). Here, where the lane bends left, a grassy track (yellow arrow) continues uphill. Parking with care, start up between fields, swinging west then south on the deep-rutted track (I found the field alongside easier going). Past a wooden gate/stile the track steepens through gorse to a second gate. Beyond it a path climbs diagonally west (right) to a third gate, then bears left to the exposed summit cairn (386497) with its fine panorama – from Bennachie (**68**) beyond the Foudland hills to Tap o' Noth (**51**), the Buck (**50**), Ben Rinnes, the Knock (**86**) and the Bin of Cullen (**94**).

Return as you came or, via the ridgetop track, head northwest through a metal gate past burned-back gorse almost a mile to the ridge's subsidiary crest, with fine local views all the way. From this point (397494), return as you came. Alternatively, aiming northeast at Huntly, it's possible to return by leaving the track and descending the slope east under dense gorse, then crossing fenced and ditched flats before climbing to the outgoing track just above the starting-point. However, this involves crossing awkward fenced ditches, so it's probably best to return as you came. The views are better, anyway.

82.   South of Huntly: the Braes of Gartly   *(Route, Cycle/Walk)*

From the Huntly bypass roundabout the A97 follows Strathbogie south past Gartly and the Leith Hall (**70**) turn, to Rhynie (**50**) and Donside beyond. After two miles the road descends over Preist's Water. Here two lanes break right, the first to Tillathrowie marking the start of an eight-mile cycle/walk circuit up and about the Braes of Gartly.

Parking by Tillathrowie village hall, start west past the silos of Bridgend grain mill. Amid sloping pasture above the burn in the broad valley below the lane narrows, then after a mile climbs past Upper and Lower Drumbulg and an old smiddy before levelling under Whitestones, once the schoolhouse. There was a shop here too, when the Braes were part of the Gordon Richmond estates. With these sold and forestry taking over, as elsewhere the local population declined.

Past the steading and cottages at Tillathrowie, after three miles the surfaced lane ends at Wester Tillathrowie (468347). The continuing track descends left (south) past a sign to Corrylair (pony-trekking). Crossing two burns amid rough pasture in the bed of the glen, it swings hard right up to a junction by a logged area. The track ahead continues to Corrylair: here turn left, climbing the whin-rich track steeply east round the Hill of Drumfergue. With broad views, the track passes above Drumfergue steading (471371) to the edge of the forest. Here, at a double fork, bear left and left again down to a third fork, then again left, over a cattle-grid under the steading to a metalled lane – the return route.

On the south slope of the Braes, this lane descends east through mature birchwood to Coynachie, levels over a second cattle-grid, then continues down to the glen's grassy bed. Watch for cattle on the road; and cross the fence above if there's a bull with them. Past Coynachie's fine old steading and watermill the lane crosses the burn then climbs to broad views. Nearing and now parallel to the Tillathrowie lane, past the mill at Bridgend it descends to the A97 some 50 yards south of the Tillathrowie lane, near where you parked.

Continuing south on the A97, a few yards up the brae on the left a back road to Gartly Church crosses the Bogie and climbs to the 1880 kirk, a plain Gothic rectangle dedicated to St. Andrew. Beyond, lonely lanes crisscross under forested Gartly Moor.

Bisected by river and railway, the hamlet of Gartly lies under the steep western Hill of Corskie (1368ft; 417m) two miles further south and just off the A97. Here the Barclays, Banff's hereditary sheriffs from the 12th to 16th centuries, had a castle, now long gone, which in 1562 sheltered Mary Queen of Scots from the Gordons (**23**). Opposite the Glen of Noth with Tap o' Noth (**51**) beyond, here the true uplands begin, the A97 climbing south of Rhynie then descending to Donside.

83.   North of Huntly: The Bin to Rothiemay   *(Route, Walks)*

Continuing past Huntly, shedding the A920 west (left) to Dufftown, and the B9022 north to Portsoy (**90**), the A96 runs northwest 12 miles to Keith. Two miles beyond the Huntly roundabout, under the Bin Forest to the right and just before the road starts climbing, a sign on the right to 'Bin Forest Walks' leads to a carpark. Here a board displays waymarked trails up and about this broad, low, densely-wooded hill (1023ft; 312m) and neighbouring Ordiquhill – for a Forest Enterprise map of these trails, call 01466-794161.

Next, on the left the Drumdelgie (immortalised in balladry: see **107**) turn leads to the North-East Falconry Visitor Centre (01466-760328) at Broadland, where birds of prey are flown daily. Cresting the Bin, the A96 leaves Strathbogie to descend past Cairnie, an old Gordon holding, then climbs past Mill of Botary and turns to Boghead and Windyraw – names epitomising the bare, uninviting land near

Keith. Here the A96 enters Moray, continuing through Keith, Fochabers, Elgin, Forres and Nairn to Inverness.

At Cairnie a road (482247) breaks north past ruined St. Martin's Church (1591), in it an effigy of Sir John Gordon of Pitlurg, father of 'the Great Straloch' (**7**). This road continues over poor land past Auchanachie Castle (498469; 1594) to Ruthven. Here, in a recess of the single remaining wall of the medieval kirk of St. Carol's, is the effigy in full knight's armour of Tam of Ruthven (**80**). In another mile the road meets the B9022, this by the Isla near its confluence with the Deveron by Rothiemay – our next visit.

From the A96 by Huntly the B9022 departs north past the driveway to Huntly Castle Hotel (533415), an 18th-century mansion once owned by the Dukes of Gordon, past which the drive descends over the Deveron and Castle Bridge (*c*.1800) to the Castle. Continuing north under the Bin, in three more miles the B9022 twists under the railway to meet the Deveron, take up the Cairnie road, and cross the Isla. Here entering Moray, before continuing past the Knock (**86**) it sheds the B9118 east a mile, via the Isla-Deveron confluence, to Milltown of Rothiemay (*rath a' mhaigh*; 'fort on the plain') – a pretty, granite-built, hill-hemmed riverside village.

Home of 17th-century cartographer Parson Gordon of Rothiemay (see **7**) and birthplace of astronomer James Ferguson (1710–76), snug Rothiemay has been settled since Neolithic times. With many cairns on the ridges above, Rothiemay stone circle (552487) is found by climbing from the War Memorial past council housing to the Keith-Aberchirder B9117. Turn right 400 yards to a field to the right, where a huge cup-marked recumbent, two large outliers either side, is what's left of the original 12-stone complex (see **60**). Rothiemay was also an early Christian centre. St. Drostan (**98**) built a chapel by Kirkton Burn in the 6th century, while St. Nathalan is remembered by his kirk and well.

Not far east of the circle by the B9117 is the 1906 baronial gateway to now-vanished Rothiemay Castle, first mentioned in 1264 and in the 16th century rebuilt as a Z-plan tower. Visited by Mary Queen of Scots in 1562 and during the Civil War garrisoned by Cromwell's troops, it survived until, some 50 years ago, it was bought by a Mr. Ward who felled the timber, sold the contents, and let it fall into ruin.

Above the Deveron and under Gallow Hill and Catstone Hill the pretty, well-wooded B9117 continues east and north above Mayen five miles past Old Marnoch Church (597501). Here amid St. Marnan's riverbank kirkyard stand unusual monuments like the Meldrum Memorial; while just north of the road the plain 1792 parish kirk occupies a stone circle, St. Marnan's Chair. Soon after the road meets the Huntly-Banff A97 opposite Kinnairdy Castle (619498), an Innes seat high on the Deveron's north bank. Sold to the Gregory family in the 17th century, this tall, narrow old L-plan tower is where David Gregory (1627–1720) invented the barometer and fathered 32 children. Which was the more laudable effort?

Back at Rothiemay (from which the Keith-bound B9117 climbs northwest over the B9022 three miles south of the Knock), nearby Fourman Hill offers grand views...and a fine walk.

84.   Above Rothiemay: Fourman Hill   *(Walk)*

For this six-mile circuit by track and back-road, from Rothiemay War Memorial descend the main street past a castellated house and the Forbes Arms to cross the Deveron by the 1872 bridge. At a wooded junction on the south bank turn left, half-a-mile uphill through forestry, to a junction (553477) on the right signposted to North and South Redhill. If driving rather than walking to this point, it's possible to park on the left by the start of an old track winding east and out of the plantation to Corsekellie (557476; see below).

Start up the Redhill road, soon leaving dense forestry for dyked fields with Redhill steading (560467) now visible ahead under Fourman Hill (572458; 1128ft; 344m). With broad views opening up from Tap o' Noth to the Knock, keep left past the steading on a stony track. This climbs the open north shoulder of forestry-crowned Fourman Hill, so-named because once it marked the boundaries of four different estates. At first a shelf of land hides Deveronside below, but soon the steady climb up the gorse-banked track leads to a double metal gate at the open crest. For over a mile beyond this point the view north and east and down to the snaking, green-banked Deveron is continuously splendid.

Here to the right a fenceline climbs the hill, a there-and-back detour of about half a mile, but the fence- and view-blocked summit is hard to reach.

Over the gate past incurious cows the muddy track (the Queen's Road, as used by Queen Mary *en route* to Inverness in 1562; **23**) continues high and fine along the grassy slope past lone Scots Pine, a great bend in the Deveron under Mayen below. In time, and now over the district boundary, the forestry on the slope above descends to meet the track by a second metal gate. Beyond it, with open woodland to the right, the track becomes a metalled lane that breaks northeast (left) above rough pasture to a white croft at Fourmanhill (583457).

Here there are options. Past the gated bend ahead (585460) the continuing lane descends almost a mile to the Bognie Arms Hotel on the A97 opposite the Forgue B9001 (next chapter) – a there-and back extension of 1.5 miles involving a stiff return climb.

Or at the bend turn left through the gate, heading northwest and downhill over the adjacent pasture to a muddy descending track.

Or, by the croft, cross a stile onto the pasture and follow the edge of reedy scrubwood north 500 yards to this track (585465). Turn left downhill under silver birch half-a-mile to a gate onto the south bank Deveronside road from Marnoch Lodge, three miles northeast. Turn left on this pretty road, west past Corniehaugh and Woodfold, *en route* recrossing the district boundary. Climbing steadily above the river, in two miles the road bends through Corskellie steading, where cup-and-ring-marked boulders line the roadside. With Rothiemay visible ahead the road enters forestry past a first then second turn left up to Redhill, the second marking the start of the outgoing route, so completing the circuit.

132

85.   Forgue & Inverkeithny   *(Route, Walk)*

From the A96 just east of Huntly the A97 breaks north to Banff, soon shedding a lane left to Rothiemay and continuing under Cobairdy Wood four miles to Bogniebrae. Here, opposite the Fourmanhill lane, the B9001 turns east a mile to Forgue, a hamlet and parish in a land of wooded hills and hidden vales. Dominated by the elegant spire of St. Margaret's (1856; photo below), Forgue makes Rip Van Winkle look energetic. But don't nod off, for here starts a varied five-mile (minimum) walk which, via Inverkeithny and the Deveron, returns over or round Boghead Hill, and which may be extended to Glendronach Distillery.

Park by the old Forgue Emporium, now closed. Start northwest up the B9001 past the recreation park – there's room to park here too – 200 yards to a bend and junction (607453; left to Huntly, right to Banff). Turn right, then right again on the narrow road to Haddo, up past a steading at a left bend, then right at the Mid Muirtown junction. Over an open brow and past Muirtown (on the right), descend round a left bend.

Just past it, a stony track (616458) descends between fields to a wooded junction. With the right fork overgrown, past an iron gate and decayed, Tudor-chimneyed lodge the left turn leads to another wooded junction. Under tall beech trees the right turn crosses the stone-bridged Burn of Forgue *en route* to Inverkeithny, while the left turn leads to a tree-shrouded ruin – Haddo House, last used as a World War II PoW camp then left to rot. Unlike the *other* Haddo (**76**; the name from *half-a-dabhach*; a measure of land), this *c.*1836 Italianate mansion with its grandiose

entry-tower is *very* spooky – and unsafe. Beyond it the track climbs past the semi-derelict 1831 Haddo Home Farm steading to the road which, continuing north from the stony track, has since bent east and downhill.

Here, by Haddo Home Farm House (617466), the road again bends sharply, north. From the bend a track descends the wood's edge to a crossing near the ruin, an old oval walled garden ahead, and to the left a burnside path to Inverkeithny. Also from the bend, the beech-hedged road runs half-a-mile north to a junction (621471) above the Deveron. Turn right, down over the Burn of Forgue past the entry to the Haddo tracks, and on through tumbledown Inverkeithny to a lane on the right up Boghead Hill (631461; 630ft; 192m).

With the continuing road climbing to a fine viewpoint over the Deveron before joining the Glendronach-Turriff B9024, turn right up Boghead Hill. A half-mile up the steep brae, a right fork (626464) descends a tree-lined mile south to Mill of Forgue, where a right turn over the burn joins the B9001 just above Forgue – the shorter, easier, and prettier return route.

If climbing on up Boghead Hill, from the open top the road descends a mile to a track (628444) breaking west then north past Balnoon over open hillside down to Mill of Forgue.

At the B9024 junction just south of Balnoon, a right turn leads past Glendronach Distillery (01466-730202; call first) up to the B9001. Licensed in 1826 and using traditional techniques (malting-floor, peat-fired kilns, coal-fired stills), Glendronach was founded by James Allardes (d.1849). It's told how, dining at Gordon Castle by Fochabers, he drank too freely of another malt and offended the duchess. Next day he explained to the duke: 'Well, Your Grace, it was just that trash of Glen***** you gave me yesterday that did not agree wi' me. If it had been myn ain gweed Glendronach, I would not have been ony the waur.' Whereupon, it's said, the duke promptly ordered a cask of The Glendronach...

Taking up the B9024 the B9001 runs north a mile to Forgue, and south a half-mile over the Glendronach burn. Here a lane forks right (Colpy 8) past Frendraught (621418), a restored 17ʰ-century mansion on the site of an earlier castle. Visited in 1535 by James V, who granted a charter to Sir James Crichton, here in 1630 a violent feud between the Crichtons and Gordons of Rothiemay climaxed in a fire in which Rothiemay, four followers, and the the Marquis of Huntly's son died, their 'ashes and brynt bones' being interred at Gartly parish kirk (**82**). Later Frendraught became, and remains, a Morison house.

Past the Frendraught turn the B9001 climbs southeast over bleak higher ground through Rothienorman *en route* to Inverurie (see **64**).

86.   Forgue to Fordyce via the Knock   *(Routes, Walk)*

West of Forgue the Banff A97 continues north over the Deveron past Marnoch, Kinnairdy (**84**), and a left turn to Cornhill. Crossing the Burn of Auchintoul, the road bypasses Aberchirder (pop. 1213), a grid-plan village founded on a broad hillside in 1764 by Alexander Gordon of Auchintoul, who unsurprisingly had trouble attracting folk to this remote moor. Originally called 'Foggie' or 'Foggieloan' after a croft on the site of the Fife Arms Hotel, this plain but spacious village boasts Britain's squarest square, but in no way can be called energetic. From it, with the B9025 breaking east six miles to Turriff (**87**); the A97 continues over hilly open land to Banff, while the B9023 turns northwest four miles over high pasture (sea-views) to Cornhill, a single-street farming village on the A95. With the old Gordon mansion of Park – originally a Z-plan tower dating from 1536 – nearby, Cornhill's main annual event is the race up the Knock, three miles to the southwest.

Returning now to the Huntly-Portsoy B9022 (**83**), on crossing the Isla and shedding the B9118, north of Rothiemay Crossroads (B9117) it traverses a stony plain dominated by the Knock's bald heather-dome (537552; 1412ft; 430m). Past the hamlet of Knock and Knockdhu Distillery, it joins the A95 at the district boundary by Glenbarry. For the main track up the Knock, turn right on the A95 past Glenbarry Inn some 400 yards, and left at a cottage on a bend. This lane runs west a mile through Swilebog to a junction: park left by a pond. The way up starts from a gate a few yards right of the junction, and climbs straight up the hill's east flank.

In another mile the northbound A95/B9022 intersects a crossroads. Here a right turn leads past Ordiquhill kirk (1805; built on an old raised circular graveyard) up to a high backland above Crombie Castle (590623), an eldritch L-plan tower a mile north of Marnoch (**83**). At Gordonstoun just beyond the Ordiquhill turn, the roads fork, the A95 continuing northeast through Cornhill three miles to the Banff-Portsoy A98, the B9022 running north five miles under Durn Hill's Iron Age fort (571638; see **69**) to Portsoy. *En route* it picks up the B9023 from Cornhill, then sheds a back road west to Deskford, a hamlet on the Keith-Cullen B9018.

The first right turn on this back road leads two miles north to Fordyce. A mile south of the Cullen-Portsoy A98 and west of Durn Hill, with its pocket-sized 1592 L-plan towerhouse and the flanking ruin of St. Talorgan's Church (originally 13th century) this village – made a burgh of barony by Bishop Elphinstone (**2**) of Aberdeen in 1499 – is a hidden delight. Flanking the street, the castle was built by an ex-Provost of Aberdeen, Thomas Menzies of Durn; and amid a creepy graveyard with Ogilvie altar-tombs the kirk's western tower and 1661 belfry survive. With conservation awards heaped on it, its Academy, founded in 1798, was once renowned.

From the village a public footpath follows the Burn of Fordyce north over the A98 and past Glenglassaugh Distillery to the graceful beach at Sandend (**91**). Also, three miles northeast is the coastal village of Cullen (**93**) – jewel in the crown of the 'Banffshire Riviera', and our final visit in this section.

87.   To Turriff   *(Routes, History)*

Past Inverkeithny (**85**) and in a series of steep-banked loops the Deveron winds on six miles northwest almost to Turriff (pop. 4255), where it breaks north to Banff and the sea.

Bisected by the Fyvie-Banff A947, from the west this red sandstone town is reached by the Glendronach B9024 and the Aberchirder B9025. Running northeast seven miles through a hilly backland, the B9024 picks up the scenic Inverkeithny lane and passes Muiresk House (a medieval English barn re-erected by the Deveron) before meeting the A947 by the Burn of Turriff under the town.

From Aberchirder, the B9025 climbs past rural turns, including the B9121 north to the hamlet of Alvah. Soon after, at Scotston (683520), two lanes break north and east to wooded Deveronside slopes – north to Mountblairy Home Farm (1800; 691544), the steading with its doric portico all that remains of the house of Mountblairy; and east past Forglen House (695517), an 1845 Gothic extravaganza containing parts of the ancient castle of Forglen. This area exudes an intense sense of privacy, but combining these two lanes makes for an interesting loop.

Beyond Scotston the B9024 descends a wooded brae past Forglen's prominent gateway to cross the Deveron. Here the Dunlugas/Eden road (see below) breaks north up the wooded riverbank, while the B9024 enters Turriff past solid red stone villas, mostly built during the burgh's 19th-century farming prosperity.

On a bluff sloping east-west down to the Deveron, and perhaps the site of an early Celtic Christian community, in 1512 Turriff became a burgh of barony with two fairs; Lammas and St. Congan's. Later the site of a major cattle mart rivalling Keith, today the Agricultural Show early each August attracts folk from all over Buchan, on the west edge of which it stands. 34 miles from Aberdeen and 12 south of Banff, here in 1639 occurred the Trot of Turriff, the Civil War's first battle, in which Royalists routed Covenanters. Here too in 1913 occurred a famous riot involving 'the Turra Coo' – a white cow poinded (legally confiscated) when farmer Robert Paterson of Lendrum refused to stamp his employees' new insurance cards 'unless they asked him to do so'. When the cow was put up for auction in Turriff Square on 9 December 1913, a riot ensued. Eight men, Paterson included, were tried for inciting the riot but acquitted for lack of evidence. Returned to Lendrum by farmers who clubbed together to buy it back, the now-famous cow had its portrait painted, a memorial being erected at Lendrum years later in 1971.

With the octagonal pre-1557 Market Cross, the ruin of medieval St. Congan's Church, and its many large buildings of striking red sandstone from nearby Delgatie, the old prosperity of Turriff and the area about is highlighted by the number of castles and great houses nearby – Towie Barclay and Hatton (**78**) to the south, Forglen to the west, Delgatie to the east, and Craigston to the northeast.

For Delgatie Castle (755506; 01888-563479, open April–Oct.), take the A947 north out of Turriff, and in under a mile turn right on a road running due east 1.5 miles to the wooded drive. Celebrated in the bothy ballad 'The Barnyards of Delgatie', this five-storey tower on an 11th-century base is the Clan Hay Centre, having belonged to the Hays of Erroll (**111**) since 1314, when after Bannockburn they took it from the Earl of Buchan.

In another mile north up the A947 the B9105 breaks northeast past junctions at Fintry; just beyond which on the right is the wooded drive of Craigston Castle (761552; 1604–07); a tall white-harled Renaissance house of red stone with later extensions by William Adam – the architect responsible for Duff House in Banff.

88.   North to Banff: Macpherson's Rant   *(Routes, History)*

Of two routes from Turriff to Banff the A947 is more direct, but its endless twists and turns frustrate, until near Banff it straightens at last. Nor is it scenic, though by Castleton Farm (722563) four miles north of Turriff is a remnant of the Castle of King Edward (or *Kin-edar*; 'head of the valley'), sacked amid the 1308 Harrowing of Buchan.

More relaxing is the riverside route via Dunlugas and Eden. Leaving the B9025 by the riverbridge just west of Turriff, from a wooded bank the lane climbs open slopes past Dunlugas, a 1793 Ogilvie house, and in two more miles descends to then climbs from the lovely den of Eden. At a fork atop the brae by the ruined Z-plan tower of Eden Castle (698587), a 16th-century Meldrum seat, turn left, north, to a junction by estate woodland. With Eden House (an 1828 Grant-Duff seat above the Deveron) ahead, turn right past a steading, right again at another Eden House entry, and east to a fork 400 yards short of the A947. Here, three miles south of Banff, join the A947, or turn left (north) 1.5 miles to a junction east of Montcoffer House (below); then right a mile to the A947. Descend left under the Hill of Doune to the A96, and cross Smeaton's seven-arched Deveron Bridge (1779) past the golf-course and the Duff House drive into Banff (pop. 4024).

From its east-facing slope above Banff Bay and opposite the bare Hill of Doune above Macduff (**96**), this Royal and Ancient Burgh (as titled in 1372 by Robert II) is historically and architecturally richer than any other Moray Firth town. Sited where bleak Buchan begins to give way to more fertile coastland, here in 1163 Malcolm IV lived, presumably in the old castle replaced by Banff Castle, built in 1750 by Lord Deskford. By then Banff was already a Hanseatic port, trading with the Baltic and Mediterranean. From that time survives the tomb-dense Old Kirkyard round the ivied ruin of St. Mary's Kirk; and the Great Garden by Low Street, site of a Carmelite monastery created in 1321 by Robert I but fired 'under sylens of nicht' in 1559.

Later, long spared any more mayhem, Banff's mild air and status as county town drew local gentry – Abercrombies, Bairds, Forbeses and Ogilvies – to build town houses. These in winter they occupied amid a social whirl about Duff House that in 1777 led the burgh to be described as 'perhaps the gayest little town in Scotland'. Some survive: a stone by the Market Inn on High Shore is dated 1585; No. 1 High Shore dates from 1675. Then Banff lay about Low Street. Today, from the burgh's Mercat Cross, steep wynds climb above the 1764 steeple to the old Cullen road, now the High Street, from the north end of which and opposite the castle the A98 departs west. Below the castle, the growing Seatown remained separate.

137

With its harbour built as late as 1775, for decades thereafter Banff fishermen landed herring, but in time the trade went to neighbouring Macduff.

Here on 7 November 1700 the fiddler-brigand James Macpherson was hanged, the clock on the tower being advanced to deny a last-minute reprieve approaching. Caught in Keith by agents of sour Lord Braco (see below), this Scots Robin Hood spent his last night composing the rant, and on the scaffold played it, then (it's said) broke the fiddle over the hangman's head and leapt to his doom. It seems first he offered his fiddle to anyone in the crowd who'd take it, but nobody dared. The ruined fiddle is in the Clan Macpherson Museum at Newtonmore; the clock, or one like it, graces Dufftown's Clock Tower; and it's said that, when Macduff folk built Doune Church on Doune Hill, they left the west face of its tower clockless so Banff folk couldn't tell the time. Later, visiting Banff in 1780, Burns rewrote the original rant:

> *O, what is death but parting breath?*
> *On many a bloody plain*
> *I've dared his face, and in this place*
> *I scorn him yet again!*

With Banff's many riches protected by the Banff Preservation Society, the information centre (01261-812419; April–Oct.) is in Collie Lodge by the carpark at the south end of Low Street, opposite it by the golf clubhouse the entry to Duff House (shown opposite).

89.   Round Duff House & Alvah Bridge   *(Walk, History)*

This varied six-mile circuit begins at Duff House (692634; 1261-818181; open daily April–Sept., Thur.–Sun. Oct.–March). Some 400 yards south of the A98, this vast baroque palace was built 1735–37 by William Adam for William Duff of Braco, later Earl of Fife,. The original plan involved balancing the main block by colonnades curving to wings either side, but Adam and Braco fell out over costs, so the colonnades and wings were never built. Successively ducal palace, hotel, hospital and prisoner-of-war camp, today Duff House serves as principal outstation of the National Galleries of Scotland, and offers a wide collection of paintings, furniture, tapestries and artefacts.

From Duff House carpark walk south past playing fields on the old toll-route. Through Fife Gates enter Wrack Wood past 'Orchard', a cottage on the right, once Duff House Laundry. The woodland track above golf course and river continues south past the domed Ice House – Duff House's 18th-century fridge. Below it and above a loop of the Deveron, a path winds parallel to the main track: follow either on to the spooky Duff family mausoleum. Built in 1793 by James Duff, 2nd Earl of Fife, on the site of a chapel erected in 1324 by Robert the Bruce, in its south wall is recessed the recumbent effigy of Provost Douglas of Banff, complete with carved skull, crossbones, and hourglass.

With the A97 nearby, continue on the main track, or follow the path along the beechwood slope past Hospital Island to a meadow and junction by a water-treatment plant. To rejoin the main track, here bear right up a bank to the bridge carrying it, and continue south, past a left turn to a fork where fields begin. Keep left, south, another mile to a white house with a wedding-cake tower: once a Carmelite retreat. The Douglas Fir nearby is a wishing tree – stick a penny in it, circle it thrice clockwise, make a wish, then descend left to the single-span Bridge of Alvah (680611). Soaring over the wooded red sandstone gorge two miles south of Duff House, it was built in 1772 to link Duff properties each side of the Deveron. It's said to contain a secret chamber where a deserting soldier boy once hid, protected by the Laird of Montcoffer's daughter, until one day she found him gone...

Over the bridge, climb left past a (lucky) Chinese Yew east to Montcoffer House (685614; after 1670), briefly home of Edward VII's grand-daughter, Princess Arthur of Connaught. Past a fine circular doocot and with wide views over the Deveron, continue east on the now-surfaced road one mile to a junction (698617).

Turn left 40 yards then, by a grey-harled cottage, left again onto a track rising gently past rough pasture, gorse and silver birch – the remains of Montcoffer Wood. Near the crest, look out for an old milestone on the left. By an old drystane dyke and its drainage portholes, descend past Gaveny Cottage to views of Banff and the sea, past Macduff Distillery to the A947 pavement, and 400 yards to the A98 under Doune Hill. Turn left over Deveron Bridge, hugging the parapet as juggernauts thunder past – a rude return to the present. Continue past the golf course and turn left to Duff House.

90.   Whitehills & Portsoy   *(Routes, History)*

West from Banff the A98 runs past right turns to Swordanes, Inverboyndie and, by the old hospital at Ladysbridge, over the B9121 north to Whitehills and south to the A97 by the Hill of Alvah. Following the Burn of Boyndie through open land under low hills past the Keith A95 and the B9025 before looping northeast, after seven miles it takes up the Huntly B9022 and enters Portsoy.

As so often, the back route holds more interest. Leaving Banff with Boyndie Bay below, turn first right past the Swordanes Hotel (visible from the A98), and bear left past roofless St. Brandon's Church and its raised circular graveyard to a staggered crossing. Turn right on the B9038 past the B9139 half-a-mile northwest to Whitehills (pop.1048), a straggling shoreline village with its own fleet and fish market. Created in the 18th century with inland additions after 1824, its sea-front cottages are, as usual hereabouts, gable-end on to the sea. Of the folk, the 1845 New Statistical Account notes that they were: 'cleanly in their habits', so their cured fish had: 'a superior reputation'. The women, of: 'superior comeliness', dominated the men, claiming all annual fishing profit and wielding: 'an influence which in any other condition of life would appear little consistent with either feminine propriety or domestic order' – so the Rev. A. Anderson stiffly observed.

Just before Whitehills a lane on the right descends to the beach and the Red Well (663654), a chalybeate spring in a beehive-shaped enclosure and once thought Roman in origin. You're advised not to drink the water.

From Whitehills take the B9121 south a half-mile to Whitehills crossroads, and turn west (right) on the B9139 three miles over open ground. Past a fork the road descends over the Burn of Boyne at Scotsmill (610655), this near Boyne Castle (see next chapter), then climbs past Cowhythe and down to the A98 at the edge of Portsoy, *en route* offering fine views of the village, the Knock and Durn Hill (both **86**) and the Bin of Cullen (**94**)

Made a burgh of barony for the Ogilvies in 1550, today a holiday village and craft centre which each July hosts the Traditional Boat Festival, Portsoy (pop. 1840; *port saoi*, 'warrior's harbour': see **92**) is a well-preserved fishing village, much of it a conservation area. Little in the A98-bisected upper town suggests this, nor is there any evidence of its former wealth. This came from the herring trade, and earlier from its export of thread and linen to England, also the sale to France of 'Portsoy Marble' – the local serpentine which, over 300 years ago, was used to build chimneypieces in Louis XIV's great palace at Versailles.

To discover old Portsoy, from the A98 near the village's west end turn right to the Square, then past Boyne Hotel (mid-18th century) descend narrow North High Street past restored merchant houses to the Old Harbour (1692). Here, ranged about the double basin and huge breakwater, are old grainstores and warehouses, many restored, with arched doorways, forestairs and crowstepped gables. On the west side of the basin is the vast warehouse containing Portsoy Pottery and Marble Workshop, where today the hard serpentine found along the shore nearby is still cut and polished. As for the atmospheric Shore Inn, it's reputed to be an old smuggling haunt (**99**), but you're unlikely to find contraband Dutch gin in the bar these days...

91.   Boyne Castle & Beyond   *(Routes, Walk)*

To walk to the hidden ruin of Boyne Castle from Portsoy, from the harbour follow Shore Street east past the fish merchants and caravan park. Over a bridge follow the shore track past an old ropeworks to a path on the rocky eastern side of Links Bay. At a fork, take the higher path up to the clifftop, skirting fields above a rocky cove and through a gate descending to a shore strewn with rose-coloured serpentine. At East Head, the path gets faint and rough as seaward views open up – Scar Nose to the west, Troup Head (**96**) 15 miles to the east. Now rounding a buttress above Strathmarchin Bay, climb diagonally east up the grassy slope to the plateau of Cowhythe Hill, aiming for a gated track bearing south (607662). Following the slope too far west leads to a quarry at the mouth of the Burn of Boyne, and no easy way round or down.

With the views wide and spectacular, follow this track south over open fields a half-mile to the B9139 by Cowhythe's wind-bent grove, and turn left down to the burn at Scotsmill (1626). Boyne Castle lies over a wooded bank the far side of the sloping field opposite. Climb the brae to the top of the field and follow the fence-line some 300 yards to the ruin on its crag above the burn.

Built 1575–80 by Sir George Ogilvie of Dunlugas (**88**); forfeited and abandoned after the '45, this four-storeyed courtyard palace with its round corner towers is unsafe, due in part to the poor mortar used in its construction. Yet, brooding above a bend in the foaming black burn opposite a dark, steep-sloped and raucous rookery, Boyne is as ominous as Gight (**77**) and Findlater (**93**). As for the wild garlic growing all about, allegedly it was brought from France by Mary Beaton or Bethune – one of Mary Queen of Scots' 'Four Maries', as in the famous song:

'Yestreen the Queen had four Maries,
This day she'll hae but three;
There was Mary Beaton and Mary Seaton
And Mary Carmichael and me.'

To complete the four-mile circuit, return up the quiet B9139 and continue west past Cowhythe, enjoying the views. After a mile, with Portsoy below, a gorse-fringed track on the right (596656) descends to a fork east of the village by Seatown Cemetery. The right turn climbs to the A98; so turn left under the village past St. Peter's Well (596663). Like the Red Well at Whitehills, this lies within a stone beehive in a grassy bank. Beyond this the track drops to the outward route. Turn left back to Shore Street and the harbour.

From Portsoy the A98 continues west over level ground past a left turn to Fordyce (**86**), then past Glenglassaugh Distillery to a staggered crossing – south to Fordyce, north a half-mile down to Sandend, a fishing village by the Scattery Burn, which over a broad, locally popular beach here enters Sandend Bay. Here, where fish are still cured, the seatown dates back to at least 1624. With coastal paths running northeast from the beach to caves by craggy Redhythne point, from Sandend a lane climbs west a mile past a right turn to Barnyards of Findlater, a steading with public parking, from which a short walk north past the cone-shaped Findlater Doocot leads to Findlater Castle (**93**).

The continuing A98 passes two turns signposted to Findlater before, crossing the district boundary into Moray, it takes up the Keith B9018 then descends into Cullen via broad Seafield Street, its foot dramatically framed by the old railway viaduct, beyond it the cliff-hemmed curve of Cullen Bay – above which, on the Bauds of Cullen, the Battle of the Three Kings was fought over a millennium ago.

92.   The Viking Wars   *(History)*

For centuries Viking raiders from Norway and Denmark plagued this coast, at last settling peacefully, or being driven off, or again invading as barons descended from those Norse who, seizing 'Normandy' in France, in 1066 took England then, via Canmore kings like David I, imposed themselves on the older Scots population – a complex tale.

Leader of the first Norse attacks was Sigurd, Earl of Orkney, who *c*.800 occupied Burghead (see *Round Moray…*). Thereafter battles were fought all round the coast to repel the marauders, who seized land from the Orkneys to East Anglia, Dublin to Normandy and Malta. Energetic sons of a hard land, their naked berserker warriors charging into battle intoxicated by the hallucinogenic fly agaric toadstool, they were feared from Cromarty to Constantinople. 11th-century Viking graffiti in Orkney's Maes Howe tomb, built four millennia earlier, boasts of a trip to Jerusalem, adding that 'Ingigerth is the most beautiful of women' and that 'Tryggyr carved these runes' - evidently Kilroy is immortal...

Already they'd colonised Greenland, visited North America, and gained power in Russia as far south as Kiev in the Ukraine, where *c*.988 a monarch descended from *Rus*, the Norse conqueror who allegedly gave Russia its name, accepted Christianity – on his own terms. Violent and smart, these were folk to be reckoned with. Not until the defeat of King Haco's fleet at Largs off Scotland's northwest coast in 1253 were they driven out or assimilated. By then the raids and resulting battles had lasted over 400 years.

The name Cruden Bay (**111**) is derived from *croju-dane* ('slaughter of the Danes'), after the 1012 battle where Malcolm's Scots drove Canute's Danes into the sea (maybe giving Canute his complex about commanding the sea). Eight years earlier, the Battle of the Bloody Pits fought above Gamrie Bay (**96**) had also led to a Norse defeat, while, fought near Burghead in 1040 the Battle of Torfness, against the Norse under Thorfinn, led to Duncan's death and Macbeth's accession (**25**).

But earlier than any of these, just west of Cullen and south of Portknockie on Bauds Moor, or Moor of Rannachie, the year 961 saw a rout of the Danes. In terms of slain leaders it was 3-1 to the Scots, the dead Danish kings still commemorated by the Three Kings Rocks on Cullen Beach. A local rhyme claims *'Between Rannachie and the sea, Three kings there buried be'*; and many gravemounds were once found on the high ground above Findochty. As for the mortally-wounded Scots king Indulph, he was carried to Cullen, where he died. Various sites near Portknockie are claimed as his final resting place, including the King's Cairn (494656) east of Woodside under the Bin.

Once seizing Portknockie, the Danes held it until, 600 years before *Macbeth* was written, the Scots cut down trees and came up behind them. As Macbeth was shocked to see Birnam Wood march on Dunsinane, so the pirates fled on seeing the walking forest. It's said many jumped into the sea and drowned off Scar Nose. Buckie men used to dig up bones from what is now Strathlene golf course. Only a century ago lived some old men who when young had played football on the Links, the ball a human skull they kicked all the harder in the belief that it had once belonged to a Viking...

93.   Cullen: from the Crannoch to Findlater   *(History, Walks)*

Cullen (pop. 1410; maybe *cuilan*, 'little nook') is in Moray – but only by yards, and with so much to offer. Above Cullen Bay near the Bin's elegant dome, this old royal burgh began as Invercullen, a 12th-century settlement which by 1618 hosted 16 alebrewers, a gallow tree, stocks and a 'common executioner'. By then the Ogilvie

Earls of Findlater had built Cullen House (506664), a mansion which, after its 1858 extension, had 386 rooms – big enough for hide-and-seek. Between it and Cullen is the high-walled Old Kirk, in 1327 dedicated to St. Mary of Cullen and, amid 'mad mourning and woe', endowed with a chaplaincy by Robert the Bruce after his wife Elizabeth died here.

From the top of broad Seafield Street the new town, began by the Seafield Earls in 1820, descends under the railway viaduct to the compact Seatown, running

from the 1817 harbour to the Three Kings rocks and the long, broad beach beyond. With 'Cullen Skink', a soup based on smoked haddock, the legacy of the vanished fish-curing business, this postcard-pretty place has attracted many artists. Two George MacDonald (**81**) novels – '*Malcolm*' and '*The Marquis of Lossie*' – were set here, and there are many fine local walks: up and about the Bin, west along the beach past Jenny's Well and the Bow Fiddle Rock to Portknockie; east to Findlater Castle; southeast to Fordyce; or up Crannoch Hill.

For the latter, from Cullen follow the A98 east half-a-mile. Just past the Keith B9018, by the Portsoy 5 sign turn left to a small carpark (518663). Over the old road bear right through beechwood to the old railway bridge. Keep left, up the wood's edge above rolling fields with fine views to the Bin and the sea. Below, the boggy Hough of Gillyfurry may be where in 1562 Sir John Gordon beat back Mary's forces before he was beheaded in Aberdeen (**23**). Further up (with the continuing track rising then descending past ruined Logie House to Sunnyside Bay: below), a path on the right climbs the wood to the Crannoch; a lochan, dry in summer, its 18th-century islet created by the Seafields. From it descend to the old King's

Highway, and turn left up to views past Durn Hill; or right down to the old railway bridge, and so back to the carpark.

More dramatically, follow the coast east past Sunnyside Bay to Findlater Castle. From the harbour start past the old curing stations and boatyard, then via the rough Portlong road past an old salmon bothy, closed in the 1970s. Beyond the bay the cliff-hugging track climbs to Logie Head, where a rough, rocky path twists up to the Giant Steps, which descend the far side. Until 1989 in ruin, that year local resident Tony Hetherington rebuilt them singlehanded, levering up huge blocks from the rubble below. Killed in a canoeing accident in 1993, a cairn (528681) at the foot of the steps remembers him.

The path continues to Sunnyside Bay, an enchanted cove of sand and rock pools. From it a path climbs the grassy cliff: see below. At the bay's east end a second path climbs to a viewpoint above Findlater Castle (543674), reached via a narrow spur. Take care! As for the castle's interior, one slip in its open-windowed, sand-filled halls could land you on sea-lashed rocks below. Why aren't they protectively barred? With the tide out, the cove below allows access over slippery rocks to the huge Doo's Cave. Here the strata stand vertical, wrenched by ancient cataclysm.

From the viewpoint a track runs south past the doocot to the carpark at Barnyards of Findlater (**91**). Returning to Sunnyside Bay, from its west end climb the path mentioned above to a well in the grass inscribed: REST, DRINK & THINK 1895. Here a tiny gate leads to a wide field. Hug its edge inland to ruined Logie House (526673), past the track south to the Crannoch, then return west to Cullen, visible most of the way. In time a track on the right to a caravan site leads to a left turn past playing fields to Seafield Place, and so back to Seafield Street. About five miles, for this walk you need good boots.

94. The Bin of Cullen *(Routes, Walks)*

Two miles south of the coast, the landmark Bin of Cullen (480643: 1050ft; 320m) rises from the Bauds of Cullen above Portknockie. Flanked to the east by the forested Little Bin (802ft; 244m.) and to the west by the Hill of Maud (900ft.; 274m), from much of the coast the Bin resembles some final graceful, emphatic flow of the land into the sea. Isolated and so near the sea, its summit offers remarkable views.

From Cullen, start east on the A98 and turn south on the Keith B9018. Crossing the Burn of Deskford at Lintmill, in two miles the road passes Nether Blairock steading. With the B9018 continuing on past Deskford's ruined Ogilvie tower and medieval church, here turn right (west) another two miles into forestry south of the Bin and park by a gated track (492633) just before Braidbog.

Beyond the gate start north. Soon on the right another track breaks northwest, continuing two miles through Shirrald's Wood to Lintmill. Under mature wood continue straight, curving down over Glen Burn to a main crossing (489635). Here the right turn follows the burn northeast. The track ahead also heads northeast, but higher, circling the Little Bin. Almost a mile up this central track and just before a main forest junction (497646), to the left under gnarly beeches a rough but pretty path climbs over the Little Bin's heathery, pine-clad south slope, in a mile joining the track now described.

This, breaking left from the crossing, is the main way up the Bin. Climbing steadily, its bracken, heather banks, beech, silver birch and old Scots Pine make it one of the area's prettiest woodland walks. The forest was planted over 200 years ago by Lord Deskford, an unpopular Improving innovator and epileptic said still to haunt Cullen House, having murdered his factor. Feeling a fit coming on, he'd lock himself in his library and drop the key from the window. The fit past, the factor would let him out, but one day the poor man came too soon. Still in a fit, Deskford chased him upstairs then down into the library again, there stabbing him to death. The incident was hushed up. *Noblesse oblige?*

Just before a fork near the crest of the saddle (484642) between Bin and Little Bin, near a beech carved with the name 'Claire' the path over the Little Bin's south face emerges invisibly from the heather bank. At the fork not far above, turn left (west), climbing from the wood to the Bin's heathery upper slopes. Here a stony track winds up to the bare round top with its white concrete cairn...and to breath-taking views.

From Cullen and Buckie streets and coastal plain below to open sea beyond, the eye runs east past Banff and Gamrie to Troup Head, sheer from the sea. Northeast lies Norway. Due north, the next direct landfall compass-wise is in Siberia, over the Pole near the Bering Straits. Far over the Moray Firth low blue Caithness dwindles past Wick to an oil-rig remote in the sea, but the dog-tooth of Morven (2313 ft., Scotland's highest peak in Old Red Sandstone) turns the eye west: past the Dornoch Firth to remote Sutherland hills; over the Laich of Moray past Covesea Lighthouse and the narrowing firth to the Black Isle and bulky Ben Wyvis; over Elgin and Culbin towards Inverness; over Moray moors to Monadhliath brows above hidden Findhorn gorges; and over Banffshire moors past Ben Rinnes to Cairngorm ramparts above the Spey.

Then south over Strathisla and Strathbogie to Tap o' Noth (**51**) and the Buck; and east of south over glacier-scrubbed rough land to the Bin's sister-hill, the Knock (**86**) and, (on a clear day) to Bennachie (**68**) in the Garioch, and even sometimes to Mount Keen south of Deeside, over 50 miles away.

Now, we turn east from Banff and Macduff into Buchan, and so start back towards Aberdeen, where we began this tour.

Section 6:

Buchan

95. Introduction: 'The Land at the Bend of the Ocean'

Buchan gets its name from the Gaelic *bou-chuan*, meaning 'the land at the bend of the ocean'. This it is. A broad, draughty plateau jutting into the North Sea and comprising the larger part of Banff and Buchan District, its coast runs east from the Deveron estuary via Macduff, Gamrie Bay (**96**) and Rosehearty to Kinnaird Head at Fraserburgh (**100**), where it bends sharply south past Peterhead (**110**) and Cruden Bay (**111**) to Collieston (**73**) north of Aberdeen.

Inland, the rolling open landscape offers few landmarks other than Mormond Hill (**106**) and the valleys of the North and South Ugie Waters. Knit by rural lanes under a huge sky, it consists of vast tracts of farmland punctuated by planned 18th century villages. With the region and climate most raw in the far northeast, stone is everywhere – megaliths, castles ruined or restored, dry-stane dykes and 'clearance cairns'; coastal cliffs, stacks and rocks thrown up in the Permian-Triassic era over 200 million years ago.

Yet Buchan was always desirable property, at least compared to the infertile Highlands beyond. First settled millennia ago when the climate was kinder, later the Romans (**16**) marched through, and later still St. Drostan founded a Celtic monastery by a bend of the Ugie at Old Deer (**103**). After *c.*790 the Norse (**92**) began their violent coastal raids; and after the Comyn Earls of Buchan fell from grace in 1308 Forbeses, Frasers, Gordons, Hays, Keiths, Leiths, Leslies and Rattrays came to dominance via rights of pit and gallows. Remote from Scone or Edinburgh and virtually above the law, these families fought incessantly, until in the 16th century their feuds took on a religious dimension.

With the Catholic Royalist cause collapsing, the lairds finally sheathed their swords and sent their sons south to learn new accent and outlook. Returning as capitalising Improvers, the new generation cleared the land for agriculture ('Weelwrocht grun', see **103**) and founded villages such as New Aberdour (**98**), New Pitsligo (**100**), Cuminestown, New Byth and New Deer (**101**), Maud (**102**) and Strichen (**106**). With local trade promoted even as Highlanders were being cleared to the coast or abroad, modern Buchan took shape via plough, harness and mill amid a diet of brose, buttery, and salted herring caught by scaffies sailing from rapidly-expanding ports.

From all this Buchan folk won a a dry wit and practical mentality; also a wealth of poetry and balladry, as annually honoured at Strichen's Doric Drama Festival. With bothy ballads like '*The Barnyards of Delgatie*', '*The Bogend Hairst*', '*Mill of Tiftie's Annie*', and '*To Roll Her in my Plaidie*' combining the bawdy and the tragic with a wit as sharp as the climate, today the Doric dialect in which they're written retains its edge (see **107**).

This last leg of the tour follows the coast east from Macduff via Gamrie Bay and the Tore of Troup to Fraserburgh; then turns southeast through the hinterland north of Ellon (**75**) and east of the A952 through Mintlaw; and lastly from

Fraserburgh follows the coast south via Cairnbulg, Inverallochy and St. Combs (**108**) past the Loch of Strathbeg (**109**) to Peterhead and Cruden Bay.

96.   Macduff to Gamrie Bay & Troup Head   *(Route, Walk)*

Crossing the Deveron from Banff (**88**), past the A947 turn south to Turriff the A98 swings under the Hill of Doune and along the shoreline into the fishing port of Macduff (pop. 3817; originally *Doune*), and as Shore Street continues under steep narrow intersecting streets to the four-basin harbour.

The focus of the burgh and expanded in 1921, it dates from 1783, when Doune was renamed Macduff to honour James Duff, Earl of Fife, who'd gained the Seatown burgh status. The name 'Macduff' was preferred to 'Douneduff' because the Earl thought the latter too close to 'doon with the Duffs'. With herring fishing expanding after 1815, by 1880 over a hundred boats worked from this port, and today fishing remains vital. There is a daily fishmarket, and also a net-making company and boat-building yard.

With fine views high above the harbour, Doune Church is reached via Station Brae. Dating from 1805, in 1865 this kirk was transformed by adding a square three-storey lead-domed tower, its west face left clockless allegedly due to Macduff's enduring outrage at Macpherson's execution in 1700 (see **88**). East of the harbour the Seatown extends to Tarlair's chalybeate well under the cliffs, where 19th century folk came to take the waters (said to be good for bairns with 'scabbit faces') and bathe in the cold North Sea. Also east of the harbour, where the A98 swings right uphill a left turn leads to 11 High Shore, site of Macduff Marine Aquarium (01261-833369; open all year). Here fish, invertebrates and seaweeds populate a vast centrepiece tank, its 'kelp reef' given added realism by simulated wave action. There is a shop and audio-visual theatre.

From Macduff the Fraserburgh A98 climbs east almost a mile past the start of the B9031 coastal route (Gardenstown 6, Rosehearty 18). This twists up and down over open windswept farmland by sea-cliffs culminating in spectacular Troup Head, two miles northeast of Gamrie Bay. Three villages hug the base of these cliffs: Gardenstown, Crovie, and Pennan to the east. Before these, after five miles the road dips into a gully above Gamrie Bay. Here, with steep-sloped Gardenstown visible ahead, a track on the left leads north half-a-mile to St. John's Chapel (792647; see photo next page) on its bluff above the bay. With fine stones in its large walled graveyard, the roofless ruin dates from 1513, but the site and its grisly history are older. Here the skulls of slain Danes were brought after the 1004 Battle of the Bloody Pits, and later fixed in the wall by the pulpit, some still to be seen as late as 1832 (**92**).

Continuing, the B9031 sheds the B9123 down to Gardenstown (pop. 802). Founded in 1720 by Alexander Garden of Troup and built on narrow terraces above the bay, this fisher-village is so steeply sited that in places the zigzag road is under the houses one side of it but above those on the other. Locally called Gamrie and

said to be Scotland's richest village, its folk are renowned for staunch religious belief, with the Closed Brethren, Open Brethren and Exclusive Brethren all represented here.

For a five-mile circuit via Troup Head, descend past Main Street's cul-de-sac to the triangular harbour, begun in 1720 and reconstructed in 1868. Park by garages at the east end of the sea-wall, built after the great 1953 gale. A sign at the start of the eastward path warns: THIS PATH IS DANGEROUS, and the crumbly pudding-stone of the cliff above suggests why. Over a shingled cove climb guard-railed concrete steps to a rocky point, beyond which a shoreline path leads half-a-mile east to Crovie (pictured on the back cover). Here some 60 cottages cling to the cliff by the high-tide mark, without room even for an access road. Almost abandoned after the 1953 gale, most of Crovie's cottages are now holiday homes.

From the turning-space at Crovie's west end, climb the steep road round a bend to a farm-track on the left (807654). For Troup Head, follow this track down then up a brae past a steading to wide views. Continue past Crovie Farm to a junction (822658). Turn left through Northfield 400 yards to a parking area (reached from the B9032 via Protston) by the gated head of a ravine. Bear right along the fence to Troup Head, with its vast views and clamorous birdlife; puffin, kittiwake, guillemot and razor-billed auk. The massive red sandstone cliff plunges 365 feet sheer to the rocks below, so take care!

Returning through Northfield, at the junction keep straight on a mile to Protston (818648) and turn right on the Stonewells track. After 200 yards, bear left on a red-earth track down to a gated field. A rough path continues down the gully back to the track and up to the Crovie road. Or follow the track past Stonewells until it winds down (left) to the road. Either way, once on the road, turn left past the viewpoints to a junction, then bear right back to Gamrie/Gardenstown.

97.   Cullykhan & The Tore of Troup   *(Route, Walk)*

Past lanes breaking south over rising fields to the Hill of Overbrae above the head of the Tore of Troup, from Gamrie the B9031 continues east three miles past Jacobshall and wooded Troup House (begun 1760, the present baronial pile from 1897) to a signposted left turn (835655) and carpark above Cullykhan Bay. Via an Iron Age causeway the path beyond descends a ravine past a gaping cave, Hell's Lum, then rises to windy Castle Point. Here ruined 17th-century Fort Fiddes occupies the site of a 13th-century castle, this built over an Iron Age fort which, palisaded *c.*700BC, in one rampart shows traces of later vitrification. With cliff-hemmed Pennan a half-mile east, below this wild, spectacular site huge rounded sea-lashed paws of rock face the opposite promontory, the Lion's Head.

Past the Fort Fiddes turn the road descends over the seaward end of the Tore of Troup, a densely-wooded ravine which, running south several miles, is home to deer, fox, badger, mink and buzzard. Rough tracks follow its flanks, at one point descending to meet and cross over, so permitting a five-mile circuit up one side and back the other.

From the carpark walk to the B9031, turn right (west) 500 yards up the road to a track on the left (833654), and above pasture follow this track south through two metal gates to a pen made of railway sleepers. Beyond this, just before a second cattle-grid start diagonally right uphill on a path through gorse, and cross a fence to a broad top track of red earth.

This track also runs from the B9031 (though starting further on; at 830653), and is an easier if longer route: at a fork by a bend soon after it begins keep left.

Continuing south into the Tore, the track winds high above the wooded, V-shaped valley to a fork. Here keep left above the steepening ferny slope, the Tore Burn at its foot, a ruin on the far slope and others below. With a forested hillock opposite, the track enters scrub oakwood and descends to the burn, meeting it by a multiple junction amid a gloomy glade (835628) two miles south of the road. Here, by a gated cattlepen, the easy return involves bearing left over the burn and starting up the opposite slope, heading north.

First, the tracks continuing south and west. From the pen the track climbing west up a subsidiary ravine to Tore Lodge soon diverges, the left fork ascending the Tore's wooded flank; the main trail continuing to a second fork. Here the left turn climbs a gully to the Hill of Troup's high pastures. With diversions round several deep west-running gullies to points where their boggy sinks may be crossed, the lane (819604) at the head of the Tore can be reached, but it's a slog. As for the track south from the pen, it crosses the burn to climb the Tore's east flank, but vanishes on a steep grassy slope. Higher up, a boggy open track continues down over an east-running ravine, south of which wet high ground makes for hard going. A final ravine

151

by Tordale forces an eastward detour involving dense fern and hidden barbed wire. For masochists only.

Choosing well, from the pen turn left over the burn, and up the cattle-churned track climb the east slope north to views of the sea. Through a gate under gorse slopes past derelict Chapelden (840635), past a cairn on a grassy mound to the left (841638), and above another large derelict at Glenquithle, the track climbs right to a tarmac lane. Now leaving the Tore, follow this lane north a mile to the B9031. Here, opposite the road down to Pennan, turn left to descend then climb the B9031 back to the Fort Fiddes carpark.

And so to a well-deserved pint in Pennan's famous inn…

98.   East from Pennan: Aberdour to Fraserburgh   *(Routes, History)*

Originally Auchmedden, or St. Magnus Haven, this single-street early 19th century sea-front village, its crescent of two-storey cottages snug under beetling crags, featured in the 1983 film *Local Hero*. Now visited as much for the grub in its pub (not the one in the film) as to call home from the phone box featured in the film, like many other Moray Firth villages Pennan once relied as much on smuggling (silk and liquor: see next chapter) as fishing.

From Pennan the B9031 continues east three miles through dreich land to draughty New Aberdour on its bare, south-sloping plateau. Founded in 1797 by William Gordon of Aberdour, this bleak village of broad parallel streets will not detain you. From it, the B9031 continues northeast to Rosehearty and Fraserburgh while, from the bottom of the long south street, lanes break south to New Pitsligo (**100**) and southeast to Strichen (**106**).

On a bend just before New Aberdour a lane (885636: signposted to Aberdour Beach) breaks left down to a second junction (886643). A left turn here leads to St. Drostan's Church, a 16th century ruin sited on one of North Scotland's first Christian settlements. It's said St. Drostan landed here in AD575 and that his bones, once kept in the surviving font, worked miracle cures. The road ends at a pebble beach and carpark, just east of it St. Drostan's Well. A chalybeate well nearby, Mess John's Well, named after a 17th century lay preacher called John Whyte, was also once medicinally famed.

Returning up to the junction at 886643, turn right for New Aberdour, or continue east above the shoreline. In under a mile this eastbound lane passes the mouldering clifftop ruin of Dundarg (895649). Fortified since Iron Age times, later a Celtic monastery, as a Comyn castle it was sacked amid 1308's Harrowing of Buchan, and not for the last time. Dundarg may be visited by permission of the owner, who lives in the 1938 Gothic gatehouse.

Two miles further on the lane meets the B9031, which in another northbound mile descends into Rosehearty (pop. 1243), an old port of broad streets and broader foreshore. Founded by the first Lord Pitsligo, this fishertoon profited from the herring boom, but the railway's arrival in nearby Fraserburgh led to the latter seizing the trade.

On flat land just south of Rosehearty, ruined Pitsligo Castle (936669) is visible from the road. Built by the Frasers of Philorth (**108**), its square, barrel-vaulted tower dates from 1424. In the 1570s Forbes of Druminnor (**53**) added a courtyard palace, sacked after the '45 by Flemish troops billeted there. Losing his estates, the Jacobite Alexander, 4th Lord Pitsligo, spent the rest of his long life (he died in 1792 aged 84) evading arrest as a cave-dwelling tramp, Sanny Brown. Unroofed by the Gardens of Troup, lately the ruin was bought by American billionaire Malcolm Forbes, who has had it consolidated.

Amid fields under a mile further east, just south of the B9031 is ruined Pittulie Castle (945671; after 1596), again built by the Frasers of Philorth. With Fraserburgh now visible ahead over the rocky foreshore, the B9031 continues through the conjoined herring-boom villages of Pittullie and Sandhaven, the latter's 18th century meal mill now a museum of rural life. So, via the Phingask Shore, into Fraserburgh. But, first:

99.   Smuggler Tales   *(History)*

With life hard and money scarce, in the 18th and early 19th centuries tax to sustain foreign wars grew so heavy that smuggling was common and no dishonour. Cottar, seaman and laird alike combined to outwit the revenue men to profit from contraband – salt, silk, lace, Louisiana tobacco, French brandy and Dutch gin.

For this activity the rugged coast from Pennan west to Burghead, and from Peterhead south to Collieston, was ideal. Many hidden caves and coves encouraged the unseen landing of illicit goods, the seatowns and inland moors provided endless hiding places, and bribery of excisemen (also called preventers or gaugers) was not unknown.

Approaching by night and signalled by shoreline lights that no preventers were about, the smuggler ship would stand by until approaching oarsmen offered a password; often a shouted: 'Devil, devil, devil' – this a name which, with the Kirk so powerful, only bold men dared speak aloud, especially at night, with Auld Cloutie (**104**) up to his tricks.

At cliff-hemmed, cave-rich Pennan, the illicit trade was so well-organised that the Quayman's Cave had landing facilities, plus a staple in the roof from which smugglers hung their lanterns. Further west, Buckie man George 'Captain' Geddes had New Orleans tobacco and rum reshipped from Amsterdam for secret local landing. Grown rich, from his smart new London address he chartered ten ships to the government as troop carriers, but failed to insure them. Ruined by the capture of eight, he smuggled himself home in a coffin on a Scots trading smack, only to find a coastguard station set up in Buckie. Repenting his evil ways, he died not only broke but teetotal. Going legal had ruined him.

South of Peterhead (**110**) are numerous caves and inlets with evocative names like the Bleedy Hole, the Auld Water Moo, the Seggie Pot and the Gin Hole. Illicit trade via this shore was well-served by two luggers, the *Crookit Mary* and the *Crookit Meg* – the latter the title of a book by 19th-century historian Sir John Skelton, who describes one landing of 'silks from Lyons, gin from Holland, lace from Brussels (and one golden cross set in pearls from Antwerp)'. He tells how this rich haul was carried inland by up to 40 hill ponies, guarded not only by the crew but by fisherfolk and cottars.

In 1830 salt cost £3 a ton, excluding duty. Fishcurers and sea-skippers each had a salt bond cellar, double-locked, one key with the salt's owner, the other with the exciseman. No salt could be removed from bond without (as with whisky today) the presence of the gauger. Yet vast quantities were smuggled. Fisherwomen bound inland hid salt under the fish in their creels. If they were intercepted, the salt was confiscated or scattered on the road. Salt on the highway then, often every 400 yards, had nothing to do, as now, with icy and treacherous roads.

Naturally the trade had its dangers and losses. A cargo of French brandy landed on the Culbin shore north of Forres was stupidly buried amid wind-shifting dunes. When the smugglers returned they couldn't find where they'd buried it. Some folk still seek this legendary cargo. More to the point (literally), a stone in St. Ternan's graveyard at the edge of Collieston (**73**) marks the grave of Philip Kennedy, who one wild December night in 1798 had his skull split open by a gauger's sword. He was 38 years old.

With the film 'Whisky Galore' on TV at least once a year, even the most law-abiding of us hosts a secret imp that delights in flouting Authority. Yet little changes. Then it was tobacco and gin. Now it's illicit drugs. *Plus ça change...*

100.   Fraserburgh: the Broch   *(Routes, Visit, History)*

Beyond the coastal B9031 turn above Macduff (**96**), the A98 (Fraserburgh 22) sweeps on past the scattered hamlet of Longmanhill to a rolling land, open but here and there interrupted by dens, gullies and windblown copses. With lanes breaking north to Gardenstown or over the Hill of Overbrae; and south towards Turriff (**87**), eight miles southeast of Macduff at Crudie (794574) there is a right turn south (Cuminestown 5, Turriff 7: see **101**). Past Crudie and turns south to New Byth (also **101**), in three more nondescript rural miles the A950 breaks southeast from the A98 into and through New Pitsligo (pop. 1145).

Bisected by the wooded Denburn and chiefly notable for its mile-long main street, this dour village was founded in 1787 by the banker Sir William Forbes of Pitsligo. With almost 2000 inhabitants by 1864, it prospered by making lace, quarrying granite, and digging peat from the moor, still-worked, that stretches towards Strichen (**106**) five miles to the east. From the village the A950 continues southeast 17 miles through Mintlaw (**105**) to Peterhead (**110**); the B9093 soon breaking east over the peat-hag to Strichen.

From the A98 and just east of the A950 turn, a north-running lane to Pennan/New Aberdour leads in two miles to a minor crossroads. Here turn right then right again to visit Northfield Farm Museum (868597; 01771-653504; open daily May-Sept.), which displays machinery and implements used on Buchan farms during the last century.

Past this point the A98 winds northeast another 11 miles through undulating open farmland to Fraserburgh (pop. 13,023), *en route* crossing the Water of Tyrie and the New Aberdour/Memsie B90322, Mormond Hill's radar arrays prominent nearby to the southeast.

Locally called the Broch (*burgh*), and described by local poet George Bruce as 'the outermost edge of Buchan', this substantial granite town began life as Faithlie in the parish of Philorth (pron. *Florth*: see **108**). Centred about Broad Street and Saltoun Square (the information office is at 3 Saltoun Square: 01346-518315; April–Oct.) above the eight-basined harbour, Fraserburgh's first harbour opened in 1546. Briefly seat of a university founded in 1595 by George Keith, founder of Aberdeen's Marischal College (**2, 13, 110**), the Broch was long quiet but, with the herring-boom in the early 1800s then the railway's arrival in 1865, the town grew so rapidly that, with 680 boats sailing from it, by 1897 it was Scotland's largest fish-

ing-port. Today, with the herring industry almost dead, it remains a major white-fish port, with nearly a hundred boats operating out of it.

North of the harbour and reached from the High Street via Barragate Road, Kinnaird Head Lghthouse and the purpose-built Lighthouse Museum (01346-511022, open daily all year) are worth a visit. Dominating the rocky tip of Kinnaird

Head where the Buchan coast bends west, the lighthouse was originally a castle built in 1570 by Alexander Fraser of Philorth. Converted into Scotland's first lighthouse in 1787 and using 20 whale-oil lamps, today all that remains of the castle is the white central tower with its 72 steps. The top (fifth) floor was converted into the lighthouse lantern chamber by the original engineer, Thomas Smith. In 1824 his successor Robert Stevenson fitted a new lantern, upgraded in 1851 by Alan Stevenson; and in 1907 was installed a massive new lens designed by another Stevenson, David. Also of this family was author Robert Louis Stevenson (1850–94), better at lighting the soul's recesses than designing lighthouses.

Automated in 1992, the original lighthouse, light and engine room remain intact, with guided tours up it from the museum nearby. Below it on the foreshore rocks is the Wine (*Wynd*) Tower (access by arrangement), a covert 16th century Catholic chapel with six finely carved pendants attached to its arched roof.

From Fraserburgh the A981 runs southwest via Strichen and Maud to New Deer; the A90 curves southeast to Peterhead and on to Aberdeen, *en route* shedding the A952 south through Mintlaw; while the coastal B9033 links Cairnbulg, Inverallochy and St Combs (**108**) and then joins the A90 near Crimond (**109**).

But before looking at these routes and the rest of the Buchan coast, we now travel west to east through the Howe of Buchan, south of the A98…

101.   Cuminestown to New Deer & Maud   (*Routes*)

From the A98 at Crudie the Cuminestown road turns south, soon crossing the B9105 which, leaving the A98 a mile east of Crudie, joins the A947 just north of Turriff (see **88**), *en route* and in three miles passing Craigston Castle (**87**). Over this crossing continue south another three miles down to the B9170 (797507) just under Cuminestown. Here a right turn west above the Burn of Monquhitter and past ruined Auchry Castle leads in a mile to a junction. At it turn right for Delgatie Castle (also **87**) and the A947.

Just past the junction at 797507 the B9027 turns left (northeast) two miles to New Byth, a pretty south-facing village of old red-rubble cottages, founded in 1763 by James Urquhart of Craigston. The continuing B9027 joins the A98 while, from a bend below and south of the village (825535), a road turns south towards New Deer. At a crossroads (836527) after a mile, the left turn up to the high Bonnykelly crossroads (862538; southwest of New Pitsligo) offers panoramic views boundaried by Bennachie (**68**), Ben Rinnes, The Knock (**86**) and the Bin of Cullen (**94**).

Founded in 1763 by Joseph Cumine of Auchry to attract spinners and weavers into the area, the Z-plan village of Cuminestown with its doglegging main street is stolid and quiet. From it the B9170 departs southeast through rolling land towards New Deer and Ellon (**75**). By a sharp left-hand bend after two miles (835481), the Greens lane continues south to the Methlick-Fyvie B9005, joining it above Gight Castle (**77**) and the Ythan – Buchan's southern boundary. Bending east, in another four miles the winding B9170 reaches New Deer (pop. 653). Dominated by the Culsh Monument to the north and laid out in its existing form in 1805 by the Gordons of Cairnbanno, this ridge-top village lies at the junction of numerous routes over the Howe of Buchan: north to New Pitsligo; northeast to Strichen and Fraserburgh; east to Maud, Old Deer and Mintlaw; southeast through Auchnagatt to Ellon (**75**); and southwest to Methlick (**76**) and Inverurie (**62**).

For the direct route to Maud, on reaching New Deer turn left over the Burn of Auchreddie, past Main Street, and right up Fordyce Terrace (A981/B9029). To get there via the Culsh Monument and Fedderate Castle, turn left up Main Street. Leaving New Deer, fork left up the low rise of the Hill of Culsh. At the cemetery wall bear right to the monument's steepled ashlar tower (882483), erected in 1876 in memory of William Dingwall-Fordyce, MP (1836–75). With wide views over the land about, the continuing road twists down then up a brae to a junction at Loanhead of Fedderate (887497). Turn right (east) towards Maud past the ruin, in a field left of the road, of Fedderate Castle (896498), a four-storey L-plan Crawford tower dating from 1474. Held for James VII and besieged by government forces after the 1690 Battle of Cromdale, it resembles a decayed tooth due to an attempt to blow it up, not in anger, but to clear the ground.

Reaching a crossroads, a left turn onto the A981 runs a mile northeast to the A950 (Peterhead 14, New Pitsligo 4); for Strichen and Fraserburgh turn left then right on the continuing A981, climbing to wide views before in three miles descending to Strichen.

Over the crossroads on the left a lodge guards the wooded drive to ruined Brucklay Castle (911502), a 16th-century tower. Continue east two miles through wooded land, Mormond Hill prominent to the north, and so into Maud (pop. 877) via Castle Road.

102.   Maud & Aikey Brae   (*Walk*)

By the South Ugie under beech-topped Bank Hill, and once called Bank, Maud came to life on becoming a railway junction in 1863: here the line north from Aberdeen forked; north to Fraserburgh and east to Peterhead. By 1866 the vast Buchan Poorhouse, now a hospital, was established here, and the livestock market every Wednesday is among Buchan's best. As for the dismantled railway, all three forks are now on the Formartine-Buchan Way (**75**), part of which we follow on this seven-mile circuit. Though scenically tame, it reveals the heart of Buchan – a vast plateau under a huge sky.

Park by the post office opposite the Station Hotel. Descend through a tunnel under the old railway. Turn right up to the station and follow the trackbed south through scrub wood, then past dyked or fenced fields. From a wooded cutting under a bridge by Mains of Oldmaud, continue past Denbrae (917464) under a second bridge carrying a lane east past Gilkhorn to the east. This is the way to go for a shorter three-mile circuit.

Amid open views, a mile further on pass under pylons to a white cottage by an old level-crossing (916458). Here turn left up a track 200 yards southeast past Greenbrae. Where the now-gravelled road swings right, continue straight on under the pylons, the track soon bending right and climbing through Kiddshill to a lane atop the rise (928438).

Turn left past the vanished or overgrown path shown on the OS map as breaking northeast to Meikle Kirkhill. Bare winter fields may allow a short-cut northeast; otherwise follow the road east, almost a mile, to a crossroads (944442) under Jock's Hill. Here turn north (left), and so back over two miles to Maud on this quiet road. With big skies above low round ridges, dairy herds in the fields about, crows cawing and distant tractors revving, this has to be the very heart of Buchan. Cresting a rise at Backhill of Clackriach (927463), with the Culsh Monument to the northwest and Maud now visible below and ahead, the road descends past a right turn up to Mains of Clackriach (934472).

I climbed the half-mile to this steading, seeking the remaining angle of Clackriach Castle, a 16th-century tower in scrubwood nearby. From it with difficulty I found a way northwest to the beech copse atop Bank Hill then, with even more difficulty (cattle and fences) descended to Maud. It may be best to follow the road all the way back.

To reach Old Deer three miles to the east, from Maud take Deer Road East/B9029 along the south bank of the South Ugie Water (little more than a burn) through hilly green land, the white tower of Drinnies Wood Observatory (**105**) prominent atop the wooded ridge diagonally left ahead. After two miles a right turn (954477) zigzags up Parkhouse Hill to Aikey Brae, once site of Aikey Fair, northeast Scotland's greatest horse fair, and also scene of the final Comyn defeat at the hands of Robert the Bruce in 1308 (**64**). And there's Aikey Brae stone circle (958472). At a sharp bend above Parkhouse a grassy track on the left (956471; room to park) climbs to a copse. Bear right on a path through this copse to the circle with its massive recumbent, single flanker and three remaining outliers.

A mile on along the B9029 a lane on the left crosses the Ugie to ruined Deer Abbey, on the banks of the South Ugie under the Peterhead-New Pitsligo A950.

103. Deer Abbey, Old Deer & Aden   (*Route, History, Walk*)

Hidden behind a long high roadside wall just northeast of Old Deer and two miles west of Mintlaw, Deer Abbey was a Cistercian house founded in 1218 by William Comyn, Earl of Buchan, as a daughter-house of Kinloss in Moray. Abandoned after the Reformation, in 1854 it was plundered by Admiral Ferguson of Pitfour (**105**) to build the Ferguson Mausoleum. Yet enough of its roofless halls, a maze of ruddy stone, remain to evoke the Cistercian spirit. Founded *c.*1120 at Cîteaux in Burgundy by St. Bernard of Clairvaux, by his death in 1155 they'd established some 300 monasteries from Ireland to Lebanon, Sicily to Scotland. Developing agriculture, fisheries, crafts and trade, they were a vital civilizing influence amid hard times. But they were not the first Christians at Deer.

Just past the abbey, the B9029 enters sleepy Old Deer, where *c*.575 St. Drostan founded one of the Northeast's first monasteries (see **58**). Long-gone, once it housed the Book of Deer, the earliest-known text in Scots Gaelic (9th–10th centuries). A small illuminated gospel-book chronicling land-holdings, this invaluable treasure is held in Cambridge's Fitzwilliam Library, with efforts to get it back it to Scotland to date unsuccessful. As for Old Deer itself, dominated by the pyramid-spired 1789 parish kirk, here in 1711 occurred the Rabbling of Deer, a riot caused by villagers resisting the imposition of a Presbyterian minister.

Under the kirk the Maud road meets the B9030 from Auchnagatt, a hamlet on the A948 five miles to the southwest. Here the B9030 continues over the Ugie to the A950; this just east of the abbey and Saplinbrae House Hotel, built in 1756 as a dower house for the Pitfour Estate, its 30-acre trout loch set in 400 acres of park, woodland and garden.

At the junction turn right, not far, to the entry south of the road (985484) to Aden Country Park and Heritage Centre (01771-622857 or 01261-812521; park open all year 7am–10pm: centre open daily May–Sept.; weekends Oct.–April). With its name (*Aaden*; 'bonny burn', or 'bonny brae') recorded in the Book of Deer, this 230-acre park is the remnant of a 31-square-mile estate developed by the descendants of Alexander Russell of Montcoffer (**89**), who in 1758 bought the land from the Keiths, who'd held it since 1324. In 1937 the last Russell laird sold Aden, much of Old Deer, and the last of the estate's 52 farms; and in 1975 the district council began restoring the remaining grounds. Now, amid nature trails and woodland walks, the elegant semi-circular steading houses a multi-media exhibition; 'Weel Vrocht Grun' (*'well worked ground'*: **107**), which shows how, after the '45, new villages were built, land cleared, crop rotation introduced, and forests planted.

For a local circuit, and armed with the 'Walks and Wildlife' leaflet and map, from the steading follow a path (NATURE TRAIL > MANSION HOUSE) south-west past the gutted 1832 mansion to a woodland ice house and a footbridge over the Ugie. Under beech and monkeypuzzle continue south past the kirkyard wall of Old Deer parish church. Where the main track swings left, continue straight, again crossing the Ugie. At the edge of a field, a wooded dell below, bear left (east) to a crossing at 'Cattle Creep'. Fork right (south) along a main pine avenue, the 'Bridle Path', to Twin Lodges and a back road. For a short circuit, here turn right to the B9030, and right again to Old Deer. By the kirkyard a shady path descends to a left turn over the Ugie under the ice house.

For a longer circuit via Stuartfield a mile south, at Twin Lodges turn left (east) up the lane, open fields to the right. In 200 yards, turn right (979472) onto a track past Mill of Aden and again cross the Ugie, here reed-choked, to a track-junction (977470). Bear left, up past Knock. With Stuartfield ahead to the right, keep straight along a wooded bank, and at Quartalehouse bear right, southwest, to a back road. Turn right 500 yards to Stuartfield.

Here bungalows surround 19th-century cottages about a broad square amid ripe fields under low hills. Not all Buchan is harsh. From the Square, return to Old Deer by the B9030. I continued west, turning right (967459) to Brae of Biffie but, past this empty steading, a path shown on the map as running north to Biffie (972474) vanishes, fenced ditches prevailing. Yet, as Aden shows, once here there were neither farms nor roads…

104. Life & Beliefs   *(History, Folklore)*

That life was always hard in these parts is a cliché, but one brought to life in Flora Garry's poem about life on a Buchan fairm-toon, *Bennygoak* (see **107**)

It was jist a skelp of the muckle furth,
A skylter o roch grun,
Fin grandfadder's fadder bruke it in
Fae the hedder an the funn (whin).
Grandfadder sklatit barn an byre,
Brocht water to the closs (steading),
Put fail-dykes ben the bare brae face
An a cairt road tull the moss.

Bit wir fadder sottert i the yard
An skeppit amo' (kept) *bees*
And keppit fancy dyeuks an doos (ducks and doves)
'at warna muckle eese.
He bocht aul' wizzent horse an kye
An scrimpit muck an seed;
Syne, clocherin wi a craichly hoast (wheezing cough),
He dwine't awa, an deed.

160

Amid such everyday hardship, no wonder folk sought the consolation of religion; and clung to imaginative beliefs and customs. Some of these, like the Stonehaven Fireballs ceremony (**14**) survive, but many others have died out. The latter include, as elsewhere in the world, the customs surrounding the last sheaf of the harvest, the *hairst*.

In Aberdeenshire this was called the *clyack sheaf* or Maiden. Cut by the youngest girl present and carried home in triumph, then dressed with ribbons, it would be kept until Christmas then offered to a mare in foal, or to the oldest cow in calf. To fail to do this was thought likely to be fatal, both for foal and farm.

Supernatural danger lurked everywhere. It was believed that witches (like the celebrated Isobel Gowdie of Auldearn; see *Round Inverness...*) could raise winds, shapeshift into cat or hare, cast the evil eye, ruin crops by yoking toads to tiny model ploughs driven twice about a field, or kill by sticking pins into clay images which then they burned. The curse of wizards like Thomas the Rhymer (**78**) was feared even by the powerful. There were mad lairds a-plenty in league with Auld Clootie, like the Laird of Skene (**11**), or the Wizard of Gordonstoun near Elgin, or various 'black colonels'; and local ministers were grimly glad to remind folk that Satan lurked everywhere, waiting to trick them as he'd tricked Janet Maitland (**67**). Iron repulsed the wily fairy folk, called the 'good folk' or 'men of peace' as a guard against their mischief. Rivers and burns were haunted by the kelpie or water-horse, a wild-eyed black horse browsing by a ford which, tempting the weary traveller to mount it in hope of a dry crossing, would throw him off to drown in the flood.

Offshore, from the Bullers of Buchan (**111**) to the Black Isle mermaids (dolphins?) drew unwary mariners onto the rocks; and no sensible fisherman would continue if, bound for his boat, he met a minister, or an 'ill-footed' man or beast, or anyone who asked where he was going, or a rabbit, dog or hare which might be a shapeshifted witch.

These fearful beliefs only gradually faded. As much as anything, it was the coming of the roads, meaning greater communication with the outside world and modern ideas, that ended them. First there were the military roads (**45**), then in 1795 the Turnpike Act was passed, so that by 1811 Aberdeenshire had more than 300 miles of turnpike, and then came the railway. The modern world was born, and gradually the fey folk faded out of human ken and returned to their ancient knowes...

Still, it's said the devil's best served by folk that don't believe in him...

105. Pitfour, Fetterangus & White Cow Wood   *(Routes, Walk)*

From Aden the A950 continues east a built-up mile to the vast A952 roundabout that ruins the diamond-shaped central square of Mintlaw (pop. 2963), a village laid out in 1813 but now little more than the roundabout plus housing estates. From it the A950 runs seven miles east past burns and broken hillocks to Peterhead (**110**) via Longside (pop. 815), a substantial village laid out in 1801 by the Fergusons of

Pitfour. It extends downhill from the now-roofless old church, built in 1620 when the parish was created out of the neighbouring parishes of Peterhead and Crimond. Here, marked by an 1861 obelisk and in response to his prayer, 'Dinna bury me like a beast', is buried Jamie Fleeman, the Laird of Udny's Fool (**72**). Here too lived the Reverend John Skinner (1721–1807), lyricist of the famed 'Reel of Tullochgorum' (**32**) and Longside's episcopalian minister for 64 years.

With their estate once known to some as 'the Blenheim of Buchan', the Fergusons of Pitfour spared no expense in making their mark. With Pitfour House (demolished in 1927) guarded by South Lodge (1816), and to the west by Bruxie Lodge (1850), they built an observatory tower (1845) atop Drinnies Wood, from which they watched horse-races on the 'Ascot of the North' below. They created Pitfour Loch to build bridges over it and boathouses about it, one a miniature replica of the Temple of Theseus at Athens; and in 1798 began digging a canal from the sea to it. Ostensibly they did this to boost the local economy, and to drain the South Ugie when it flooded, but they were playboys, among the first the hard Northeast had known and, as such, were thought very odd indeed.

From Aden and Mintlaw there are three ways north to Strichen and Fraserburgh. Most obvious is the A952 which, running north past Fetterangus (below), continues past the B9093 turn to Strichen then through New Leeds, a hamlet that failed to realise the industrial ambitions of its founder, Captain Fraser of Strichen. Rounding Mormond Hill, it joins the A90 from Peterhead, and so reaches Fraserburgh.

Or via the A950 return west two miles past Deer Abbey to a road climbing right, (Strichen 4; White Cow Wood 1.5). This is the direct way to White Cow Wood and its waymarked trails.

Of more interest are two lanes turning north from the A950 opposite Aden. To Fetterangus and Drinnies Wood, these meet at a crossroads in a half-mile. Continue due north up a fine beech avenue a mile to a second minor crossroads (982505), this by the ruined old kirk of Fetterangus. Founded in 1752 by James Ferguson of Pitfour, with its broad main street the neat little village is just to the east. At this crossing turn left past Den o' Howie a half-mile to Drinnies Wood, part of the old Forest of Deer, and left again to a carpark (974506; open 10-5 mid–May–Sept.). From it a path leads south a half-mile to the Fergusons' white battlemented octagonal three-storey 1845 tower. Beyond it the road soon fades to a track running north into forestry adjoining White Cow Wood, close by to the west.

Back at the crossroads at 982505, turn left (north), keeping left at and bearing west past Auchryne, and in 2.5 miles reaching the Strichen road just north of White Cow Wood. Turn left to a car-park (956514) on the right, this offering entry to forestry walks.

Combining waymarked routes: take the main track west past two left turns to a junction. Swing right then left (yellow arrow) to open ground west of the wood by stands of splintered pine, the view south leading to Bennachie (**68**). Turn right (north) up the perimeter track through a logged area, then right again (east) on a rough, waymarked path over the heath. With views northeast past Mormond Hill, this leads to a recumbent circle (947519). The stony path continues past it back to the wood. Turn right onto a main forestry track and continue south through the airy, half-grown plantation, ignoring a red arrow pointing east (left). Back at the junction where the waymarked paths diverged, keep left a half-mile back to the carpark. Turn left, north, some two miles down the brae to Strichen, beautifully sited on the North Ugie Water under Mormond Hill.

106.   Strichen: Stone Circle & Mormond Hill   *(History, Walk)*

Better-sheltered than most Buchan communities, Strichen (pop. 1159) is named after Lord Strichen, who in 1764 began building it over older Mormond so as to 'promote the arts and manufactures of this country'. Offering a prize to the first householder with a 'reekin lum' (smoking chimney), he succeeded, for today Strichen is a centre of Buchan culture, each May hosting the Doric Drama Festival and the Buchan Heritage Festival.

Straddling the Fraserburgh-New Deer A981 and hugging the east bank of the North Ugie, its most prominent building is the battlemented, turreted 1816 Tower House on the High Street; and its oldest the ruin of Mormond Parish Church (1620), sited above the village where the White Cow Wood road descends to the A981.

Opposite this junction is a carpark by Strichen Community Park, just north of which Bridge Street enters the village. Nearby, between the old railway (Formartine & Buchan Way: see **75**, **102**) and the riverbridge, Brewery Road breaks west towards New Pitsligo (**100**) past Strichen stone circle, a mile southwest of and above the village. To walk to the circle, from the carpark follow the wooded railway bed west. Soon after Strichen's last houses, a pedestrian gate allows road-access. Walk on a few yards to a right-hand bend and bear left down a track under the old railway bridge and embankment to a busy burn. From this point a south-bound track bears left then right between rising fields up to a gate. Beyond it turn diagonally left over pasture to a crest, on it the circle (936545; see photo next page).

Overlooking the shell of Strichen House (1821), and with wide views over rolling land to Mormond Hill, this circle has been through the wars. Visited in 1773 by Samuel Johnson, who was typically unimpressed, in 1830 the stones were flattened by a tenant farmer. Furious, Lord Lovat insisted they be restored, which they were, but in the wrong place. With further vandalism in the 1960s, in 1978 the local council restored the circle. Kerbed by a stone bank, like Easter Aquhorthies (**60**) and Loanhead of Daviot (**66**) the grey granite recumbent and its flankers may be used to sight on the moon. With the cremated remains of a woman found in the bank, and most of the other stones again in place, the site lacks the over-protected look of some others, but is no worse for that.

Nearby is a round stone tower with a triangular window – once a doocot?

Return as you came, or descend past the unsafe shell of Strichen House to Strichen Mains, thence northeast up the farmtrack to the community park.

From Strichen the A981 runs north over windswept land some seven miles to Fraserburgh, *en route* crossing the B9032 at Memsie, birthplace of Buchan poet John C. Milne (below), and site of the Memsie Cairn (974622), a burial mound 15ft high and 60ft round. A longer but interesting route to Fraserburgh means taking the B9093 east a mile to a left turn (964548) north to a maze of lanes south of bare Mormond Hill (753ft; 230m); Buchan's Bennachie, being so visible so far.

Though less elegant, in its way Mormond Hill is as interesting. On this southwest side, under the ruined 1779 hunting lodge built by the imaginative Captain Fraser, six years earlier (after Boswell and Johnson's visit) he'd had carved into the slope a huge white horse. A mile to the east and less conspicuous, the imitative White Stag was cut into the slope by William Fraser of Cortes in 1870.

More prominent than either, on the summit is a modern installation, perhaps 'the hub of military communications in Scotland'. Here are the gleaming dishes and masts of a long-range surveillance centre serving NATO, the USAF North Atlantic Relay System (NARS), and the US Navy's Microwave System (UKMS). You thought Mormond Hill was in Scotland? From Strichen there are paths up and about Mormond Hill but, as McKean puts it, 'care will have to be taken to avoid the military'. It sounds like fun.

These high rural lanes run east then north to the A90 to Fraserburgh, six miles to the north, and so to a walk round Cairnbulg, Inverallochy & St. Combs...but first:

107.   The Doric   *(Dialect, Poetry, Ballad)*

It's no coincidence that Strichen hosts the Doric Drama Festival. Spoken in varied forms throughout the Northeast, this Scots dialect is most distinctive in Buchan, home of most of the writers, poets and balladeers who work and have worked in it. Called by Boswell a 'strange sharp accent', characteristics distinguishing it even from other Scots (let alone English) include substituting 'f' for 'wh' (English 'why'; Scots 'wha'; Doric 'fa'), altered vowels (E 'good'; S 'guid'; D 'gweed'), and hard consonants (E 'father'; S 'faither'; D 'fader; and again: E 'wrought'; S 'wrocht'; D 'vrocht'); these suggesting Norse/Germanic influence (as in German *Die Tochter milchte die Kuh*; Doric *the dochter milkit the coo*). Another characteristic is use of the diminutive 'ie' (as in 'beastie' for 'beast'),

Many unique Doric words (see Glossary) relate to rural life and wildlife ('doo' or 'cushie-doo' for 'pigeon') Doric traditionally being less urban than rural, so for longer denying outside influences. This can lead to parochialism (as in the hopefully-apocryphal *Aberdeen Press & Journal* headline: *NORTH EAST MAN DROWNED – Titanic sinks*), but also helped create that sense of identity so vital in the hard Northeast. Drawing on the harsh Buchan climate and the dry wit of the *fowk*, this expressed itself much in the jingles of untaught poets (*Our feet's cauld, our sheen's thin/Gie's a piece an' lat's rin*) as in the protests of the bothy balladeer suffering under: *a fairmer up in Cairnie/Wha's kent baith faur and wide/Tae be the great Drumdelgie* (see **83**):

> There's sax o you'll gaun tae the ploo,
> An twa will drive the neeps, ...
> But when that we were gyaun furth,
> An turnin out to yoke,
> The snaw dank on sae thick and fast
> That we were like to choke ...

Writers in Doric have included Charles Murray, the Alford poet (**54**), William Thom, the 'weaver poet' of Inverurie (**62**), and the Huntly-born novelist George MacDonald (**80**). Here, in 'yon braid Buchan land', and either side of Mormond Hill, were born two of the finest Doric practitioners. One of them, John C. Milne of Memsie, wrote of Fraserburgh (**100**):

> O Tam, gie me auld Faithlie toon
> Whaur trees are scrunts for miles aroon
> And nae a burn wad slake or droon
> A drunken miller;
> But sands and bents that wear a croon
> O' gowd and siller

The other, Flora Garry, was born at Mains of Auchmunziel, from which she could see the Hill of the Cuckoo, *Bennygoak*. The first two verses have been quoted earlier (**104**); the third runs:

> *I look far ower by Ythanside*
> *To Fyvie's laich, lythe lan's,*
> *To Auchterless an Bennachie*
> *An the mist-blue Grampians.*
> *Sair't o the hull o Bennygoak*
> *An scunnert o the ferm,*
> *Gin I bit daar't, gin I bit daar't,*
> *I'd flit the comin' term.*

108.   Cairnbulg, Inverallochy & St. Combs   *(Walk)*

For Cairnbulg and Inverallochy, from the A90 roundabout just south of Fraserburgh turn east, not far, then right onto Cemetery Road/B9033. From the centre of town follow Harbour Road south past Fraserburgh Bay's broad beach and turn left on the same road. Continue two miles past the golf course, past a right turn to the Nature Reserve carpark, and over the sluggish Water of Philorth. Turn left onto the Rathen Road/B9107 to these siamese-twinned villages, which face each other over a shared main street – Cairnbulg to the west, Inverallochy to the east. Residents of one are *Bulgers*; of the other, *Cottoners*. Rivalry between these two villages, which to the outsider seem as one, was once intense.

With the street widening, the unseen boundary continues to the baker/butcher. Here turn left along Cairnbulg's Main Street to Shore Street and curve west round the windy point to Cairnbulg harbour, facing Fraserburgh over the sandy bay. For this six-mile, mostly back road circuit, start southwest along the rocky shore to the shallow, bird-rich, dune-hemmed estuary of the Water of Philorth. Over it the beach curves two miles to the Broch. Following the estuary's east side to grassy dunes, where these diminish as high spiky grass meets the fading shore, bear diagonally left on a short path through grass and thistle to a fence, its topmost barbed-wire strands tied to let folk duck through.

With no true path, bear southwest away from the water over dunes and rough cattle pasture, aiming at old army buildings by the B9033, Cairnbulg Castle's (016640) turrets above trees under Mormond Hill beyond. At the ruined buildings (023646), over a gate pass left through a double gate and over the old railway track. Cross the B9033 to the southbound lane opposite and continue a mile past Cairnbulg Mains, the castle to the right.

Originally the Comyn-owned Castle of Philorth, from 1375 to 1615 it was Fraser property. Abandoned in 1799 with the block linking its two towers demolished, in 1896 the towers were restored and the central block rebuilt for Sir John

Duthie. The castle is private, but parties can book visits: call Fraserburgh information centre (01346-518315).

Under a big sky the lane crests, bends, climbs, then dips to a junction (022630). Turn left 100 yards to a crossroads by a fancy new house with a vast lawn, ornamental pond and wrought-iron gates. Keep left past Moss-side, right at the next fork, and so east on flat ground past cottages and bungalows over a crossroads (Cortes 3, St. Combs 2), With the stump of Inverallochy Castle (041630; after 1504, once by the now-drained Loch of Inverallochy) to the right, a mile on from Moss-side the lane reaches the B9033.

Turn right a few yards to a lane on the left. This runs past Craigiepots and Hallmoss a mile to St. Combs (pop. 833), a fisher village at the head of beach and dune extending south to Peterhead. Laid out in 1764 by Charles Gordon of Cairness, here a Temperance March is held on 2nd January each year. From this lane St. Combs is reached from a crossing (052637) above the sea. As for Cairness House nearby (038614; 1791–7), it has been called: 'arguably the finest neo-classical mansion in Scotland'.

Visiting St. Combs (or not), from the crossing turn north on a track through the golf links now shared by Inverallochy and Cairnbulg. At an unusual half-timbered ranch-style house ('Ranch Whitelinks Bay'), cross the links to the broad sandy bay. Follow the beach round a stony, muddy point, then climb rough steps to a track along the edge of the links. Watching for mishit drives, enter Inverallochy. Past a net and clothes-drying green follow Shore Street, its houses with names like Galilee and Creel Cottage gable-end on to the sea, many costly, with elaborate porches. Look out for Maggie's Hoosie at 26 Shore Street, a mid-17th century rubble-built cottage with earth floors and timber box-beds.

Again, where does Inverallochy end and Cairnbulg begin? Yet, despite satellite dishes, the Sleepy Hollow old-time feel is reassuring, as in Cromarty on the Black Isle.

Following Shore Street back to Cairnbulg harbour, return to the B9033 and turn left, southeast, to the main St. Combs entry road. Here the B9033 breaks south three miles to the A90 west of Crimond, so passing Cairness east of the Loch of Strathbeg, and alsothe elegant 1825 mansion of Crimonmogate (038587).

109.   Loch of Strathbeg to Inverugie

From Fraserburgh the A90 runs south past ruined Philorth House towards Mormond Hill (**106**). After three miles, passing through Rathen with its high-steepled kirk and Mormond House, formerly Cortes (**106**) nearby, the road Y-forks, the A90 shedding the A952 to Mintlaw. The A90 turns east over flat, fertile wooded land past a crossroads (St. Combs 4, Mintlaw 7) with, to the left, the 900ft-tall masts of the Crimond RN/NATO communications station, opened in 1978 on a disued airfield.

Beyond the masts is the Loch of Strathbeg, open to the sea before in 1720 a storm blew sand so violently that the sea was shut out. Britain's largest dune loch

(550 acres; 220 hectares), its surrounding wetlands about are managed by the RSPB. With geese, duck and swan wintering alongside lapwing and curlew, hides surround the visitor centre at Starnafin (057581) south of the loch. To find it, enter Crimond (pop. 926), a village lending its name to the tune to which the 23rd psalm is usually sung, composed by Jessie Seymour Irvine, a daughter of the manse. By the spired 1812 parish kirk (its clock shows 61 minutes, not 60) is signposted the way to the nature reserve, open daily dawn to dusk.

Just east of Crimond a left turn (065564) off the A90 leads, via an increasingly potholed road, past yet another Haddo House (*c.*1750: see **76, 85**) to the barren east end of the Loch of Strathbeg. Here at Old Rattray is the ivied ruin of St. Mary's Chapel (085575), founded in 1220 by William Comyn and the remnant of

the Burgh of Rattray, its harbour abandoned after the storm of 1720. Nearby lie the earthworks of a Comyn fortress destroyed by Robert the Bruce amid the Harrowing of Buchan in 1308. This spooky place has coastal dunes 75 feet high, these running north and south from Rattray Head, beyond it on an offshore rock the lighthouse, its foghorn lonesome on wild North Sea nights.

So from ancient to ultra-modern. Two miles further southeast the A90 runs past the vast sci-fi sprawl of the Total Gas Terminal (1976). Set on the links of St. Fergus, this complex provides almost half Britain's current natural gas demand. A single street of cottages, St. Fergus itself lies by the main road, which continues south another three miles to Peterhead, the landscape increasingly industrial.

At a bend two miles further south, under a hilltop motte (103487) by a steading with a large silo, is a right turn: Inverugie 1.5. This leads immediately to a

168

fork, the left turn soon passing ruined Inverugie Castle (103484), a Cheyne fortress later converted into a Renaissance château by George Keith, 5th Earl Marischal (**2, 13, 100**). As at Fyvie (**78**), Thomas the Rhymer allegedly visited Inverugie during the time of the Cheynes. It's said he stood on a stone and predicted that, as long as it rested in peace, Inverugie's future owners, the Keiths, would prosper, but its removal would see the family fall.

Dispossessed for supporting the Old Pretender, who landed at Peterhead on 22 December 1715, with the cause lost James Keith (1696–1758) and his brother George, 10th and last Earl Marischal (1693–1778), fled to Europe. Serving in Spain then (like General Patrick Gordon; see **75**) in Russia, James led the Russian army against the Swedes and in 1747 became field-marshal to Frederick the Great of Prussia. Made Governor of Berlin in 1749 and by now joined by George as one of Frederick's ambassadors, he won the early battles of the Seven Years War, but was slain at Hochkirch. The Keiths made peace with George II in London in 1740, but their estates were not returned. The fate of the stone is unclear; more certainly, in 1868 William I of Prussia presented Peterhead with a statue of James Keith, now found in Broad Street in front of the 1788 Town House.

Continuing on this lane over the Ugie, turn right to a sharp left bend. From it a short riverbank walk reaches a crag, on it ruined Ravenscraig Castle (096487), a four-storey L-plan tower built in 1491.

South of the bend under the motte (see above) the A90 crosses the Ugie, here entering an estuary opening to the sea below and north of Buchanhaven, an 18th-century fishertown, now part of Peterhead. The A90 breaks south past the burgh; the A982/North Road continues to the town centre.

110.   Peterhead   *(Visit, History)*

Scotland's most easterly and Buchan's largest town, Peterhead (pop. 18,801) occupies an exposed promontory ending in Keith Inch, once an island and now linked to the town by its piers. Yet again it was George Keith, 5th Earl Marischal (see above), who in 1593 founded the Harbour and Barony of *Keith Insche commonly called Peterhead*, northeast of Peterugie parish church. The town developed uphill from the shore to Longate, the main street until Broad Street was developed in the late 18th century. By then already a fishing town, the harbour was expanded, and by 1820 Peterhead was Britain's main whaling port. The herring boom (by 1850 over 400 boats fished from here) led to further expansion, with elegant houses, assembly rooms and baths being built, while in 1886 the great breakwater all but enclosing Peterhead Bay and the vast Harbour of Refuge was built by convicts from the grimly notorious prison sited just south of the bay.

Today Peterhead remains the UK's largest white fish port (the fishmarket, held daily, has 78 loading bays) while also profiting from North Sea oil and gas by servicing offshore rigs and pipelines. Frigg Field gas is piped ashore at St. Fergus to the north, and Forties Field oil is landed at Cruden Bay (**111**) to the south – facts doubtless irritating to Brochers, given the traditional rivalry between the two towns. As John Milne (**107**) put it:

> *Hae a' the toons and coonties in ye heid,*
> *For, loshtie man, I doot there's naething waur*
> *Then mixin up the Broch and Peterheid!*

More functional than cheery, and though its red granite houses give it character, it's hard to see Peterhead as a popular spa, yet in the 18th century this is what it became, the mineral waters of the Wine (*Wynd*; see **100**) Well by the shore being so popular that in 1759 the masons built Assembly Rooms by it. To add sea-bathing, near the well in 1799 James Arbuthnot excavated from solid rock a vast basin, filled each tide with fresh sea water. With warm baths also available, in 1804 Robert Forsyth remarked that the burgh's facilities made it: 'the most fashionable resort as a water place in north Britain'.

Of the baths and well little remain. The fisheries are what's remembered and, by the shore above the Marina and below South Road/A982, the Maritime Heritage Museum (1779-473000; April–Oct; phone for winter hours) graphically presents its tale: one of whalers, fisherfolk and navigators risking the open sea in small boats; of the 'scaffies' and 'fifies' that preceded the 'Zulu' drifter designed in Lossiemouth in 1879 amid the Zulu wars; and of the arrival soon after of the steam trawler that put paid to line fishing.

From here the A982 runs south past Peterhead Prison to the bypass round-about, from which (Ellon 16, Aberdeen 32), the A90 continues past the huge stack of Peterhead Power Station and a left turn to Boddam and Buchan Ness. Behind an RAF compound, Boddam (pop. 1505) on its rocky promontory dates from the 1830s. Just offshore, linked by a bridge to the mainland, is the 1824 Stevenson light-house (**100**), and on a crag to the south are the remains of Boddam Castle, a 16th-century seat of the Keiths of Lundquharn.

The road climbs south above the coast, here deep-cut with gullies, crags and caves, and in three miles passes through tiny Longhaven. Just beyond, the A975 (Newburgh 12) turns left 2.5 miles to Cruden Bay via the Bullers of Buchan.

111. Slains Castle & the Bullers of Buchan   *(History, Walk)*

From the A982 follow the A975 under a mile to a carpark 300 yards from the Bullers (110380; Old Scots, 'rushing of waters'; or French, '*bouilloire*, 'cauldron'). A path leads past cottages (one named 'Breathing Space') to the lip of a vast, 200 foot deep pit pierced by an arch through which the sea surges violently. Gulls squall above the roar of the waves. This place is potent, and for once even Doctor Johnson was impressed, insisting on sailing into this 'monstrous cauldron'. Take care, especially if you dislike heights.

Continue round a bend past a track to Slains Castle, visible ahead, to Cruden Bay (pop. 1817). The name, from *croju-dane*; 'slaughter of the danes', recalls a 1012 rout of Canute's Danes (**92**) by the Scots. Bisected by the Water of Cruden, the village dates from 1830 when the Earl of Erroll, owner of Slains, built Port Erroll by the estuary at the sandy beach. Dry at low water, the harbour was a failure; but after 1897 the Great North of Scotland Railway established a resort here. By 1932 the 55-bedroom hotel was closed, yet this Victorian seaside town remains popular with golfers, and remains associated with the Irish author of the classic horror tale *Dracula*, Bram (Abraham) Stoker (1847–1912).

From the harbour may be seen the Scours of Cruden, the rocks off the headland to the south. The legend that the bodies of those shipwrecked and slain on them emerged from the sea visibly to join their souls in heaven or hell led Stoker to write his *Mystery of the Sea*. On the cliff-edge above is Whinnyfold (*Finnyfaul*), a windswept cluster of cottages built *c.*1860. Here, just north of the district boundary, Stoker had a house.

To visit eerie Slains (102362), from the carpark between hotel and harbour follow a path through a stunted, wind-torn wood, then along a bare ravine, rock-faces grimacing above the sluggish, weed-choked burn where Stoker had Dracula land in Britain...

Past a brick tower the path climbs northeast to a grassy clifftop, fulmar and gannet wheeling over the crags. Roofless, Slains perches a quarter-mile ahead on the clifftop, its walls, as Johnson noted in 1773: 'a continuation of the perpendicular rock'. Ancient seat of the Hay Earls of Erroll, it's like a deserted eyrie.

Wiith Old Slains (**73**) near Collieston five miles to the south sacked in 1594 by James VII after the 9th Earl joined Huntly (see **80**) in Catholic revolt, when in 1597 Erroll returned from exile he built this courtyard palace, each room opening to the next. With additions thereafter, in 1836 it was largely rebuilt and faced with granite. Here, a century ago, the 19th Earl held parties for the Bohemian avant-garde, including Stoker. Maybe here Bram read *Dracula* to shaky guests as the sea boomed on the rocks below.

Sold in 1916 and abandoned in 1925, its roof removed to avoid tax, the castle, its site and the approach to it remain alarming. A sign at the fenced edge of castle and cliff warns: *These cliffs are dangerous*. Quite so.

Beyond this brick and granite maze of roofless rooms and vaulted dungeons is a grassy promontory, on one side the foaming sea below; on the other a deep and narrow gorge. From this wild place, return as you came, or follow the well-dyked old estate road east, turning left at a junction and so back to Cruden Bay.

From Cruden Bay the A975 passes the Whinnyfold lane, bends right then left past the pinnacled tower of St. James' Church, built in 1842 and a landmark for miles about, then runs over bare Lochlundie Moss past the Meikle Loch and the Collieston (**73**) turn, before crossing the Ythan past Newburgh joining the A90 for its final run into Aberdeen.

112. The Final Run   *(Route, Farewell)*

From the A975 turn to Cruden Bay the A90 continues over scrappy land, then via Z-bends past a left turn to Cruden Old Church (St. James), prominent on a knoll to the east. It runs on through rolling open land to a crest from which Bennachie (**68**) appears on the horizon. Soon after, four miles north of Ellon and 20 north of Aberdeen, the A90 is joined by the A952 from Mintlaw, so continuing past Ellon and Newburgh and back to Aberdeen, where we began this journey.

That seems like a long time ago, and I hope you've enjoyed the trip. So, goodbye for now, an' lang may yer lum reek!

Bullers of Buchan

Glossary of common place-name prefixes and suffixes

Key to abbreviations: B = Brythonic/Brittonic; E = English (OE = Old English); G = Gaelic; L = Latin; N = (old) Norse; S = Scots

Aber	Brittonic/Welsh	'estuary', 'confluence' (*see* inver)
Ach	Gaelic *achadh*	'field'
Allt	Gaelic *allt*	'burn', 'stream'
Aonach	Gaelic *aonach*	'ridge'
Ard	Gaelic *aird*	'height', 'high place', 'promontory'
Auchter	Gaelic *uachdair*	'upper part of', 'high ground'
Bal	Gaelic *baile*	'town', 'village', 'enclosure'
Ban	Gaelic *ban*	'white'
Bealach	Gaelic *bealach*	'pass'
Beg	Gaelic *beag*	'small', 'little'
Ben	Gaelic *beinn*	'mountain', 'horn'
Blair	Gaelic *blar*	'battlefield', 'cleared ground'
Bodach	Gaelic *bodach*	'old man'
Buidhe	Gaelic *buidhe*	'yellow'
By, Bie	Norse *byr*	'farm', 'hamlet'
Cardine	Brittonic *cardden*	'copse', 'thicket'
Clach	Gaelic *clach*	'stone'
Corrie	Gaelic *coire*	'hollow', 'kettle'
Craig	Gaelic *creag*	'cliff', 'crag'
Darroch	Gaelic *darroch*	'oak'
Dearg	Gaelic *dearg*	'red' (pron. jarrag)
Drum	Gaelic *druim*	'back', 'spine', 'ridge'
Dubh	Gaelic *dubh*	'black'
Dun	Gaelic *dun*	'fortress', 'castle', 'hill', 'mound'
Eagach	Gaelic *eagach*	'notched'
Eas	Gaelic *eas*	'waterfall'
Eilean	Gaelic *eilean*	'island'
Ey	Norse *Ey*	'island'
Firth	Norse *fjordr* (art;G)	'sea-estuary'
Fuaran	Gaelic *fuaran*	'spring'
Garbh	Gaelic *garbh*	'rough'
Gart	*gardr* (N); *garth* (B); *garradh* (G)	'garden', 'enclosure', 'yard'
Glas	Gaelic; Brittonic	'grey' or 'green' (G); or 'water' (B)
Gorm	Gaelic *gorm*	'bl;uish green'
Gowrie	Gaelic *gowrie*	'goats'
Hope	Norse *hop*	'bay', 'refuge', 'valley'
Inch	Gaelic *innis*	'island', 'meadows by a river', 'field'
Inver	Gaelic *inbhir*	'estuary', 'confluence' (see aber)
Iolaire	Gaelic *iolaire*	'eagles'
Kil	Gaelic *ceall, cill*	'monastic cell', 'church'
Kirk	Scots (*kirkju*:N)	'church'
Knock	Gaelic *cnoc*	'round hillock'
Kyle	Gaelic *caol*	'slender', 'thin, 'sea-strait'
Lairig	Gaelic *lairig*	'pass'
Liath	Gaelic *liath*	'grey'
Linn	Gaelic *linn*; Brit. *llyn*	(1) 'pool', (2) 'lake'
May	Gaelic *magh*; *moigh*	'field', 'plain'
Meall	Gaelic *meall*	'knob', 'hump'
Moine	Gaelic *moine*	'mossy land'
Monadh	Gaelic *monadh*	'moorland', 'flat-topped ridge'
More	Gaelic *mor, mhor*	'great', 'big'

Ness	naes (OE); nes (N)	'point', 'headland' (L. nasus, 'nose')
Pit	Pictish	'part', 'share', 'piece' (?)
Rath	Gaelic rath	'fort'
Rathad	Gaelic rathad	'road'
Ruadh	Gaelic ruadh	'red', 'reddish'
Sgorr	Gaelic sgorr, sgur	'sharp peak'
Shee	Gaelic sithe, sidhe	'fairies', 'fairy hills'
Shieling	Norse skali	'hut' (usually on high pasture)
Stob	Gaelic stob	'point'
Strath	Gaelic strath	'river valley', 'fertile valley'
Tobar	Gaelic tobar	'well', 'source'
Tom	Gaelic tom	'conical hillock', 'mound', 'knoll'
Tor	Brittonic tor	'hill'
Uaine	Gaelic uaine	'green'
Uisge	Gaelic uisge	'water' (whisky)

A Brief Doric Glossary

Doric	English	Doric	English	Doric	English
aa	all	aabody	everyone	aathing	everything
aawye	everywhere	ae	one	affa	awfully
afore	before	aifter	after	alivven	eleven
athoot	without	avaa	at all	aye	always, still
ayont	beyond	baa	ball	baillie	farm steward
been	bone	beerial	funeral	biggin	building
bizzard	buzzard	bleckie	blackbird	briks	trousers
byordnar	extraordinary	byre	cowshed	caal	cold
chuckneys	chickens	claes	clothes	coo	cow
cratur	creature	cushie doo	woodpigeon	crubbit	bad-tempered
deuk	duck	drouth(y)	thirst(y)	echt	eight
ee(n)	eye(s)	faa(s)	who(se)	fae	from
fairm toon	farm	feart	afraid	fir yowie	pine cone
fit	what	fleg	scare	fower	four
gaar	cause to	gey	rather	gled	hawk
gomeril	fool	gowk	cuckoo	greet	weep
grieve	farm manager	grun	ground	gweed	good
hallyracket	boisterous	heelster-gowdie	head over heels	heid	head
hingin-luggit	droopy	hinna	have not	hoolet	owl
hunner	hundred	ilka	each, every	jaloose	guess
jeelt	frozen	ken	know	kist	chest
limmer	loose woman	loon	boy	lum	chimney
mappy	rabbit	messages	shopping	moose	mouse
neep	turnip	peelie wally	sick	peesieweep	lapwing
puddock	frog	pyet	magpie	quine	girl
roon	round	rype	search	sark	shirt
sax	six	shank	leg	sheen	shoes
skelp	smack	skurri	gull	snaa	snow
speir	ask	spik	speak	thole	endure
thrawn	stubborn	twa	two	twal	twelve
vratch	wretch	waa	wall	waabit	exhausted
waallie-draigle	tramp	wecht	weight	weet	wet
wifie	woman	win	leave	winner	wonder
wrang	wrong	wrunkled	wrinkled	wyver	spider
yark	wrench	yoke	start work	yon	that
yowe	ewe				

Bibliography

Some books and other publications I've plundered or which you may find useful in following up topics are as follows (some out of print or hard to find):

Bord, Janet & Colin, *Sacred Waters,* Paladin, London 1986

Clayton, Peter, *Guide to the Archaeological Sites of Britain,* B. T. Batsford, London 1985

Dorward, David, *Scotland's Place-Names,* William Blackwood, Edinburgh 1979

Graham, Cuthbert, *Portrait of Aberdeen and Deeside,* Robert Hale, London 1980

Ives, Edward D, *The Bonny Earl of Murray: the Man, the Murder, the Ballad,* Tuckwell Press Ltd., East Linton 1997

Jackson, Kenneth, *The Symbol Stones of Scotland,* Orkney Press, Kirkwall 1984

Kay, Billy, *Scots - The Mither Tongue,* Grafton, London 1988

Keay, John & Julia, (eds.), *Collins Encyclopaedia of Scotland,* HarperCollins, London 1994

Laing, Lloyd & Jennifer, *The Origins of Britain,* Granada, London 1982

Lockhart, J G, *Curses, Lucks & Talismans,* Geoffrey Bles, London 1938

Lynch, Michael, *Scotland: A New History,* Pimlico, London 1992

Mackie, J D, *A History of Scotland,* Penguin Books, London 1964

Marren, Peter, *Grampian Battlefields,* Aberdeen University Press, 1990

McDowell, R J S, *The Whiskies of Scotland,* John Murray, London 1975

McKean, Charles, *Banff & Buchan: An Illustrated Architectural Guide,* RIAS, Edinburgh 1990

Oram, Richard, *Scottish Prehistory*, Birlinn, Edinburgh 1997

Ritchie, Anna, *Picts,* HMSO, London 1989

Shepherd, Ian, *Gordon: An Illustrated Architectural Guide,* RIAS, Edinburgh 1994

Smith, John C. (ed), *Old Aberdeen: Bishops, Burghers and Buildings,* Aberdeen University Press, Aberdeen 1991

Smith, Robert, *Discovering Aberdeenshire,* John Donald, Edinburgh 1988

Spaven, Malcolm, *Fortress Scotland,* Pluto Press, London 1983

Spence, Lewis, *Magic Arts in Celtic Britain,* Aquarian Press, London 1970 (1946)

Stott, Louis, *The Waterfalls of Scotland,* Aberdeen University Press, 1987

Towill, Edwin Sprott, *The Saints of Scotland,* Saint Andrew Press, Edinburgh 1983

Watt, Archibald, *Highways and Byways Round Stonehaven,* Gourdas House, Aberdeen 1984

Wightman, Andy, *Who Owns Scotland,* Canongate Books, Edinburgh 1996

About the author

Born in Banff in 1947 and since 1970 (writing as Stuart Gordon) author of some 20 titles of fiction and non-fiction, when Richard Gordon returned to north Scotland in 1988 he realised he knew little or nothing of the region and its history, and set about changing that. In 1992 he published *The Complete Moray Rambler,* some of it incorporated in this book, which is a sequel to *Round Inverness, The Black Isle and Nairn* (1998), and *Round Moray, Badenoch & Strathspey* (1999). He lives near Buckie and is now working on a history of the Northeast.